6396
NL

Signed by Author

17.50
Americana
W. VA.

Senator Henry Gassaway Davis

Davis & Elkins College

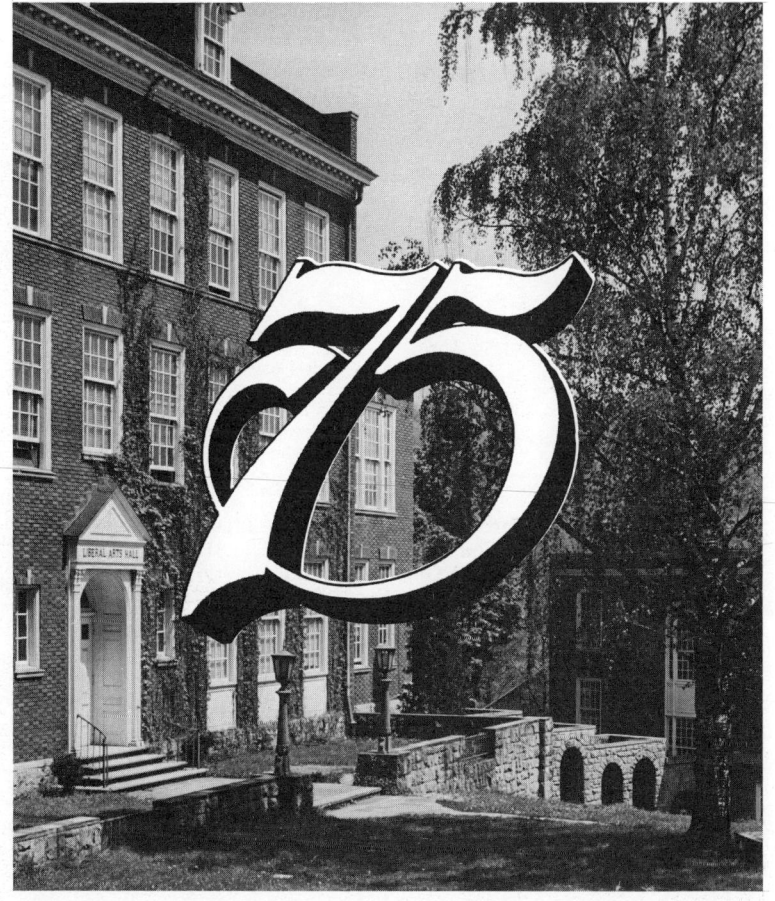

The Diamond Jubilee History

by

Thomas Richard Ross

Standard Book Number 87012-381-5
Library of Congress Card Number 80-81342
Printed in the United States of America
Copyright © 1980 by Davis & Elkins College
Elkins, West Virginia
All Rights Reserved

This book is dedicated to

JENNINGS RANDOLPH

As a Faculty Member, Trustee, Honorary Trustee, Congressman, Airline Executive, Member of the Board of the Benedum Foundation, and Senior United States Senator from West Virginia, Jennings Randolph has for more than fifty years rendered distinguished service to Davis and Elkins College as well as to his state and nation.

Contents

Foreword		ix
I	In The Beginning: 1891-1904	1
II	The Infant Survives: 1905-10	15
III	Growing Pains on Sally Mike Hill: 1910-20	29
IV	The Roaring Twenties and the Scarlet Hurricane: 1920-29	56
V	D&E in the Depths of the Depression: 1930-35	86
VI	Struggling for Survival: 1935-43	112
VII	Years of Achievement and Frustration: 1943-53	143
VIII	Retrenchment, Reform, and Renewal: 1953-64	185
IX	Years of Expansion and Innovation: 1964-79	244

Foreword

To be invited to write the history of the college which one has served for most of his professional life (and for more than two-fifths of the institution's existence) is an honor greatly to be appreciated, but it is also a humbling responsibility. Each member of the faculty and board of trustees, each alumnus, student, employee, and constituent has had a particular perception of the ideals, personalities, and events in the life of the college. What to one may have seemed significant may have appeared trivial to another. What may have loomed large in the memory of some, others may have been unmindful of at all times. Thus, it is impossible for one historian to present an account of the incidents and the people associated with the long period herein considered in a manner universally acceptable. The writer, therefore, is obliged, in the words of one university research director, "to go where your facts lead you even if they take you out of a second story window."

It is natural that each person should love most the times he knew best. Those who knew the college in the 1960s or 1970s very likely have quite a different "image" of D&E from those who were here in the 1940s or 1950s, just as the memories of the latter group differ from those for whom "College Days" were pre-World War I, or the glorious era of the Scarlet Hurricane in the "Roaring Twenties," or the desperate days of the Great Depression in the 1930s. In truth, "the good old days" were perhaps not so "good" as they often appear in retrospect and certainly not "old" at all, when one lived them.

This history is written from the viewpoint of one who holds with Shakespeare that "what's past is prologue." The hopes and the dreams, the accomplishments and the failures, the good fortune and the mistakes of each era combine to make the college what it is today and what it may become tomorrow. The success and the progress of the present were made possible by the struggles and the sacrifices, the vision and the effort of those who led and taught and studied and labored in more distant and often very discouraging times, as well as by those of the present. Regardless of how seriously and sincerely those associated with the college over the years—faculty, trustees, students, staff—may occasionally have differed over issues, rules, methods, or personalities, my conclusion is that few, if any, have disagreed about ultimate goals. Most have sought, in accordance with their lights, to improve the college and to keep foremost the aim of her being of the greatest possible service to students, community, state, and nation by offering sound liberal education and career preparation under Christian auspices.

My obligations for assistance in this undertaking are manifold. President Gordon E. Hermanson, who conceived the idea of a Diamond Jubilee History, not only arranged for the necessary financial and other support but has given encouragement on many occasions. His able administrative assistant, Elizabeth Guye Kittle, has borne with infinite patience the almost daily burden of providing minutes, catalogs, and other documents and records from the security vaults in her office and has been ever gracious and helpful in seeking other sources of information for my use. Miss Anna Parmesano, for forty-five years Mrs. Kittle's predecessor in the president's office, generously permitted me to use her scrapbook of newspaper clippings about the college and sought to supply answers to my queries about her memories of days long gone.

I must acknowledge, too, the valuable assistance afforded by Vice-President Nevin Kendell and his secretary, Robin Price. His staff in the development office, John Frost, Ann Stottlemyer, Barbara Schulz, and Becky Bisgood, were especially helpful in providing photographs, old college publications, and information about alumni. Several people in the business manager's office also cooperated in various ways—notably Vicki Evans, Harry Thompson, and Brenda Moore and her assistants in the Office Services Center. The same is true of librarians such as Mary Margaret Woodward and Douglas Kranch, and of Registrar John Neill and his secretaries.

Although an effort has been made to give credit in footnote citations to everyone who has provided information through interviews and letters, I want to express my special gratitude to the following: Mrs. Charles E. Albert, Dr. David K. Allen, Robert

A. Allen, Miss Emily Barry, Dr. S. Wilds DuBose, Mrs. Claire Fiorentino, Dr. Margaret Goddin, C. A. ("Bill") Gross, Mrs. Tatiana Jardetzky, Stuart L. Johnson, Mrs. Bruce Lee Kennedy, Mrs. Thomas Davis Lee, Dr. Robert T. L. Liston, Edward and Nancy McFarlane, Fred A. Miller, Michael Pedretti, Harry L. ("Bud") Shelton and his wife, Kathryn, Charles A. Stevenson, Dr. Jean Tallman, Harry Whetsell, and Frank C. Wimer.

Before her death, Miss Virgie Harris gave me her collection of materials related to the history of D&E, a thoughtful act from which this book has benefited.

Acknowledgment is due also to Kent Kessler who granted permission to quote from his book *Hail West Virginians!* which is a storehouse of data relative to athletic history.

George Smith and the skilled craftsmen of the McClain Printing Company have been cooperative and helpful throughout the tedious process of seeing the copy through the press and Mrs. Dorothy Winkler's advice, meticulous attention to editorial detail, and care in proofreading have been of inestimable value.

Those who have read part or all of the manuscript and improved it by their criticisms and suggestions include Ralph R. Booth, Phillips V. Brooks, Margaret P. Goddin, Gordon E. Hermanson, Ann and Evan Kek, Nevin Kendell, William E. Phipps, Jean, Laurie and Tom Ross, and Harry L. and Kathryn Shelton.

My obligation to my secretary, Linda S. Marsh, is immeasurable. She has not only deciphered my handwriting in order to prepare the first draft but has typed and retyped subsequent revisions with great care, patience, and good humor. Much of the work involved in the preparation of the index was done by Cammie Joan Parker, a student assistant in the History Department.

Finally, I am especially grateful to my wife, Jean McCorkle Ross, not only for enduring without complaint the numerous inconveniences which are the usual lot of the spouse of a professor writing, but also, in this instance, for re-living with me many of the experiences we have shared at D&E during the last thirty years covered in this book.

Thomas Richard Ross

Kerens Hill, Elkins

Senator Stephen Benton Elkins

I

In the Beginning: 1891-1904

In September 1904, as the presidential election campaign began to warm up, President Theodore Roosevelt and his Republican running mate were confident of victory. This electoral canvass was of special interest to the people of Elkins, West Virginia, because of the fact that former Senator Henry Gassaway Davis, founder of the city, was the nominee of the Democratic party for vice-president of the United States. Although eighty years old, Davis traveled about the country speaking several times a day and keeping the name of his hometown on the front pages of the nation's newspapers.

A major topic of speculation in the booming little mountain town, then only fifteen years old, was how United States Senator Stephen Benton Elkins was going to vote in November. Elkins, for whom the city was named, was the son-in-law and business associate of Henry Gassaway Davis. Earlier in the summer there had been frequent mention in the leading newspapers in the East of the possibility that the Republican party might nominate Elkins for vice-president. Twenty years earlier, he had come into national prominence as campaign manager for James G. Blaine, the 1884 Republican presidential nominee. After serving as Secretary of War in the cabinet of President Benjamin Harrison, Elkins had been chosen United States Senator from West Virginia in 1895. By 1904, he was a Republican leader in the Senate and the dominant figure in his party in the state.

Would Senator Elkins support Roosevelt and the Republicans or vote for the ticket headed by Alton B. Parker and Henry Gassaway Davis, his father-in-law, closest neighbor, and revered friend? An experienced and prudent man, Elkins did not respond directly to the newsmen's persistent queries. He did, on occasion, observe that if the Democrats had been wise, they would have named Davis instead of Parker "for the first place on the ticket," but otherwise he made no effort to satisfy the curious. One journalist, with more imagination than poetic talent, depicted Senator Elkins sitting on the porch of his summer mansion, Halliehurst, looking across the yard at nearby Graceland, the Davis home, and pondering:

> Eenie, meenie, meinie, mo!
> What's the answer, yes or no?
> Ought I vote for Theodore?
> Or cast my slip for Pop-in-lawr?
> Pop-in-law's a Democrat,
> Hence, I'm not for him, that's flat!
> But, even though a Democrat, he
> Has always been a Pa to me.
> How I'd hate to hear him say:
> "Steve, you knifed your Gassaway!"
> Hence, I'm where I was before,
> Pop-in-law or Theodore?
> Eenie, meenie, meinie, mo--
> Why does fate pursue me so?[1]

Undoubtedly, Senator Elkins supported and voted for the Republicans. Senator Davis enjoyed the attention given him as a vice-presidential candidate and was amused at the charges that at eighty, he was too old to serve if elected—he lived on in good health until 1916. A realist and a sophisticated politician, he appreciated Senator Elkins's political position—just as he understood very well why the Democrats had nominated a wealthy "elder statesman" for vice-president when everyone knew they had little chance to win the election. Indeed, he once humorously observed: "They just wanted to tap my barrel!"

Though they might differ mildly and good-naturedly about politics, Senators Davis and Elkins were in harmonious agreement in regard to another major topic of conversation in their hometown in September of 1904—the establishment of a Presbyterian college, named in their honor, which began its first academic session on September 21. For many years, Senator Davis had shown his concern for education by providing money to build elementary or high school facilities in various towns and villages such as Piedmont, Gassaway, Davis, and Henry.

---

1. From an unidentified newspaper clipping in a scrapbook belonging to Mrs. John A. (Bruce Lee) Kennedy which she kindly allowed the author to use.

Graceland and Halliehurst.

Early indications of Senator Elkins's interest in promoting higher education include his tentative offer to help the Baptists establish a college if they would locate it in Elkins and his statement to a Buckhannon minister that:

> It has been in my mind for a long time to establish a college at my own town, and if so I could not make a large contribution towards helping your college. If the Methodists had done half as much at Elkins towards establishing a school, Senator Davis and I would have given $50,000 in aid of it. It is our purpose to build a substantial college at Elkins, and I only wish it could be under the auspices and control of the Methodist church.[2]

Fortunately, the interest in higher education of these two wealthy businessmen-laymen coincided with that of a number of clergymen in the Lexington Presbytery of the Presbyterian Church in the United States, who, in the 1890s, recognized the need for a Presbyterian college in West Virginia.

From colonial times, the Calvinist denominations had led in

---

2. S. B. Elkins, Washington, D.C., to the Reverend S. L. Boyers, Buckhannon, W.Va., December 27, 1899. Elkins Papers, Letterbook No. 58, Davis and Elkins College.

the establishment of schools and colleges in the United States. There was at least one Presbyterian college in every state except Maryland which touched the borders of West Virginia, but since the state had separated from Virginia and had been admitted to the Union as recently as 1863, there was no Presbyterian college in the Mountain State at the end of the nineteenth century.

As early as 1891, the Lexington Presbytery of the Southern Presbyterian Church had appointed a committee, under the chairmanship of the Reverend C. S. Lingamfelter, pastor of the Presbyterian Church in Elkins, to "consider the propriety of establishing a first class school at Elkins."[3] At a meeting of the committee on November 25, 1891, the following proposal was presented on behalf of the donors for consideration of Presbytery: "that the Honorable S. B. Elkins and H. G. Davis will place in the bank at Elkins, W.Va., to the credit of the Presbyterian Church, subject to the order of its treasurer, twenty thousand dollars ($20,000) and will deed to the church for grounds and buildings for a school, twenty-five acres of land, and will furnish transportation over the West Virginia Central and Pittsburgh R.R. for all freight necessary for the building and founding of said school, at one-half regular rates, provided the church will raise an equal amount of money ($20,000) for the same purpose." The committee recommended that the Lexington Presbytery request the Winchester Presbytery to "unite with us" in the effort "to establish a college at Elkins, W.Va., and in the event the effort is successful, to join with us in the ownership and conduct of said college." A message of appreciation was dispatched to Messers Davis and Elkins, and a committee to solicit funds was appointed.[4]

The way was not clear in the 1890s for Winchester Presbytery to join in supporting this effort, but in the spring of 1892, the Lexington Presbytery appointed a special committee "to formulate some plan of action in regard to a college at Elkins." Captain H. L. Hoover, a ruling elder, was appointed to serve as an "agent" of Presbytery to solicit funds, and the other presbyteries of the Synod of Virginia were asked to give him "permission to labor in their bounds." Reports of the special committee at subsequent meetings of the Lexington Presbytery in 1892, 1893, and

3. *Minutes of Lexington Presbytery*, 1891, vol. 18, p. 510.
4. *Ibid.*, p. 527.

1894 indicate continued interest in the project, but not much success on the part of those seeking funds. The "Panic of 1893," a serious economic recession, was doubtless a major reason that the special committee finally advised Presbytery on May 9, 1894, that "there is nothing left for your committee but to say that nothing has been accomplished because there was nothing that could be done."[5] Indeed, 1894 was the darkest year Americans had known for thirty years. Half a million laborers were on strike. Prices and wages hit rock bottom. Few workers made as much as six hundred dollars a year, the corn crop was a failure; wheat sold for less than fifty cents a bushel; cotton prices fell to six cents a pound; and "Coxey's Army" marched on Washington. Few West Virginians or Virginians, Presbyterian or otherwise, had any money to give to start a college.

Nevertheless, the idea of a "college at Elkins" did not die. In October 1895, the Lexington Presbytery was informed that Senators Davis and Elkins had made a revised proposition. They had increased the sum offered from twenty thousand to thirty thousand dollars plus the "suitable site" and agreed to pay the first five thousand dollars whenever the Presbytery could match that sum and thereafter to match "dollar for dollar," in units of five thousand dollars, the sums Presbytery could raise until the whole thirty thousand dollars had been paid. They further agreed to give the Lexington Presbytery "exclusive control of the institution when established." Presbytery voted unanimously to accept this offer and also to ask the Synod of Virginia "to give the college its approval, and to assist Lexington Presbytery in raising the funds necessary for the endowment." The plea to the Synod was for help in establishing a Presbyterian college in West Virginia "which shall do for the people of the state what Hampden-Sydney, Washington and Lee, and Davidson Colleges have done for Virginia and North Carolina."[6]

The Synod gave its "hearty endorsement" and recommended that the churches provide "liberal support." The session of each congregation was asked to appoint a "local agent" to seek funds from members, but, sad to say, Presbytery was later informed that "comparatively few of the sessions responded." By May

---

5. *Ibid.*, 1892, 1893, 1894, *passim.*
6. *Ibid.*, 1895, *passim*; and Minutes of the Board of Trustees of Davis and Elkins College, 1902-55 (Introduction), p. 1. (Hereinafter cited as Trustee Minutes.)

1896, only $3,760 had been subscribed. However, a group had visited Senator Davis in Washington and reported he "manifested such a deep interest in the scheme and such liberal views in relation to it as greatly to cheer your committee."[7] Though some enthusiasm was regenerated at Presbytery meetings, very little tangible support was forthcoming in the mid-1890s. The economic depression continued and, though the clergy and ruling elders who attended meetings of Presbytery and Synod might make or listen to fervent addresses on the need for a Presbyterian college and pass resolutions designed to promote that goal, the farmers, laborers, small businessmen and professional people in the pews often had barely enough income to live on—and none to pledge for building a college.

Thus, it is not surprising to discover that in May 1897, the special committee on "a college at Elkins" reported that they had found themselves "confronted by such obstacles, especially the continued depression of the business interests of the whole country as to prevent the accomplishment of any special results." Presbytery did not give up, but decided to establish an "Academy" at Elkins hoping that it would later grow into a college. This school was started in 1898, but due to an epidemic which struck the principal and most of the students, the project failed. At its meeting in October 1899, the Presbytery decided "after trying one plan after another through the whole term of seven years" that it was only "honest and just" to inform Senators Davis and Elkins that "we are unable to raise the money upon which their offer was conditioned . . . and that we are compelled . . . to give up such a greatly needed work in our West Virginia territory."[8] Thus, the nineteenth century ended without further effort to establish a college in Elkins.

With the general improvement of economic conditions in the country early in the new century, the project was revived. This time the initiative came from the Presbytery of Lexington rather than from the Senators. At a meeting at Franklin, West Virginia, on September 12, 1901, the Presbytery adopted a resolution offered by the Reverend A. H. Hamilton of Steele's Tavern, Virginia, asking Senators Davis and Elkins to contribute "at

---

7. *Minutes of Lexington Presbytery*, May 5, 1896, report of the "Committee on the College at Elkins."

8. *Ibid.*, October 20, 1899.

least $30,000" and to "donate suitable grounds" for a college at Elkins. The Presbytery promised to contribute to the undertaking $30,000 of its share of a "20th Century Million Dollar Fund" then being raised in the Southern Presbyterian Church for Christian Education and Church Expansion. Within six weeks, Mr. Hamilton was able to present to the Presbytery a communication from Senator Davis renewing the offer he and Senator Elkins had made in October 1895. Lexington Presbytery, on October 23, 1901, voted to proceed to raise the $30,000 and to appoint a committee composed of A. H. Hamilton, G. A. Wilson, and L. H. Paul (ministers) and J. A. Patterson and J. N. McFarland (elders) "to take this matter in charge." At a subsequent meeting, Presbytery empowered A. H. Hamilton "to vacate his pulpit for a season" and appointed him to be "Presbytery's agent to raise $30,000 to secure the College at Elkins," guaranteeing him a monthly salary of $133.33 plus his expenses. Winchester Presbytery was asked to cooperate and agreed to do so, though at first no arrangements were made for it to share in the ownership or management of the college.[9]

After a year of soliciting, A. H. Hamilton reported that he had cash and pledges totaling $23,607. Of this, $10,000 came from citizens of Randolph County and $5,000 from Winchester Presbytery with the remainder from "churches East of the Alleghany Range" in Virginia and "other parts of West Virginia." After receiving this report, the Lexington Presbytery elected a nine-man board of trustees for the college. These included: Ex-Senator Henry Gassaway Davis, Senator Stephen Benton Elkins, the Reverend Frederick H. Barron, and C. Wood Dailey of Elkins; the Honorable John J. Davis of Clarksburg; the Reverend F. M. Woods, Martinsburg; G. W. Finley, Fisherville, Virginia; the Reverend A. H. Hamilton of Steele's Tavern, Virginia; and the Reverend A. M. Fraser, Staunton, Virginia.[10]

The board of trustees met for the first time on December 4, 1902, at the home of C. Wood Dailey in Elkins, with six members present. A. H. Hamilton, the temporary president, announced that the purposes of the meeting were to adopt a name for the college, select a site for the campus, make plans for erecting the first building, and effect a permanent organization of the board. Neither Senator Davis or Senator Elkins was present at the

9. *Ibid.*, September 12, October 23, November 12, 1901.
10. *Ibid.*, October, 1902, and Trustee Minutes (Introduction), p. 4.

meeting as they were in Washington, D.C., during the winter months. President Hamilton stated that Senator Davis wished to inform the board that he was giving fifty thousand dollars for an endowment and an additional five thousand dollars for clearing and improving the college grounds. The secretary, C. W. Dailey, read a letter from Senator Elkins offering to give for a campus as much land as was needed from the "Sally Yokum Farm" on the Beverly and Fairmont Turnpike, south of Elkins, overlooking the Tygart Valley River.

So far as can be determined, the first motion ever adopted by the board of trustees was offered by G. W. Finley to provide "that the college to be established be called *The Davis and Elkins College.*" That the vote was unanimous is not surprising! Then, in typical Presbyterian (and academic) fashion, the board of trustees appointed a committee to have the land surveyed and described, a committee to plan the buildings, a committee to draw up a constitution, and a committee on finance to assist the Agent of Presbytery in raising the balance of the thirty thousand dollars not yet pledged. Finally, having voted to elect the Honorable H. G. Davis to be permanent president of the board, with the Reverend F. H. Barron as secretary, and Major W. J. Armstrong as treasurer, the board adjourned to meet at the call of its president. As 1902 ended, the dream of establishing a Presbyterian college in Elkins seemed nearer to becoming a reality than ever before in the eleven years since the Senators' first proposal was presented to the Lexington Presbytery.[11]

The excavation for the foundation of the administration building began in May 1903 on a site known as "Sally Mike Hill" where later in the century Judge Robert E. Maxwell would build his house. The cornerstone was laid by Senator Davis at six o'clock in the evening, August 12, 1903, following an address by the Honorable C. Wood Dailey. In the spring of 1904, the board appointed a committee of its members, chaired by Senator Elkins, to select a president for the college at a salary "not exceeding $2,500 per year." At the same time, the board empowered the building committee to "furnish the college and prepare it for occupancy." The first gift for instructional use, "a Cabinet of Minerals," had already been received. It was from the widow of Jedediah Hotchkiss, of Staunton, Virginia, one of the

---

11. Trustee Minutes, December 4, 1902, p. 5.

The "Old College Building": 1904-26.

ruling elders whom the Lexington Presbytery had appointed in 1892 to the first committee named to seek to raise money for the college.[12]

By the late summer of 1904, shortly after the nomination of former Senator Davis for vice-president of the United States, the trustee committee had selected Joseph E. Hodgson of Keyser, West Virginia, to be the first president of Davis and Elkins College. Prior to appointing him, Senator Elkins's committee had considered at least four other candidates—a Dr. Finley, who was rejected for "lack of administrative ability"; a Colonel Edgar, who was considered to be too old; a Professor John I. Armstrong, who "wanted an arrangement for three years and certain guarantees as to endowment which the trustees could not give"; and a Rev. A. D. Light who had a "lack of business prudence." President Hodgson's salary was fixed at fifteen hundred dollars for the year "with the privilege of residing in the college building free of charge." A native of Virginia and a graduate of Washington and Lee, with some advanced study at the Johns Hopkins University, President Hodgson was responsible for teaching mathematics and physics in addition to his administrative duties. The Reverend Frederick Henry Barron, pastor of the

12. *Ibid.*, March 24, 1904, p. 10.

President Joseph Hodgson and the 1904 D&E football team. *Back row:* President Hodgson, coach; H. Irons, Marstiller, Maxwell, Baker, Ward, and Harwood. *Front row:* Hilliary, Halderman, Crickard, Knote, C. Irons, and Johnson.

Davis Memorial Presbyterian Church and secretary of the board of trustees, was employed part time to teach philosophy and biblical literature. He had been educated at the University of Toronto and had earned a B.S. degree at Knox College Seminary in Canada. The only other faculty members appointed for the first academic year were two alumni of Hampden-Sydney College, the Reverend Malcolm G. Woodworth (B.D., Union Theological Seminary) who offered courses in English and modern languages at a salary of twelve hundred dollars and John Calvin Wolverton who taught Latin, Greek, and history for the princely stipend of eight hundred dollars per year.[13]

Although the financial failure of the construction contractor,

13. *Ibid.,* January 10, 1905, p. 11; S. B. Elkins, Elkins, W.Va., to J. E. Hodgson, Keyser, W.Va., June 30, 1904; S. B. Elkins, Washington, D.C., to Dr. G. W. Finley, Fisherville, Va., April 6, May 22, 31, July 6, 1904; S. B. Elkins, Washington, D.C., to Judge T. P. Jacobs, New Martinsville, W.Va., April 14, 1904; S. B. Elkins, Washington, D.C., to C. W. Dailey, Elkins, W.Va., May 11, 1904. Elkins Papers, Letterbooks Nos. 64 and 65, Davis and Elkins College.

Hobbs and Company, delayed the completion of the college building until early autumn, the receiver was able to have it ready for the opening of the first academic term, September 21, 1904. Three stories high with exterior walls of red brick, foundation and trimmings of West Virginia sandstone, and a red tile roof, the first college building was an impressive edifice. The basement housed the dining hall, kitchen, and gymnasium. The chapel, library, office, president's room, reception room, and some classrooms were provided on the first floor, with additional classrooms, suites for resident professors, and some dormitory and bathrooms on the second floor. The third floor contained most of the student rooms. In all, there were quarters for fifty students. Steam heat and both gas and electric fixtures were features. Rooms were furnished with a single iron bed, dresser and washstand, table, towel rack, and chairs. "Modern" apparatus for heating and lighting were included in each room, but students had "to furnish bedclothing, towels and napkins"—all plainly marked with the student's name.

The calendar for the first academic year provided for three terms beginning respectively, September 21, 1904, January 4, and April 5, 1905, with the session closing on June 13, 1905. Christmas vacation was from December 21 to January 3 and there was a week's vacation between the second and third terms —March 30 to April 5. The first catalog, printed in Elkins by the *Inter-Mountain* early in 1904, stated that students "may enter the College at any time, but it is highly advantageous to enroll near the beginning of the school year." No persons under the age of thirteen were admitted.

The first student to matriculate at D&E was Stuart L. Johnson who was one of the forty-two to enter the Preparatory School. He was still living in 1979 and visited the college during the Diamond Jubilee to receive special recognition on Alumni Day. While in the Preparatory School, he played on the football team (coached by President Hodgson) and won the nickname "Skeeter" because he could run so fast that another player said he was harder to catch than a mosquito. He did not live at the college, but roomed with his brother, the late Herman Johnson who was then editor of the *Inter-Mountain*.[14]

14. Stuart L. Johnson interview with Thomas R. Ross (Elkins), September 24, 1979.

Approximately thirty-five students, freshmen and Preparatory School students, registered for the first term and the number was increased to fifty-two on January 4. Three entered later and the total enrollment for the year in the college included nine freshmen (seven men and two women) and four male special students. Two of the freshmen, Davis and Elkins Read of Cumberland, Maryland, were the twin sons of a railroad attorney employed by the Senators. Davis soon dropped out and Elkins attended only one year during which he played on the first football team.[15] There were forty-two in the Preparatory School (twenty-six boys and sixteen girls). President Hodgson's first report to the board stated frankly that most of the work was preparatory, "very few students being prepared for college work"—a lament relative to freshmen which would often be heard during the next seventy-five years!

When one glances at the curriculum offered the entering class in 1904, it is not difficult to understand that few students might have seemed to be "prepared for college work." The faculty stated that the courses of instruction offered "are those of a well organized college preparatory school and of the freshmen year of the high standard college." After the first year, the college courses were to be expanded to include full work for the sophomore, junior, and senior years. The scope of academic work provided in 1904-1905 may be summarized as follows: three courses in Greek (including reading of the *Anabasis,* Lysias's orations, Homer, Thucydides, and Greek history); four courses in Latin (including reading of Caesar's *Gallic War,* Cicero, Vergil's *Aeneid,* works by Ovid, Sallust and Livy, and Roman history); two courses in French and two in German (including readings in French and German history; five courses in English (including grammar, composition and rhetoric and English and American Literature, and the *Bible* as literature); three courses in history (including English and American history, Ancient, Medieval and Modern European history, and Bible history); five courses in mathematics (from arithmetic to analytic geometry and calculus); a general course in physics; and "elementary" courses in physiology, in philosophy, and in geography.

As could be expected, much emphasis was placed on the fact that D&E was a church-sponsored college. The catalog from the

15. *The Forward,* Spring, 1963.

beginning and for many years thereafter carried on the first page the slogan: "Erected for the Advancement of Christian Education." Likewise the "purpose" included the statement: "Education should be based on the fundamental principles of the Christian religion, and so the Bible shall have place in the curriculum of the College, but no sectarian instruction shall be given. The great aim and object will be to furnish a broad and thorough training in literature and science, under proper religious influence. It is a false conception of education that fosters only the intellectual side; there are the moral, spiritual, and physical sides as well, and a correct system of education must recognize these." In the early years, students were required to attend chapel daily. These services included singing, reading of scripture selections, prayer, and sometimes sermons or talks by faculty members or visitors.

Students were warned that they were "expected to conduct themselves" as gentlemen and ladies at all times, "to conform strictly" to the rules of the college and "by all proper means to promote its best interests." Monthly reports of "the deportment and class standings" of students were sent to parents or guardians.

By late twentieth century standards, the cost of attending Davis and Elkins College was modest in the extreme. Tuition was $50 for the *year* for students in the college and $40 for those in the Preparatory School. Board was $110 for the year, and a room in the college building rented for $36, approximately $1 per week for the academic year. Fees totaled $10 a year and laundry $15. The first catalog statement regarding "Expenses" included the observation that "the liberality of Honorable Henry G. Davis and Senator Stephen B. Elkins makes it possible to offer the best instruction at a merely nominal figure."

It is undoubtedly true that the two senators were of crucial importance in the establishment of the college and did much in their lifetimes to keep it from failing. They and the leaders of the Lexington Presbytery, especially the Reverend A. H. Hamilton, and numerous now forgotten Presbyterians who contributed money and efforts to establish "the College at Elkins" laid the foundation for the developments of later years. Ever to be remembered, however, are the sacrifices of several generations of faculty members and administrative officers who, like the first four mentioned above, faithfully served the college at shamefully low salaries in order that tuition and fees could be kept at a "merely nominal figure."

One can but regret that Senators Davis and Elkins did not heed the advice of C. A. Campbell of Charleston, a Presbyterian educator, who wrote to Senator Davis in 1902 that the Senator ought to provide the proposed college with an endowment of at least "two million dollars."[16] The lack of adequate endowment has been one of the chief obstacles hindering the realization of the original goal of establishing a Presbyterian college in West Virginia "which shall do for the people of that state what Hampden-Sydney, Washington and Lee, and Davidson colleges have done for Virginia and North Carolina." Perhaps by 1904, it was already too late for any college to play the role in West Virginia that those older and wealthier colleges had had in those states. The important fact is that Davis and Elkins College from the beginning has sought to be of service to her students, and through them to the state, the nation, and the world—meeting the perceived needs of each generation to the best of her ability.

16. C. A. Campbell, Charleston, W.Va., to H. G. Davis, Washington, D.C., January 19, 1902. H. G. Davis Papers, West Virginia University Library, Morgantown, W.Va.

II

The Infant Survives: 1905-10

If the goal of founding a college in Elkins which should do for West Virginia what Hampden-Sydney and Washington and Lee had done for Virginia was unrealistic without an adequate endowment, the ideal of offering only a classical curriculum was equally so by the beginning of the twentieth century. As early as the 1880s, the scientific revolution and the growing complexity of American life had given rise to demands for education more broadly based and more clearly articulated to the needs of a new age. This led, even at the oldest and best colleges, as well as in the newly established universities, to the addition of courses in natural sciences and the emerging social sciences to the traditional classical and humanistic studies characteristic of earlier curricula. Also, there was growing acceptance of the practice of allowing students to choose a major field of concentration and to "elect" some courses for their degree programs instead of having all studies rigidly prescribed as "requirements."

It is not possible to determine to what extent the academic program first announced by D&E may have affected early efforts to attract students. A new college in an isolated town in a small state with competition from numerous tax-supported colleges, as well as several already existing church-related institutions, was sure to face serious obstacles to rapid growth. Even so, a total enrollment of only thirteen in D&E's first year was a grave disappointment to the faculty and trustees. By the beginning of 1905, the "Current Expense Fund" was exhausted and even though Senators Davis and Elkins donated four thousand dollars to the fund in January, two of the professors did not receive all of their first year's salary until October of the second year. Senator Elkins had perceived, even before the college had opened in 1904, that the financial support of D&E by the Presbyteries was not going to be what had been anticipated. "The trouble is," he wrote trustee C. W. Dailey,

> the Church leaves a deficit of $7,000 of the $30,000 promised, and takes no part of the burden of maintenance. My understanding when we went into this matter was that the Church would maintain the College as well as contribute one-third of the expense of building and for this reason we have deeded the property to the Presbyterian Church. I wanted the College placed under the aegis or protection of the great Presbyterian Church, thinking it would be maintained and cared for.[1]

The senator's early concern about the failure of the church to support the college adequately proved to be a valid one—not only in the first year but thereafter.

At the spring meeting of the board of trustees in March 1905, after Senator Davis had announced his intention to build a residence for the college president, a committee was appointed to "reorganize the faculty, choose a president, and arrange salaries for one year." Joseph E. Hodgson, apparently discouraged, had decided to give up the presidency, but he was retained as professor of mathematics and French. Professors Woodworth and Wolverton were reappointed, the former to teach English and the latter German and history.

By early summer, the committee had persuaded Frederick H. Barron to accept the office of president in addition to his duties as minister of the Davis Memorial Presbyterian Church, secretary of the board of trustees, and professor of philosophy and biblical literature. The office of Dean of the Faculty was created and Marshall C. Allaben was appointed to be the first dean and to be professor of Latin and Greek. He had earned his B.A. degree at New York University and had served as principal of Allegany County Academy in Maryland for three years prior to coming to D&E.

The catalog for the second year indicates a slight change in the arrangements for freshmen. Two "sections" were provided. "Section A" required both Greek and Latin. "Section B" substituted either German or French for Greek. Anticipating that there

---

1. S. B. Elkins, Washington, D.C., to C. W. Dailey, Elkins, W.Va., May 11, 1904, Elkins Papers, Letterbook No. 65, Davis and Elkins College; Trustee Minutes, September 26, 1905, p. 13.

Dr. Frederick Henry Barron, president, 1905; professor and trustee.

Marshall C. Allaben, first dean and
third president: 1906-10.

would be sophomores, and possibly juniors and seniors by transfer, the faculty announced courses for more classes and arranged "five parallel groups" (or fields of interest) for the last three years of undergraduate study. These were numbered and named as follows: I. Classical, II. Language and Literature, III. Historical-Philosophical, IV. Philosophical-Scientific, V. Exact Science. Courses were specified for each year in each "group," but some provision for "electives" was made in the senior year. The major difference between "groups" was in the amount of language required or in the type and number of courses in science to be completed. Departments were organized and listed for the first time in the 1905-1906 catalog. Among the first created were the departments of Greek and Latin, English, history, mathematics, German, French, philosophy and Bible, geology, political science, biology, physics, and chemistry.

The final aspects of the "reorganization" involved decisions to adopt a two-semester calendar to replace the three terms of the first academic year and to provide that the annual meeting of the trustees should be held on Commencement Day at the college instead of at the call of President Davis in his Washington office.

If disappointment in an enrollment of thirteen students in the first year had been a factor in bringing about reorganization of the faculty, curriculum, and calendar, the registration figures in September 1905 must have been profoundly shocking to all concerned. There were four freshmen and two special students, but no sophomores, no juniors, and no seniors! None of those who had been in the 1904-1905 Preparatory School had entered the college. The four freshmen had been freshmen in the preceding year (Abbie and Harry Irons of Elkins and George and John Knote of Wheeling). One of the special students of the preceding year did return—Joseph Zaidan of Sidon, Syria, D&E's first foreign student. The only new student in the college was Rogers Oliver of Atlantic Highlands, New Jersey—the first student from a state from which hundreds would come in later years.

With an enrollment of six students and a faculty of five, D&E College must have had the best student-faculty ratio of any college in the nation. With a tuition of fifty dollars per student per year, it must have had the smallest income! Surely this would have meant disaster had it not been for the facts that fifty pupils enrolled in the Preparatory School and that the Senators Davis and Elkins were willing to "tap their barrels" again to provide the funds needed to balance the budget.

Needless to say, the second year was discouraging. Most of the faculty's time and energy had to be devoted to the adolescents in the Preparatory School, many of whom were only thirteen to fifteen years of age. Since the six college students were at the freshmen level, there was no opportunity for a professor to offer an advanced course in his special field of interest. On February 1, 1906, F. H. Barron resigned as president of the college, and the board named Dean M. C. Allaben to be the third president. At the same time, the board voted to abandon coeducation and to "maintain the College after June 30, 1906, for males only."[2] No

2. *Ibid.*, p. 14.

reason for this action was recorded. One can surmise that the board had concluded that public prejudice against coeducation might be a factor which accounted for the low enrollment. In that era, of course, none of the great Ivy League colleges and none of the three Presbyterian colleges, which the founders of D&E revered as models, was coeducational.

At the end of the academic year, Professors Hodgson, Woodworth, and Wolverton resigned. Thus, when the third year opened, none of the original faculty remained except Professor Barron who retained his professorship of philosophy and Bible after relinquishing the presidency. Among the four men who joined the faculty in the fall of 1906 was James E. Allen, professor of the French and German languages and literature, a man destined to play a key role in the history of Davis and Elkins College for nearly three decades thereafter. An alumnus of Hampden-Sydney College, he had pursued graduate studies at both the University of Virginia and the Johns Hopkins University and had served as a high school instructor and principal for eight years before coming to D&E. Other new faculty members included Henry A. Converse, also an alumnus of Hampden-Sydney, who had earned a Ph.D. at the Johns Hopkins University and was the first D&E professor to hold a doctorate. He was named dean of the faculty, succeeding President Allaben, and professor of mathematics and physics. Waldo H. Dunn, a graduate of Yale and author of *The Vanished Empire: A Tale of the Mound Builders,* replaced M. G. Woodworth as professor of English language and literature and served as the first secretary of the faculty. The first director of athletics, William R. Redden, an alumnus of the Bates College, completed the faculty list, he being also professor of natural science. President Allaben taught Greek and Latin and political science and Professor Allen offered Spanish as well as French and German.

During 1906, construction of the president's house was completed. A gift of Senator Davis, this twelve-room residence cost ten thousand dollars and was an adaptation of the Old English style of architecture. Located below the college hill, well back from the river near the junction of Barron Avenue and Eleventh Street, the house was still standing in 1979.

The catalog for 1906-1907 indicates an effort to broaden the curriculum by the addition of courses in most departments. For example, two courses in psychology were added to the offerings

The "President's House."

in the Department of Philosophy, and a course in sociology was included in the Political Science Department. There were two new courses in history (though no one was listed to replace Professor Wolverton to teach in that department). Eight courses were announced in biology, instead of the one previously available. Geography and paleontology courses appeared in the Geology Department, and the chemistry offerings were enlarged from three to twelve courses. Additional evidence of a desire to present a curriculum designed to appeal to students with special interests is to be found in the creation of two new "Groups" entitled "Natural Science" and "Medical Preparatory." Also, courses in mechanical drawing and physical education were taught for the first time.

Perhaps of more interest to prospective students than these changes in the academic program, were the announcements regarding plans to develop "extra-curricular" activities. These included a debating and literary society known as "The Olympian Council," a glee club, banjo and mandolin clubs, and the publication of a college paper, *The Acta*, in the early years a six-page weekly. Probably of even greater significance was the fact that the athletic field was nearing completion and was described as soon to "have a quarter-mile cinder track" and ample space for football, baseball, and general athletics. In addition, there were two "full regulation size" lawn tennis courts. A college athletic association had been organized and a director of athletics appointed. "Exhibitions and Contests" were promised "at various times throughout the year."

There had been a few football games in 1904 and 1905 with the Elkins "All-Stars" and teams from Clarksburg, Fairmont, and Grafton high schools as well as with Alderson-Broaddus and Bethany colleges and the West Virginia University freshmen. In 1906, D&E opened the season with a 22 to 0 victory over Philippi High School—despite the use of high school teachers on the Philippi team. That year President Allaben coached the D&E squad. They defeated Potomac State 13 to 6, but lost to the WVU Reserves twice and to Wesleyan. Allaben served as coach again in 1907, but if the reports of what happened to D&E at Grafton and Buckhannon that season are accurate, it was a rather hazardous job. During a game with the Grafton Mechanical School, President Allaben was assaulted by a spectator and was the "recipient of many fierce blows and kicks from the mob." The D&E players rushed to his aid and "finally managed to extricate him from the crowd of ruffians." Finally, the D&E contingent "left the field under police protection" and the game ended in a scoreless tie.

A few days later, D&E defeated Wesleyan 8 to 0 on the Buckhannon field, but that game also ended in trouble. In fact, even before the game started, someone in the crowd was heard to say that he would "kill any D&E player who scored a touchdown." After D&E blocked a punt and scored a safety, Bill Gross caught a pass and made a touchdown as the time was running out. Bill had heard the threats and had reason to believe them as someone kicked or knocked his eyebrow off just before the game ended. Eugene Arnold rushed Bill to a doctor's office where thirteen stitches were required to patch up his forehead. Meanwhile, the referee, an Elkins school principal, was chased from the field and ran all the way to the first railroad station east of Buckhannon where he jumped aboard a train and escaped. President Allaben was attacked by "rowdies, chased through a swamp and out-of-town."[3]

D&E lost only one game that season, being defeated by a Charleston team. Victories included a 17 to 0 game with

---

3. Kent Kessler, *Hail West Virginians!* (Parkersburg, 1959), pp. 251-52; C. A. ("Bill") Gross's interview with Thomas R. Ross, Elkins, W.Va., August 27, 1979.

Alderson-Broaddus (in which Bill Gross scored all the points) and a 40 to 0 win over Allegheny Academy. A writer in *The Acta* in the spring of 1908 boasted that the football team ranked "second only to West Virginia in the state. The decisive defeat which we administered to Wesleyan College was a triumph that will long be remembered. Our eleven was scored on by only one team in the whole season." Since the total enrollment of D&E College was eight, it is obvious that there were some rather husky "boys" in the Preparatory School who played football for the college. To recruit a winning team of *eleven* from a student body of eight, would have been a remarkable feat, even for Presbyterians.

The next season, Wesleyan canceled its game with D&E, "afraid of losing," the Elkins fans suggested. Perhaps so, as D&E had defeated her other opponents except for a 6 to 4 loss to Fairmont Normal. In 1910, no opponent crossed D&E's goal line, though Marshall College won a 6 to 3 victory by kicking two field goals. Wesleyan canceled out again, prompting one writer to remark: "All we can say about Wesleyan is that she's got Yellow Fever."[4] Commenting on the Wesleyan forfeiture, the editor of *The Acta* for November 21, observed that "the students and friends of the College were much disappointed when it was learned that the game would not be played. The College Y.M.C.A. had planned a reception for the Wesleyan boys and every means was being made to wipe out the old unfriendly feeling existing between the two schools. . . . It seems that the only way for the two schools to exist in peace is to cease all relations."

"School Spirit" was generally good throughout this period, even though there were few students in the college. In September 1906, the enrollment dropped from fifty to forty-one in the Preparatory School, apparently the result of the decision not to admit girls. *The Acta* for November 1906, lamented "How the co-eds are missed! Would they not feel vain did they know the longings of the lonesome." There was a slight increase in the number registering for college. Harry S. Irons had become a sophomore. There were six freshmen, including C. A. ("Bill") Gross, who was elected manager of the baseball team. Still living in 1979, he has always been a generous friend of the college. There were also three special students. Of these ten, only three (Harry and Robert Irons and Cleon Raese) were from West Virginia. In-

---

4. Quoted in Kessler, *op. cit.*, p. 252.

asmuch as the total enrollment in both the Preparatory School and college was only fifty-one, one of whom died during the year, the financial condition was unimproved and again Senators Davis and Elkins "kindly paid the deficit, thus making their gifts for the present year the magnificent sum of $8,186.44." Senator Elkins also gave the library "a sizeable collection of books."[5] There was little change in the general situation in the years from 1907 to 1910. Enrollment in the college dropped to eight in 1907-1908, rose to fifteen the next fall and reached a high of eighteen in 1909-10. That of the Preparatory School (or Sub-Freshmen Department as it was designated in 1908) had declined to only thirty-one boys by 1909-10. Tuition was reduced from $50 to $40 per year in 1909. During the period 1904-10, room rent was lowered from $36 to $25 and board charges from $110 to $108 per year.

In this era, there was some "turnover" in faculty, but Allaben, Barron and Allen provided some stability and continuity. Walter Nicholson came in 1908, being notable as the first to hold the rank of "instructor," but he remained only one year. Dr. John A. Arbuckle, another of the seemingly endless line of Hampden-Sydney alumni associated with D&E, was the first M.D. to teach at this college, serving two years as professor of natural sciences. Also, appointed in 1908 was Roy B. Hunter, a graduate of Yale, who served for four years as professor of mathematics and physics. The following year, John McKenzie (A.B., University of Toronto; and B.D., Yale), who would later become dean of the faculty, came to the college as professor of English, as did Minor C. Hubbell, professor of the French and German languages and literature, a graduate of Ohio Wesleyan.

In January 1908, A. H. Hamilton reported to the board of trustees, that the Lexington and Winchester presbyteries were more than $7,600 "short of the $30,000 pledged by them to the Building Fund." Thereupon, Senators Davis and Elkins gave the college $5,000—over and above their original pledge—to be applied to the amount due the fund by the Presbyteries. At the same time, the board adopted a resolution approving the efforts of the Presbyteries to secure the cooperation of the Synod of West Virginia of the Presbyterian Church in the United States of America (the "Northern" Church) in "the control, support, and

---

5. Trustee Minutes, September 14, 1907, p. 15; *The Acta,* February 17, 1906, p. 3.

conduct of the college."⁶ Subsequently, in June the board appointed Senator Elkins, President Allaben, and Professor Barron to meet with a committee from that Synod to work out a plan for the consideration of the board and of the Presbyteries of Lexington and Winchester. By February 1909, what was known as the "Plan of Cooperation for The Davis and Elkins College" had been agreed to by all the parties concerned. This plan provided that "the said college in all its interests shall be under the joint care and control of the Presbyteries of Lexington and Winchester of the Presbyterian Church in the U.S., and of the Presbyteries of Greenbrier and Kanawha of the same church, if at any time they agree to join in such care and control; and the Synod of West Virginia of the Presbyterian Church in the U.S.A." Provision was made to reorganize the board of trustees, enlarging it to eighteen members, nine nominated by the Presbyteries of the "Southern Church" and nine by the Synod of the West Virginia of the "Northern Church." It was stipulated that the new board "shall conduct the said College, under the rules and regulations in force at the time this agreement is adopted, subject to amendment by the Board, provided that the purpose for which the college was founded, viz: 'to teach the higher branches of learning usually taught in colleges' and to maintain a 'high moral and Christian standard,' shall not be changed."

In return for receiving a share of the buildings, grounds, and assets of the college, the Synod of West Virginia of the Presbyterian Church in the U.S.A. promised to urge "its churches and people to throw their patronage to said college" and to do everything possible to "build up the institution and make it a college worthy of the Presbyterians of West Virginia," giving it financial support "in all practical ways."⁷

The adoption of this Plan of Cooperation seventy years ago was a significant milestone in the history of the college. It meant that D&E, unlike most of the numerous other Presbyterian colleges in the nation, would derive support from both of the major branches of the Presbyterian denomination. For several years after 1909, the "College Board" of the Presbyterian Church of the U.S.A. contributed annually sums ranging from $750 to $2,000 to the current expense funds of D&E. The first trustees

---

6. *Ibid.*, January 28, 1908, p. 16.
7. *Ibid.*, January 28, 1908; June 30, 1908; February 3, 1909, pp. 16-24.

from the Synod of West Virginia of the "Northern Church" included George Baird of Wheeling, W. G. Brown of Kingwood, Bernard L. Butcher of Fairmont, the Reverend John W. Francis of Parkersburg, Robert Hazlett of Wheeling, Professor Thomas E. Hodges of Morgantown, the Reverend Herman Stoetzer of Fairmont, and the Reverend John M. Waddell of Charleston.

In the summer of 1909, the college offered summer school classes for the first time. The suggestion for this innovation seems to have come from Professor James E. Allen and the attendance was such that the board commended him for his successful direction of this project. The following summer, ninety-two students registered for summer courses and the Summer School has continued as a means of supplementing the income of the college, making greater use of the facilities, and enlarging the opportunities for serving the needs of the community.

In October 1909, President Allaben recommended that coeducation be resumed at the college. Action was postponed on this matter, but later in the year, the board agreed to permit young women to attend classes beginning in February 1910. Also, the board voted in 1909 to instruct its Constitution Committee to make provision in the by-laws for the development of "student government at the college." Doubtless this was done on the initiative of President Allaben, who had said at the outset of his administration that the future of the college "is largely in the hands of the student body," who, he hoped, would demonstrate in their mature lives "just what things Davis and Elkins College will stand for in the years to come." The president had indicated that "we have no desire to become the greatest institution in the country, measured by the number of students, but we do wish to be great when measured by the men we send out."[8]

The first two of those "we send out" were graduated on June 9, 1910. After delivering the valedictory address, Robert Sydney Irons of Elkins received the first Bachelor of Arts degree granted by D&E. The salutatorian of the first graduating class, Allison Cochran Brooks, of Philadelphia, was then awarded the Bachelor of Science degree. These two constituted the whole membership of the "Class of 1910."

In some respects, the year of 1910 marked the end of an era of infancy and instability in the early history of the college. By then,

---

8. *The Acta,* November 1906, p. 1.

the Plan of Cooperation had been implemented, the "two-year sub-freshmen course" had been substituted for the Preparatory School, the academic departments had been established, the annual deficit had been reduced to less than five hundred dollars (which Senator Davis continued to pay), and the first commencement ceremony for graduating seniors was held. Also in that year, the third president of the college, Marshall C. Allaben, having served four years, decided to resign to resume graduate study. In accepting his resignation, the board of trustees expressed "very sincere thanks" and "high appreciation for the services that he had rendered" during his five years as dean of the faculty and president of the college. The board stated that "it is not too much to say that whatever progress and development the college has made up to this time, must be linked with President Allaben's name."[9]

The committee to select a new president reported on February 15, 1910, that it wished to nominate "Professor James E. Allen, for three years one of the most faithful and efficient Professors of the College," to be the fourth president, effective July 1, 1910. At the time of his appointment, Professor Allen was serving as principal of the Nicholson School in Richmond, Virginia, after having been professor of French and German at the college from 1906 to 1909. His decision to return to Elkins was to prove to be of great significance and led to a presidency lasting a quarter of a century—the longest in the history of the college.

9. Trustee Minutes, February 15, 1910, p. 27.

Dr. James E. Allen, president, 1910-35.

III

Growing Pains on Sally Mike Hill: 1910-20

It was Sir Winston Churchill who wrote: "No one can understand history without continually relating the long periods which are constantly mentioned to the experiences of our own short lives. Five years is a lot. Twenty years is the horizon to most people. Fifty years is antiquity."[1] In the life of Davis and Elkins College, the twenty-five years of the presidency of James E. Allen, 1910-35, were in 1979 beyond "the horizon" to most people reading this history—indeed they almost qualify as "antiquity." Those who remember the days when the campus was above the river in South Elkins and the college building was on Sally Mike Hill refer to it as the "Old College" and to that period as the "era of the first President Allen."

Shortly after his appointment as fourth president of the college, James E. Allen was described by the Elkins *Inter-Mountain* as "one of those finer types of men whose services to the higher ideals of Christian Education and sympathetic helpfulness towards these ideals are ever being sought by prominent institutions of learning throughout this great and broad country." Devoutly religious and classically educated, President Allen was also an administrator with a saving sense of humor and a sensitive understanding of human nature. The 1919 *Phoenix*, an annual that year, was dedicated to him by the editors as follows: "To the gentleman of lofty ideals; a man of strong character; a fine scholar, cultured and broad-minded; a tireless worker." His former students, living in 1979, remembered him as a "great Virginia gentleman," a "real scholar," and an "excellent

1. Winston Churchill, *The Birth of Britain* (New York, 1958), p. 47.

teacher." At least one recounted with something akin to awe that "Dr. Allen once gave his own son an 'F' in a Latin course." Physically not a large man, the young president was somewhat thin in the face and body and was endowed with rather prominent ears. Thus, the graduating seniors in 1913 remembered him in their "Class Will" in this somewhat humorous clause: "We give and bequeath to President Allen a pair of elephant ear muffs."[2]

During the first year of the Allen presidency, Senator Stephen Benton Elkins died on January 5, 1911. His efforts in founding the college, his active service on the board of trustees, and his continued willingness to assist the college financially each year doubtless gave rise to expectations that he would provide generously for the college in his will. That he did not do so is revealed poignantly in the request formulated by the board of trustees on March 9, 1911, begging the members of the Elkins family "to remember this College which he has helped to bring to its present condition of usefulness and to carry out his plans for its perpetuation and growth. May we not ask you as the heirs of his noble estate, to apply to this worthy object such a sum as will, in connection with Mr. Davis's gift, place the College upon a surer foundation and thus make it a memorial to their names to which coming generations may point with pride and recognize in it a source of untold blessing to themselves and to the state in which it stands." Specifically, the board asked the Elkins family "to make permanent Mr. Elkins' contribution of two thousand dollars a year" and to establish an endowment sufficient "to lift the College to its proper place among the great Colleges of the land."[3] This petition fell on deaf ears so far as an endowment is concerned, and although Mrs. Stephen B. Elkins continued to give annual support and later donated Halliehurst Hall and the surrounding land to the college, no "sufficient endowment" was forthcoming. In June, Davis Elkins, the senator's eldest son was elected to fill his father's term on the board of trustees. He had been chosen to succeed his father in the Senate a few months earlier. By coincidence, the topic for debate at the April meeting of the Olympian Council was "resolved, that United States Senators should be elected by direct vote of the people."[4]

   2. *The Acta* (Commencement No. 1913), p. 9; W. R. Cromwell, Jr., interview with Thomas R. Ross, Elkins, (May, 1979).
   3. Trustee Minutes, March 9, 1911, p. 34.
   4. *The Acta*, April 3, 1911, p. 1.

On a lighter note, the beginning of the Allen era was recalled by one old-timer for a different reason:

> One fair morning in the spring of 1911, students trudging their weary way up the College path looked up to the top of the hill for the flag on the flagpole, as always. But that day they saw a three-cornered diaper! A son, Jimmy Allen, had been born to the President's family. Weariness disappeared; up the hill they scampered, formed a company, and declared a holiday.
>
> Word soon spread to the high school, at that time held in the First Ward School building. Papers, books, lunches were stacked. The high school students, too, declared a holiday, formed a group, marched up the railroad track over the bridge, down the College path, up to the Campus, and there united with the College company to give the little new prexy a rousing welcome and the parents cheers and songs. The celebration lasted all day and some say students carried the festivities on into the night. Who knows?[5]

Commencement in 1911 saw the graduation of the second senior class. As in the previous year, there were only two graduates. Eugene Hill Arnold of Elkins received the B.A. degree and Cleon W. Raese of Davis was awarded the B.S. degree. The enrollment for the year had been somewhat encouraging, there being twenty-two regular students and five special students in the college as well as thirty-nine "Sub-Freshmen" and eleven in the "Commercial Department." The latter department first had been organized to meet the needs of "those whose time does not permit them to take either a high school or collegiate course." Anticipation of an increase in enrollment for the subsequent year was one reason for changes made in the organization of the college by the fall of 1911.

Among the changes to be noted was the board's action to release President Allen from teaching duties for a time in order to "give him an opportunity to travel in the interest of the college." At D&E, as elsewhere, the money-raising and public relations aspects of the college president's role had begun to become paramount. Professor John McKenzie was elected dean by the board, and four additional faculty members were authorized. One of these, Jesse H. Riddle, was to be the first college librarian in addition to teaching commercial subjects and history. The registrar,

---

5. Charles E. Albert, "It happened at Davis and Elkins College," *The Davis and Elkins Historical Magazine,* March, 1949, p. 12.

Abbie S. Irons, was assigned to teach stenography as well as to continue her duties as secretary to the president. Although Miss Irons did not teach degree candidates, she and Fannie B. Derr, appointed instructor in elocution and oratory in 1911, were the first women members of the faculty. The most significant new appointment in 1911, however, was that of Charles E. Albert, an alumnus of Lafayette College, to teach engineering. This initiated a relationship which, with the exception of two brief intervals during which he was employed elsewhere, lasted more than half a century. He came to establish the new Department of Civil Engineering in which he offered courses in mechanical drawing, surveying, railroad surveying, descriptive geometry, and machine drawing.

In that year too, the Commercial Department was separated from the college and the Preparatory School (as the latter was again named). This department had its own "principal," Professor Harry W. French, and offered diplomas, rather than degrees, to those completing nine months of study in either "The Shorthand Course," "The Bookkeeping Course," or "The Combined Course." Training in shorthand, typewriting, punctuation, office practice, bookkeeping commercial arithmetic, penmanship business law, English and spelling was offered. The catalog emphasized that "students will not be graduated from the department whose spelling is bad."

Aside from adding these above-described vocational programs, the faculty simplified degree requirements, abolished the "A" and "B" freshmen sections, abandoned the "Parallel Group System" established in 1905 for the upperclass curricula, and sharply reduced the course offerings in the departments. Candidates for both the Bachelor of Arts and the Bachelor of Science degrees were required to complete three years of Bible, two years of English, one year of history, one year of mathematics, one year of physics, and two years of language (Latin for the B.A., French or German for the B.S.). B.A. candidates also had to have either two courses of Greek or two of French or German, a third year of English, two years of philosophy, and a year of political science. B.S. students had to have at least one additional year of mathematics, and several courses in science. Both degrees required a senior thesis, "neatly typewritten," on a subject approved by the faculty.

In this period, faculty committees were organized, the first listing being in the catalog for 1911-12. Appointed by President Allen, the initial committees were entitled "Committee on Studies and General Regulations," "Committee on the Dormitory," "Committee on Entertainment," and "Committee on Athletics." Soon a "Committee on Religious Work" was created. Thereafter, and down even unto the present day, committee work has required the attention of the faculty and has been a significant factor in the development and implementation of the policies and programs of the college.

Even before the creation of the Athletic Committee, the faculty had formulated a statement of policy regarding the purpose of an athletic program. The 1908 catalog stated that "all athletic enterprises are under the direct control of the Faculty, such sports are encouraged as will contribute most to the welfare of the student body in general, and all tendencies to commercialism or professionalism in athletics are checked in their very inception. In other words, this department is maintained solely for the purpose of providing suitable means for the proper development of the human body, and not to place a premium upon physical powers or to 'advertise' the College."

The Faculty Minutes for October 13, 1909, record the adoption of "Athletic Eligibility Rules" which required that any student representing the college in any intercollegiate game must be "taking a full schedule of work." Furthermore, these first "Eligibility Rules" included the statement that "No student shall represent the College in any intercollegiate game or contest who has at any time received, either directly or indirectly, money, or any other consideration, to play on any team . . . or any money or financial concession, or emolument as past or present compensation for, or as prior consideration or inducement to play in, or enter any athletic contest, whether the said remuneration be received from, or paid by, or at the instance of any organization, committee, or Faculty . . . or any individual whatever."[6]

Later, on December 13, 1909, the faculty voted to instruct the president of the college to apply for associate membership in the Intercollegiate Athletic Association of the United States because of belief "that the athletic activities in our schools and colleges should be maintained on an ethical plan in keeping with the dignity and high purpose of education."[7]

6. Faculty Minutes, October 13, 1909, p. 30.
7. *Ibid.*, December 13, 1909, p. 37.

Enrollment in the college having risen to thirty-seven by the fall of 1911, it was possible for D&E to begin to participate in athletic competition on more of an intercollegiate basis. From the first years of her existence, D&E's teams had included both college and preparatory school students. Athletic contests had usually involved games with high schools, prep schools, and occasionally with the freshmen or "reserve" teams of West Virginia University or other teams of nearby colleges such as Alderson-Broaddus, Fairmont Normal, and West Virginia Wesleyan. College yells and songs were composed or "borrowed" and used at games and pep rallies. "The College song of 1911, which was sung to the tune of an old church hymn sometimes called the Cornell song, seemed to arouse a loyalty and love for the school, its environs, its friendship of students and Faculty, that could hardly be surpassed anywhere. It suited the spirit of the time." The words were as follows:

> Standing on a lofty summit,
>   'Bove the river's wave,
> See our dear old Alma Mater,
>   Like a watchman brave.
>
> Chorus:
>
> Swell the chorus, every loyal one,
>   True and truer be.
> Hail her walls and towers are lifted,
>   Piercing toward the blue,
> While the future beckons onward,
>   Fairer than our view.[8]

In the beginning, sports were coached by students or occasionally by an interested faculty member such as President Allaben or by an Elkins citizen. In 1910-11, the catalog indicates that Cleon W. Raese, a senior, coached both football and basketball and that Sidney R. Gould, a freshman, coached baseball. The next year John F. Brown, a young lawyer and later a judge, coached football; H. P. Mullennex, a freshman (who later would become a faculty member and director of athletics for a brief period, and much later would be president of the board of trustees), helped Robert P. Strickler, professor of Latin and

---

8. Albert, *loc. cit.*, p. 11.

English, coach basketball. Strickler had been "one of the best basketball players ever developed at the University of West Virginia" and did much to get basketball started in a major way at D&E.[9]

Football was long the major sport at D&E and the tradition of having a "winning team" was established in the early teens under such coaches as Edward E. Tarr, professor of history and director of athletics, and his successor, Harnus P. Mullennex, instructor in English and mathematics and athletic coach. Virtually all of the schools with which the D&E teams competed had much larger student enrollments, as articles in *The Acta* repeatedly emphasized. West Virginia Wesleyan, a Methodist institution at Buckhannon only thirty miles away, early became the "traditional rival." Competitors in athletics, in addition to those mentioned, included Glenville Normal, Bethany, Marshall, Salem, Shepherd, West Virginia University, and sometimes such out-of-state colleges as Gettysburg, Muskingum, and Waynesburg.

By the mid-teens, basketball began to rival football in popularity in the view of many fans. In 1916, the D&E basketball team, coached by H. P. Mullennex and starring such Elkins athletes as David Barry, Richard Hamill, Harry E. Whetsell, and Frank C. Wimer, won second place in the state. The next year, the same coach, with a team which included Frank Wimer as captain, Paul Cutright as manager, Harry Whetsell, Walter Hoyt, Paul ("Biz") Dawson, Leon A. Willison, and David Barry, claimed the state championship for D&E—the first honor of this type won for the college. They won fifteen out of sixteen games and, as one writer put it, "as for the team itself, it is easily the best that ever wore the 'maroon and white' . . . varsity forwards, Wimer and Cutright, performed in a manner scarcely excelled. . . . Whetsell and Dawson, at guards, are a combination seldom equalled."[10] It is interesting to note that after service in World War I, both Richard Hamill and Harry E. Whetsell became members of the D&E faculty—Hamill for only a brief period, but Whetsell served the college with distinction in various capacities for more than twenty years. He and Frank C. Wimer, who later was to become a

9. *The Acta*, November 6, 1911, p. 5.
10. *The Phoenix* (Easter Number, 1917), p. 23; Frank C. Wimer interview with Thomas R. Ross, Elkins, August 2, 1979.

Victory banquet for the 1917 D&E basketball team, the West Virginia Champions. Arrow No. 1 is Harris Jones, 2 is Lee Crouch, 3 is Governor Herman Guy Kump, 4 is Robert Jones, 5 is Dr. James E. Allen, Sr., president. *Seated,* third from right is Frank Wimer; second, Harry Whetsell; at front table on left is Eugene Daetwyler.

famous coach at Elkins High School and would be named to the West Virginia Hall of Fame for Athletes, still lived in Elkins in 1979 and were long loyal supporters of D&E.

The first women's basketball team was organized in 1914, but it did not "appear publicly" until the 1916 season and then lost every game but one. Win or lose, however, the student body, though small in number, gave enthusiastic support to the various teams. One of the college songs popular in the teens included these lines of verse:

"You may sing of Yale and Harvard, of Princeton and of Brown.
You may tell of all their victories, their glory and renown.
You may sing of all their triumphs, and triumphs they may be.
But for us there's just one College, and that one is D&E."

In this period, too, students began to participate in drama and music to a greater extent than had been possible earlier. The "College Quartette" became quite well known and those with musical and dramatic interests occasionally joined forces to present operettas. Intercollegiate debate had been a significant activity for several years and R. Emmett O'Connor and Jesse H. Riddle had won the state meet for D&E as early as 1911. Although the trustees had voted in 1909 to provide for the formation of student government, the first listing of officers appears in the College Directory of 1911-12 when Samuel W. Scott was president of the student body, Sidney R. Gould, vice-president, and Leta Wimer, secretary.

The college returned to a three-term calendar in 1911-12 and also began to publish a more extensive catalog which included information concerning scholarships, student loan funds, prizes, donations, and a more detailed description of the standards and rules of the college. Among the latter mentioned were such statements as: "The college is free from fad courses." "The bookish side of college is intensified." "The college *will not admit students in the hope of reforming them.*" "The one thing we insist upon above all things else is honesty." "Fire arms shall not be kept in the dormitory at any time."

Some trustees were alarmed in the spring of 1912 to learn that Professors French and Strickler were not members of any church. Though no formal action was taken, the Executive Committee of the board advised President Allen that it was "the opinion of this Committee that the College should not employ in its faculty men or women who are not members of some Evangelical church." Both men were reappointed regardless of their lack of church affiliation.[11]

In 1912, the college began to develop a "lecture series" and to bring visiting lecturers and entertainers to the campus for purposes similar to those of the "Impact" program of the late 1970s. Among the topics listed were "An illustrated lecture on Sir Walter Scott," "Sex Hygiene," "Child Study," "George Washington," "What does College Education Mean?" and "The Birds of West Virginia."

In view of the increase in the activities sponsored by the college early in the decade of the teens, it is fortunate that the

---

11. Trustee Executive Committee Minutes, March 15, 1912, p. 11.

budget figures for 1911-12 have survived the ravages of time. Some of the items may be of interest to later generations accustomed to thinking in terms of millions of dollars annually in income and expenditures. The total income was $12,725.50 of which Senator Davis contributed $4,500.00, the Elkins heirs $2,000.00, the Presbyterian College Board $1,500.00, and the Synod of West Virginia $500.00. Tuition receipts were $2,400.00, room rentals and various fees brought in $800.00 and $625.50 respectively. Expenditures for salaries for the president and faculty totaled $8,185.00. The young lady who served as the secretary to the president and as registrar and instructor in stenography was paid $480.00 per year and the janitor's annual wages were $425.00. No provision was made for "Athletic Grants," "Travel," "Student Government," "Lectures" and "Concerts," or any of the numerous activities now found in the budget for "Student Affairs."

The financial situation of the college was apparently of increasing concern to the trustees after the death of Senator Elkins and in view of the advanced age of Senator Davis. It is obvious that from the beginning, the gifts of Senators Davis and Elkins had enabled the college to survive. The budget for 1911-12, as shown above, indicates that more than one-third of the income for that year was donated by Senator Davis. What would become of the college when he was gone? He asserted in a letter to the secretary of the Presbyterian College Board that he did not intend to "provide by will" more than $100,000 "as an endowment for the College."[12]

In the summer of 1912, the senator had informed the trustees of his intention to bequeath $100,000.00 to the college endowment fund. A few months thereafter, he announced that he would also give "an amount equal to that which the board may be able to raise from other sources, up to $50,000.00." The trustees immediately sought the aid of the College Board of the Presbyterian Church, U.S.A., in developing plans to secure the funds needed. Also a letter to Mrs. Elkins, signed by all the trustees, was presented to her urging that she contribute liberally to this effort and concluding that "we feel that it will be a hopeless task to try to secure the needed $50,000.00 unless you

---

12. H. G. Davis, Washington, D.C., to Robert McKenzie, New York, February 20, 1912; Trustee Minutes, June 11, 1912, pp. 40-41.

can see your way clear to head the list of donors." The Reverend W. A. Cook of Wheeling was appointed as "Field Representative" to solicit "matching funds" but after more than two years of work, he could report pledges totaling only $24,991.92. Of that amount $5,000.00 had been pledged by Senator Davis himself! Elkins citizens pledged $4,117.09; the Presbyterian College Board, $5,000.00, and the rest by the six supporting Presbyteries.[13] The goal was never achieved.

Meanwhile, in November 1911, realizing the need for the most effective effort to conserve and manage the finances of the college, the trustees appointed N. I. Hall, a prominent Elkins banker, as the "Official Treasurer" of the board and directed the Executive Committee to "arrange for the auditing of the books . . . and to institute a good system of bookkeeping." At the same time a "Permanent Loan Fund Committee" was created and the first "Constitution and By-laws of the Board of Trustees of Davis and Elkins College" were adopted. This constitution provided that the board must "exercise exclusive control . . . of any unusual expenditure in excess of $500.00" and reserved to the board the power to elect not only the president of the college but also "a Librarian, a Registrar and a Dean." The librarian was required to report to the board at every stated meeting and the registrar's duties included the collection of "all fees and fines from students." She was to keep "a correct account of all receipts and expenditures and make a monthly report to the Executive Committee."[14]

The first constitution is of interest in other respects besides its provision for financial control. It specified that neither the president of the college nor any professor could resign without having given "at least three months notice" and that resignation "shall take effect only at the close of the scholastic year." Each professor was to teach in "the department in which he was elected to teach" and "at the end of each scholastic year shall present to the board through the president of the college a written report on the progress of the students in his department, the subjects and books studied, the results of examinations . . . and any sugges-

---

13. Trustee Executive Committee Minutes, April 5, 1912; Trustee Minutes, June 8, 1915, p. 47.
14. Trustee Minutes, November 14, 1911-June 8, 1915, *passim*. In 1907, Mr. Hall had first been elected treasurer, but his responsibilities and duties seem to have been increased in 1911.

tions he may care to make for the improvement of his department." The faculty was made responsible for the issue each year of a catalog and for arranging for commencement and was authorized to adopt such rules and measures "as they may deem proper" to achieve the purposes of the college. These "laws so adopted by the Faculty and not in conflict with these By-Laws or with the laws of the state shall have all the force and effect of laws of the College." The dean of the college was given "such duties as are usually assigned to that office" and was to act as president in the absence of that officer. The constitution provided that the president should be chairman of the faculty, should conduct instruction in such department as the board might assign him, be "bound to promote and maintain by every means in his power" the interest and reputation of the college, and "provide for the students daily devotional exercises and systematic instruction in the Bible." Of course, at each "stated meeting" of the board, the president was to "make a report on the administration and condition of the institution" including suggestions that "he may deem wise for the improvement and prosperity of the college." It is obvious that in many respects, the board's treasurer and its Executive Committee (which was composed of five trustees who met monthly)—and sometimes the whole board—dealt with matters and performed functions which properly belonged to and which later became the responsibilities of the college administrative officers or of faculty committees. This early inclination of the board to get involved in administrative details became a habit which occasionally resulted in unfortunate consequences and was a source of irritation to President Allen and his immediate successors, as well as to many faculty members. That President Allen allowed this to develop was undoubtedly his greatest error and his chief weakness as an academic administrator. Perhaps it is understandable in view of his relative youth and inexperience when he assumed the presidency and of the fact that the early boards were dominated by older men of great wealth and men accustomed to exercise power, but who lacked an understanding of the nature of collegiality.

An unusual characteristic of the D&E Board of Trustees in these early years was the prominence of politicians among its membership. Former Senator H. G. Davis, of course, was the "permanent president" of the board from its organization in 1902 until his death in 1916. Likewise, Senator S. B. Elkins was from the beginning until his death a leading member and he was succeeded both on the board and in the United States Senate by his son, Davis, in 1911. In addition, Congressman Howard Sutherland of Elkins served as chairman of the board's Executive Committee for several years and then, after the death of H. G. Davis, as president of the board, continuing after his own service in the United States Senate began in 1917. In the academic year 1912-13, it is interesting to note that of the eighteen members of the board, one was a United States Senator, one a former United States Senator, and one a future United States Senator. Two were congressmen (Sutherland of Elkins and William G. Brown, Jr., of Kingwood) and one a former congressman (Judge Alston G. Dayton of Philippi). Three were state or local officials and one was the president of West Virginia University (of necessity an "academic politician," at least). The remaining members, except for one businessman, were Presbyterian preachers—which need not imply that they may not very well have been adept "ecclesiastical politicians!"

By 1913, the board of trustees included members from the Greenbrier, Kanawha, and Tygarts Valley presbyteries, as well as from Lexington, Winchester Presbyteries, and from the Synod of West Virginia of the Northern or U.S.A. Presbyterian Church. The first three Presbyteries were all within the geographical boundaries of West Virginia, as was the Synod. For this reason, as well as because there was some thought that its being named for two wealthy men might deter others from giving support to the college, Senator Davis proposed in July 1913 that the name of the Davis and Elkins College be changed to West Virginia College. The matter was referred to the Executive Committee since some trustees felt that members of the founding families, less broad and generous in their views than Senator Davis, might be offended and since they feared other "possible difficulties which might arise in changing the name."[15] The committee allowed that matter to die and ignored the instructions that it bring in a report at the next stated meeting of the board.

At the 1912 commencement, one B.A. and two B.S. degrees were awarded and ten students received diplomas from the "Commercial School." Also, for the first time, D&E conferred honorary degrees. The recipients of Doctor of Divinity degrees

15. Trustee Minutes, July 19, 1913, p. 43.

were Professor Frederick Henry Barron, minister of the Davis Memorial Presbyterian Church of Elkins, a longtime faculty member and trustee, and the Reverend John Young of Pittsburgh, Pennsylvania.

In 1913, the college awarded three B.A. degrees—one of which went to Velma Belle Currence, the first woman graduate of D&E. She was the president of the class of 1913 and was notable as the leader of the "Suffragettes" on the campus. Shortly after her election, in an interview published in *The Acta*, the male members of the class emphasized that their unanimous support of this "follower of Mrs. Pankhurst" was "due rather to her position as the first girl graduate than to her conviction concerning women's rights, and that their action does not necessarily set a precedent for succeeding classes." Commenting on the possibility that the suffragettes might demand that the deity be referred to as "She," Professor Barron facetiously remarked that "already some of them want me to conclude my prayer with "Awomen" instead of "Amen." In her address at the "Class Day Exercises," Miss Currence asserted that "our Alma Mater needs many, many things, but there is one preeminent need which towers above all others. As we know, D&E is coeducational but where are we to place our girls? This great need is for a girls' dormitory, why shouldn't we give the girls equal advantages with the boys."[16]

Certainly the point regarding the need for housing for female students was pertinent. Subsequently, in 1918, the college rented the old hospital building, located next to the courthouse on Randolph Avenue, and converted it into a dormitory with facilities adequate for twenty-five women students. It was described in college catalogs as being "little more than one-fourth of a mile from the College, not too far to walk, and far enough to give ample exercise in going to and from the main building." Presumedly the boys, whose dormitory was *in* the main building, got sufficient exercise in escorting the girls to and fro and from such escapades as the following recorded by a contemporary:

16. *The Acta*, January, 1913, p. 7; and Commencement Number, 1913, p. 3. (Mrs. Pankhurst was the leader of the women's suffrage movement in England at that time.)

Early one morning a group of college girls on their way to the first class hurried up the college path. As they rounded a curve in the path, out from behind the pine trees emerged an apparition. It reared up to a height of six feet or more. The girls ran helter skelter down the path, with the apparition—whatever it was—hard after them.

"It's Santa Claus," said one, "it has long whiskers."

"It's Satan," said another, "it has horns and hoofs."

As a matter of fact, it was a big buck angora goat escaped from a nearby farm. The boys, of course, soon arrived on the scene and by coaxing, pulling, and driving, finally pushed old Satan into the building. Pandemonium broke loose, for old Satan took after any one in sight. After much excitement, enough boys arrived to hold old Satan and he was gradually backed out of the front door and down the hill. His presence, however, lingered for a few days in the form of a pungent smell.[17]

In addition to concern for provisions for housing for women, serious efforts were made in those years to increase the library holdings. Senator Elkins had given some books and various individuals occasionally donated volumes from a deceased relative's collection, but there was no systematic purchase of reference and periodical materials. As a result of the efforts of Congressman Sutherland, the D&E Library was designated as a Government Library Depository in 1913, but inadequate library facilities and budgets long remained a major weakness of the college. There were by actual count 1,624 volumes in the D&E Library in 1913. By 1920, the total was 3,408, an increase of 1,784 in seven years.[18]

A new degree, the Bachelor of Literature, was announced in 1914 and the academic departments were reorganized that year. A Department of Education was added (courses in education had been taught since 1911), as was a Department of Music. Latin and Greek were included in a Department of Ancient Languages, German and French were offered in a Department of Modern Languages (Spanish being omitted from the curriculum). The Department of Science administered the courses offered in chemistry, physics, astronomy, geology, and biology. History and political science were combined into one department. The

---

17. Albert, *loc. cit.,* p. 17.
18. Daybook used as an accession book, 1913, and College Catalog, 1919-20.

other departments were English, expression, mathematics, Bible studies, philosophy, and civil engineering. The Commercial Department remained separate from the academic departments and the name of the Preparatory School was changed to "The Academy."

The graduating class of 1914 had the unique distinction of receiving more bachelor's degrees than there were seniors. The reason for this was that one student was awarded both a B.A. and a B.S. degree and one was awarded both a B.A. and a B.L. degree. Also, Velma Belle Currence, B.A., 1913, had spent a fifth year to earn a B.L. degree with the class of 1914, a diploma in the Commercial School, and doubtless also to continue her leadership in the local "suffragette" movement and to agitate for a "dormitory for girls."

It is interesting to note that the D&E students were aware of and vocal about many of the major issues of the second decade of this century. Not only was the question of votes for women being heatedly discussed at D&E, as in the rest of the country and in England, but the students were also writing about or debating such then current topics as President Wilson's policy of intervening in Mexico, the abolition of capital punishment, prohibition, the adoption of "progressive" measures such as initiative, referendum and recall, the control of big business, evolution, tariff reform, government ownership of public utilities, and of course, the World War.

The editor of *The Acta*, writing in November 1914, some three months after the outbreak of the war in Europe, observed, prophetically as we now know, that "the civilization of yesterday is gone. Man descends to the level of the savage. The lust for blood overwhelms palace and hovel, and millions prepare to conquer or die." Like most Americans in 1914, the D&E community was horrified at the news from the battlefields and, though hopeful of an allied victory, was convinced that "as Americans, it is our duty to be neutral." Unlike many hysterical citizens who regarded German-Americans as dangerous subversives, the enlightened *Acta* editor urged respect for them and reminded the college community that while "it is but natural that the good wishes of millions of Americans should go to that British Empire of which we were once a part . . . we owe, also, a tribute of respect to the German Empire from which so many of our citizens come. The contribution made by the land of Luther and Goethe to the world is a vital factor ... the rich and vigorous character of that nation had infused itself into our national life, and it is well to bind citizens of that race to us as fellow Americans by respecting their opinion on the great war."[19]

Other students looked at the war less seriously, of course. One wrote:

> "Oh, save us from the woes of war
> And all its desolations
> And all those awful foreign names
> And their pronunciations!"[20]

Within less than three years, however, neutrality would end, tolerance of things German would largely disappear, and the "woes of war" would directly affect D&E.

In the autumn of 1914, the editor of the *Randolph Review*, noting that a decade had passed since D&E had begun its first academic year, wrote of the college:

> First and most important of all, it has gained its place in the hearts of the citizens.... Elkins feels that the College is one of her institutions and is not a thing separate and apart ... internally, the College has made progress, has grown. The number of the Faculty has been increased and consists of instructors of large caliber. The number of students enrolled showed a large increase over any previous year, and prospects are very bright for a still greater increase next year ... in fact, everybody connected with the College, either closely or remotely, is enthusiastic about its work and its future ... and it is most gratifying that ... the College is growing as an institution for Christian Education should grow.

The new faculty referred to included three women, Eloise Cleveland, professor of modern language, Bertha Johns, professor of expression and dramatic art, and Winifred Gross, instructor in voice. Louis K. Koontz, a graduate of Washington and Lee University with an M.A. from the Johns Hopkins University, former president of Frederick College, joined the faculty as professor of history and political science and "Principal of the Dormitory." The following year, he was elected vice-president and dean of the faculty.

Although total enrollment for the institution (the college, the

---

19. *The Acta,* November, 1914, p. 17.
20. *Ibid.,* p. 31.

academy, the Commercial School and such special departments for part-time, non-degree candidates as the "Department of Expression," "The Teachers' Review Department," and the "Music Department") numbered 168, only 35 were college students—11 more than in the preceding year, but two fewer than in 1911-12. Tuition was still only $50 per year and the total cost for a resident student was estimated at $225 to $231 per year.

New courses, especially in the Department of History and Political Science and in English, tended to emphasize more "modern" subjects such as "Europe 1788-1915," "History of Latin America," "Comparative Government," and "American Poetry," "The Short Story," "Tennyson," and "Browning." Dean McKenzie offered "Kantian and Post-Kantian Philosophy," and Professor Barron added "A Study of the Life of Saint Paul," and "Christian Evidences—What Christianity is, What it does, How superior to other beliefs," to the previous courses in the Department of Biblical Studies.

The Library Committee and a Committee on Advertising were created in 1914. The statement of "Purpose" was expanded in the catalog and it now included the observation that "the College is generally credited with having the most highly trained teaching staff of any of the smaller colleges of the State." The city of Elkins was described as having "seven thousand people" and as being "one of the most prosperous and attractive cities of the State," with sixteen passenger trains arriving and departing daily. "If one can get to a railroad, he can get to Elkins," was the proud boast of the D&E catalog sixty-five years ago—one which no one could make in the 1970s!

Special lectures for the year included such topics as "The American Indian" by Captain W. H. Cobb of Elkins, and "Equal Rights for Women" by Miss Eudora Ramsey of Greenville, South Carolina. Only three seniors were graduated in 1915, but the entering freshman class the following September numbered twenty-five—the largest so far, thus bearing out the prediction made in the *Randolph Review* the preceding year.

In 1914 and 1915, the first two permanently endowed scholarships were established. Dr. S. M. Scott, Sr., of Terra Alta, West Virginia, donated one thousand dollars in memory of his son, the income from which was to be used to provide a scholarship. Mrs. C. M. See of Philippi established a five hundred dollar trust fund to help provide scholarship assistance to pre-ministerial students. The college also began to offer "Service Scholarships" to students who were candidates for the ministry and to the sons of ministers.

Without question the most notable event of the 1915-16 academic year for D&E was the death in Washington, D.C., of Senator Henry Gassaway Davis, president of the board of trustees, on March 11, 1916, two days after the death of Congressman W. G. Brown, also a trustee. No person had contributed as much money and few had given more time and encouragement in the effort to establish and sustain "The College at Elkins" than had Senator Henry Gassaway Davis. Perhaps one cannot do better than to quote from the memorial adopted by the board of trustees and recorded in the minutes for June 13, 1916, as a tribute to its "venerable and esteemed President":

> Having exceeded the span of life alloted to man by more than a score of years, he did not spend these additional years, as some men are wont to do, in passively waiting the summons, but, on the contrary, the years from seventy to ninety-three in his life were years of active participation in his business and philanthropic work.... In these years, he planned and caused to be built, largely from his own means, the College which bears his name, and he cheerfully assumed active interest in its management as well as a large part of the obligation for its maintenance, and in his will bequeathed for permanent endowment the substantial sum of One Hundred Thousand Dollars.
>
> To no man in his adopted State was opportunity given to serve it actively so long and so well. While he was known as a railroad builder to his associates and to the public of his time, the Senator did not fail to realize that with material development must come intellectual and religious development....
>
> Commanding in physique, forceful in character, optimistic in his outlook upon life, devout in his religious faith, genial to all, and hospitable in a marked degree in his beautiful home, the Senator's personal life and character were enriched by vastly more than ordinary attributes of the successful businessman. This Board realizes that in the death of Senator Davis, the College and the community in which he lived have sustained a great loss. Not only this community, but the state at large, has lost its most distinguished citizen.[21]

---

21. Trustee Minutes, June 13, 1916, pp. 51-52.

In less than six weeks after the senator's death, the board appointed a committee "to wait upon the Trustees of the Henry G. Davis estate, Mrs. S. B. Elkins, and others and take such steps as may be necessary to raise the $1,200.00 needed for the balance of the College year." Apparently they were not successful for in mid-June, the board authorized "the borrowing of $1,200 for the purpose of paying the salaries now due to the teachers of the College." With the death of the old senator, the "Davis barrel" was no longer an easy one to tap. For years, he had given at least $4,000 annually, but in 1916 and 1917, the executors of his estate disallowed the college's claim for interest earned from the $100,000 bequest on the grounds that the $100,000 did not belong to the college until the estate was settled and thus that the interest earned should go to the estate, not the college, until October of 1917.[22]

Disappointed by the efforts to raise even half of the money needed to match the $50,000.00 mentioned above, and facing annual deficits, as well as a total accrued debt of $16,672.86 as of Commencement Day, 1916, the board of trustees decided in October to enter into a contract with the Wards Systems Company to plan a "Quick Fund Raising Campaign" for the sum of $150,000.00. Meanwhile, action was taken at subsequent board meetings to borrow $20,000.00 from Elkins banks to pay debts, meet expenses and provide initial financing for the fund-raising campaign.[23] Headquarters for the statewide undertaking were established in the Gassaway Hotel (now the Tygart Hotel) in Elkins. J. C. Spiker, the proprietor, donated the use of the hotel auditorium for this purpose as a token of his support of the college. A "Committee of One Hundred" prominent citizens of the state, with Dr. F. H. Barron as chairman, was organized to help promote the campaign. Serving on the Executive Committee with Dr. Barron were several Elkins businessmen, including Richard Chaffey, president of the Peoples National Bank; W. G. Wilson, president of the Davis Trust Company; Lee Crouch, president of the Elkins National Bank; A. E. Dann, of the Elkins Furniture Company; Troy Hardman, president of the Hardman Lumber Company; William Gullard, president of the Gullard-Clarke Company; and, of course, President Allen, Senator-elect

22. *Ibid.*, June 12, 1917, p. 56.
23. *Ibid.*, June 13, 1916, and October 6, 1916, pp. 51-56.

Sutherland and N. I. Hall, president and treasurer, respectively, of the board of trustees.

The purpose of the campaign was stated as being "to pay off the present indebtedness, and to erect a Girl's Dormitory and a Science Hall which we hope will prove beneficial to the paramount interests of the state of West Virginia." The Elkins *Inter-Mountain* gave extensive coverage to the campaign from the beginning as did the *Randolph Enterprise,* the *Randolph Review,* and various Presbyterian Church publications. The "Grand Opening Banquet" at the YMCA in mid-December featured U.S. Senator-elect Sutherland as toastmaster and included the reading of numerous telegrams of endorsement from such men as Thomas R. Marshall, vice-president of the United States (otherwise famous for his observation that "What this country needs is a good five-cent cigar!"); Champ Clark, Speaker of the U. S. House of Representatives (former president of Marshall College in Huntington); John J. Cornwall, governor-elect of West Virginia; Carl R. Gray, president of the Western Maryland Railroad; and several college and university presidents. A copy of the menu, which was printed in Old English style, is interesting. Beginning with an oyster cocktail, the meal included "Soup Elkins," "Mountain Olives," "Celery Tygarts Valley," "Roast Turkey with D&E Sauce," "Allegheny Peas," "Randolph Potatoes," "West Virginia Salad," "Presbyterian Ice Cream," "Synodical Cake," and "Moderator Coffee 'A La Barron."

On the night preceding the dinner, the college drama students presented a "Big Benefit Performance" in support of the campaign. Staged in the Opera House, Megrue's comedy, *It Pays to Advertise,* was a sellout at fifty cents per person. One of the most famous plays of the war era, it had run for seven hundred consecutive nights at George M. Cohan's Theater in New York City. The D&E production, directed by Professor Bertha May Johns, was acclaimed by the *Inter-Mountain* critic to be "the best home talent play ever offered in Elkins." Among the star performers were Harry E. Whetsell and Eleanor Cody of Elkins and Boyd May of Raywood.

Enthusiasm was great at first and $15,000 was pledged by Elkins citizens on December 15 in the first two hours of the campaign. Thereafter, however, frustration and disappointment characterized the efforts of the money-raisers. By early March 1917, only approximately $30,000 had been pledged. With the entrance of the United States into World War I in April, the D&E campaign was suspended for several months. Headquarters were reopened on July 11 with the announcement that a check for $1,000 had been received from a large corporation "through the personal efforts of Senator Sutherland" and that the trustees "confidently expected" to find a very competent field expert to carry on the solicitation in the near future.[24] In fact, the "Quick Fund Raising Campaign" ultimately fizzled out without even coming close to the $150,000 goal.

Whether or not the financial campaign would have been successful had the nation not gone to war cannot be known. Perhaps its failure was merely the first of the "woes of war" to be felt by D&E. At any rate, as the commencement issue of the 1917 *Phoenix* (the student publication which replaced *The Acta* in 1916) emphasized, "military drill" had become the "order of the day" on the campus. "Practically all the students and some of the members of the Faculty are taking part." On April 13, 1917, just seven days after Congress declared war on Germany, "the Davis and Elkins Military Company" was organized with John W. McGlamery, a sophomore, being chosen as captain. One writer noted that McGlamery "bears himself in a military manner, and although there has been some mutiny among the ranks, he has suppressed all uprisings with a firm hand." There was great difficulty in obtaining guns for use in drill at D&E (as elsewhere throughout the country), and Captain McGlamery was praised for his initiative in procuring a few from "the wilds of Pendleton County" despite the fact that "these guns answer the description of those which General Washington used to cross the Delaware on Christmas night a few decades ago." A bugle was presented to the company by George Coffman, an Elkins merchant, and a flag by Mrs. F. H. Barron and Mrs. M. W. Wilson. The students had also organized a Belgian Relief Club and most of the women students enrolled in a course in Red Cross work offered at the Davis Memorial Hospital under the direction of Dr. W. W. Golden. By the beginning of the fall term in 1918, a Student Army Training Corps had been organized under the command of Lieutenant P. V. Campbell and almost every college man and many of the students of the academy joined, and a number of

---

24. *Elkins Inter-Mountain*, November-December, 1916, *passim*.

S.A.T.C. inductees were sent from "all sections of the East for training at D&E."[25]

At commencement in 1917, seven B.A. and two B.S. degrees were awarded (as compared to two of each in 1916) to the largest class to be graduated prior to 1921. However, enrollment for the following year dropped drastically from fifty to thirty-one in the college, with only sixteen entering freshmen in contrast to twenty-five and twenty-six, respectively, in the two preceding years. There was no football team in 1917-18 and not much prospect for basketball. One unforeseen result of D&E's having won the state basketball championship in 1917 was that West Virginia University employed H. P. Mullenex as basketball coach and several D&E champions transferred to the university in the fall of 1917, among them Harry E. Whetsell, Frank C. Wimer, Paul Cutright, and "Biz" Dawson.

Undoubtedly the failure of the financial campaign and the exigencies of war combined to produce an exodus of faculty members from D&E. Seven of the eleven faculty members of 1916-17 left before the end of the summer of 1917, including Dean Louis Koontz, and Professor Robert P. Strickler, S. G. Moore, Bertha Johns, Frank Corrington, Norman Beglen, and H. P. Mullennex. In a front-page article, the *Inter-Mountain* lamented the loss of the popular Louis Koontz, professor of history and political science since 1914 and dean and vice-president since 1915, stating that "he was recognized as a man of profound scholarship, a splendid teacher, a man of the highest general culture and Christian influence. The trustees have never elected a man who seems to have given more satisfaction than Professor Koontz."[26]

Inasmuch as Professor Albert, who had left in 1913, had not yet returned, only President Allen and Professor Barron and two junior faculty members who had come in 1916 were left to launch the 1917-18 academic year. The office of dean and several professorships were left unfilled or filled with temporary or part-time faculty until after the war. Professor Willis H. Wilcox, later to be dean, did come in 1918 to teach English, history, and education, and his wife was appointed professor of vocal music.

25. *The Phoenix* (Commencement Issue, 1917), pp. 33-34; and (Annual Issue, 1919), pp. 31, 65.
26. *Elkins Inter-Mountain,* July 12, 1917, p. 1.

Dewey L. Fleming, then editor of *The Phoenix,* described the situation in the autumn of 1917 as follows: "We realized that the old order had changed when school opened for the Fall Term and a great majority of the old familiar faces were missing. A short time after the opening of school, it was observed by members of the Faculty and the student body that the old 'spirit' was lacking. Little or no interest was manifested in athletics. Everyone ... found it very difficult to settle down and do good work ... with the departure of more young men for training camps, the apathy became more pronounced." Pride was expressed, however, in the fact that one hundred D&E men were then in military sevice, "four of whom are now Captains and twenty Lieutenants."[27] One of those captains was Richard K. Sutherland, son of the Senator, an Elkins boy who made a career in the army and who, in World War II, was to be a lieutenant general and chief of staff for General Douglas MacArthur. Another, Robert Emmet O'Connor was promoted to major and later became a D&E trustee.

Despite the fact that the college and the academy had been in existence less than fifteen years by the end of World War I and had never had a large enrollment, 180 former students of the prep school and the college, including 13 of the 29 male graduates of D&E saw military service in the Great War. William Roscoe Gould of the class of 1917 was the first D&E graduate to die in the service. Subsequently, his parents gave the college a sum of money and some coal land in his memory.[28] The great influenza epidemic struck the campus in early October of 1918 and classes were suspended from October 5 until October 16. Apparently everyone recovered for by October 22, *The Phoenix* noted that "all students attend chapel."

The discouragement and apathy on the campus in 1917-18 seems to have been characteristic of the trustees as well. After appointing E. A. Bowers, an Elkins lawyer as the college's "permanent attorney" in 1917, and voting to leave the matter of appointing a field agent "in the hands of the Executive Committee

---

27. *The Phoenix* (Commencement Number, 1918), p. 23, and (Annual Number, 1919), p. 29.

28. Trustee Minutes, March 25, 1919, and November 25, 1919, pp. 64, 73; and December 30, 1921, p. 86. (Four D&E men lost their lives in World War I. They were William R. Gould of Weston; Claude McDaniel of Elkins; William Mylius of Alpena; and Walter Scott Hardy of Richmond, Va.)

with the power to act," the board was unable to get together a quorum for a meeting in 1918 and did not meet, as far as the records show, from June 12, 1917, until March 25, 1919.

By then, the war had ended and things were beginning to return to what Warren G. Harding would soon call "normalcy." The girls' basketball team of 1918-19, composed entirely of Elkins students, played nine games and won every game—"a one hundred per cent record"—as *The Phoenix* proudly described it. The champions included Elma Weimer, Martha Tonry, Katherine Wilhide, Okareda Ketterman, Mary Gail Tyree, Katherine Wilverdine, and Maud Crouch. Their coach was Emory Morris. The trustees began in June 1919 to discuss building a science hall and a gymnasium and to confer about the "best methods for a campaign for money." Of necessity, the board had to act *ex post facto* in approving the awarding of degrees which had been granted to seven students in 1918, but did proceed in due order in voting to award three B.A. degrees to the all-female class of 1919. At the commencement, the college issued High School Teaching Certificates and Standard Normal Diplomas for the first time. Honorary Doctor of Divinity degrees were bestowed on the Reverend G. I. Wilson of the First Presbyterian Church in Parkersburg, a trustee, and the Reverend W. E. Craig, pastor of the First Methodist Episcopal Church in Elkins—the first non-Presbyterian so honored by the college.

At a special meeting on November 25, 1919, the trustees were informed that the General Education Board of the Presbyterian Church, U.S.A., was offering to give twenty-five thousand dollars to the college provided that another seventy-five thousand dollars would be raised in addition. At the same meeting, the trustees authorized the Executive Committee to select another name for the college provided that the heirs of Senator Davis, especially Mrs. Stephen B. Elkins and Senator Davis Elkins, were "agreeable to the change."[29] Subsequently, Dr. Barron notified the board that Mrs. Elkins and her brother, John T. Davis, had not replied to his inquiry about this matter, but that Mrs. Arthur Lee had told him that "the members of the families of the late H. G. Davis and S. B. Elkins would prefer a change in name."[30] The board may have taken Mrs. Elkins's silence as a

29. *Ibid.*, November 25, 1919, p. 69.
30. *Ibid.*, September 16, 1920, p. 75.

sign of consent. If so, they were undoubtedly mistaken—as was her sister, Mrs. Lee—about the wishes of Hallie Davis Elkins, as they would discover early in the next decade.

Hallie Davis Elkins

IV

The Roaring Twenties and the Scarlet Hurricane: 1920-29

In 1920, with the ratification of the Nineteenth Amendment to the Constitution of the United States, the goal of D&E's Velma Currence and the other prewar suffragettes became a reality. Women voted that year and helped elect Warren G. Harding to the presidency. Enfranchisement of women was but one of many aspects of change at the beginning of the third decade of the century. That was the age of the "Flivver and the Flapper"—the former symbolic of the revolution which the automobile and concrete highways brought to transportation, the latter descriptive of the emancipation of women and the decline of Victorian sex mores. The first scheduled radio broadcast was made in 1920 in Pittsburgh, an event presaging the revolution in communication, entertainment, and advertising which resulted from the development of radio and television. Prohibition—the "Noble Experiment" which failed—went into effect in January 1920 and soon led to the rise of organized crime, and a breakdown not only of law but of respect for the law which adversely affected the nation, including the behavior of college students, for more than half a century thereafter.

In retrospect, one sees that the First World War was followed by an era of materialism and disillusionment. Weary of war and of the passion for reform which had characterized the first two decades of the twentieth century under the leadership of Presidents Theodore Roosevelt and Woodrow Wilson, Americans turned with unabashed enthusiasm in the 1920s to the search for riches and pleasure. Widespread distrust of intellectuals, especially college professors, was characteristic of the Roaring Twenties. In fact, Calvin Coolidge, who professed to believe that "the business of America is business," wrote, while still vice-president, that colleges and universities were "hotbeds of sedition." Subsequently, the state of Tennessee, aided by elder statesman William Jennings Bryan, a devout Presbyterian of the fundamentalist fringe, successfully prosecuted John T. Scopes for teaching the theory of evolution to his biology classes in Dayton, Tennessee. Thus, whether the economy was marked by depression or prosperity, colleges like D&E found few people interested in providing them with adequate financial support—unless it be, on occasion, for intercollegiate athletics or perhaps a building. Although in the euphoria induced by the stock market boom of the Coolidge era, some people might make generous pledges in the expectation of paying what they agreed to contribute—just as they bought stocks on margin hoping that prices would continue to rise—but when the time came to write a check, they discovered that it is much easier to promise than it is to pay. Furthermore, although it is well remembered that the 1920s ended with the Great Depression, it is also true that they began with a postwar recession and that coal mining and farming, both of vital importance in the economy of West Virginia, were in distress throughout the decade.

Nevertheless, unaware or unmindful of how both anti-intellectualism and economic factors might be great obstacles to success, the D&E trustees met several times in the summer and fall of 1920 to plan a new financial drive to raise $300,000, of which $200,000 would be endowment. There was, as has been indicated, a desire to build a science building and also to acquire $75,000 needed to qualify for the $25,000 challenge offer presented in 1919 by the Presbyterian General Education Board. When college officials learned in the autumn of 1920 of a proposal that a "Campaign for Funds" be conducted in behalf of all the Presbyterian-supported institutions in the state, the trustees decided to abandon their plans for a D&E drive and to join with representatives of those other institutions in an effort to raise $1.1 million.[1] This campaign, soon known as the "United Crusade for Christian Education," was launched under the auspices of the

1. Trustee Minutes, June 16, September 16, October 14, 1920, pp. 74-78. (The institutions involved were Davis and Elkins College, Union Theological Seminary (Richmond), Lewisburg Seminary, Greenbrier Presbyterial School, Davis-Stuart School and West Virginia Synodical School.

Committee on Christian Education and Ministerial Relief of the Southern Presbyterian Church and the General Board of Education of the Northern Presbyterian Church.

Prior to agreeing to enter the campaign, the D&E trustees stipulated that the college's share of the proceeds must "be fixed at not less than fifty per cent of the amount actually raised" and that all contributions designated by donors for D&E must be given to the college even if the result meant she got "more or less than her quota." The final version of the agreement provided "that all gifts coming to any institution in the campaign from whatever source . . . should be credited to that institution and be part of the campaign fund," and that D&E's share would be $500,000 or five-elevenths of the amount collected.[2]

At that time, there were suggestions from various sources that D&E would be better off if located elsewhere in the state and if she had a "more Presbyterian" name. T. P. Allen, field secretary of the Synod of West Virginia, appeared at an October 14, 1920, meeting of the trustees and urged that the college be moved to Clarksburg. His point of view was that more students could be served in a larger, more accessible city and thus funds could be raised more easily. Unconvinced, and apparently somewhat miffed at Allen's plea, the trustees immediately and unanimously adopted a resolution stating that "this Board looks with displeasure upon any agitation looking to the removal of this College from its present location." However, the board did adopt a motion to change the name of the college to "Westminster College of West Virginia" provided that there "be no forfeiture of endowment or other properties." The college attorney, E. A. Bowers, was directed to investigate the legal aspects and to certify in writing as to the legal implications. He subsequently did so at great length: his findings being that the trustees had the power to change the name without any risks of forfeiture.[3]

Meanwhile, in 1920, Mrs. Stephen B. Elkins gave the college eleven acres of land adjoining the southern end of the campus above the river—one indication of the renewal of her interest in D&E. Although no written evidence on the subject has come to light, it does not require great sagacity to suspect that Mrs. Elkins was not pleased with the proposal to substitute

2. *Ibid.,* June 14, December 30, 1921, June 13, 1922, pp. 82-92.
3. *Ibid.,* October 14, 1920, pp. 76, 79-80.

"Westminster" in place of her father's and husband's names for the college they had helped to found. A gracious but strong-willed woman who had been the daughter, wife, and mother of United States senators, Hallie Davis Elkins seldom failed to have things as she wanted them to be. Thus, no one should be surprised to discover in the Trustee Minutes for June 14, 1921, that those gentlemen conveniently remembered that back in September 1920, *before* their name-change vote of October 14, President Allen and Professor Barron had been appointed as a committee to correspond with alumni and friends in regard to a suitable name for the college. Inasmuch as the committee had never reported, the trustees in 1921 resolved that "the matter of change of name for the College is not properly before the Board for its full consideration . . . and that this Board postpone further consideration and action upon the matter of change of the name of the College until such report is filed."[4] Of course, since "such report" was never filed, the name remained unchanged! Manifold and manifest are the blessings of proper parliamentary procedure!

While the "United Crusade" campaign was still in its first year, Mrs. Elkins indicated that she and her children were considering giving the Halliehurst Farm to the college and she requested that the board of trustees indicate "its attitude" in regard to accepting the mansion and other buildings and some of the land. President Allen did not favor accepting this offer. Plans had already been completed for the construction of a science building at the lower level of the original campus and the president felt that it would be wise to continue to develop that campus rather than to move across town and lose the Old Building and the President's House. He feared the incurrence of a debt of the magnitude necessary to erect new buildings and start over in another location, knowing that such a financial burden might be difficult to overcome and could well endanger the future of the college.[5] Nevertheless, the board informed Mrs. Elkins on December 30, 1921, that "such gift would be of the greatest value and importance" and instructed the Executive Committee to "conduct such further negotiations as to detail as may be necessary." The negotiations were prolonged, lasting almost two years. Conducted for the board by E. A. Bowers and A. Spates Brady, both

---

4. *Ibid.*, June 14, 1921, p. 83.
5. Letter from Robert A. Allen, Saint Albans, W.Va., to Thomas R. Ross, Elkins, W.Va., March 21, 1979.

Elkins citizens and college trustees, the discussions with Mrs. Elkins and her representatives resulted in the drawing up of a detailed Deed of Conveyance, dated December 15, 1923, granting to the college Halliehurst Hall and approximately sixty acres of land with the other buildings located thereon. The trustees approved the terms of the deed and it was signed on December 31, 1923.

Especially notable were the specifications that the board of trustees must *"hold the property hereby conveyed for the exclusive use of the Davis and Elkins College, perpetuating that name for said College"* and that the Halliehurst Farm *"shall become the permanent seat of Davis and Elkins College."* If there had ever been any question as to Mrs. Elkins's desires regarding the name or location of the college, the wording of these clauses surely provided an unequivocal answer!

Another provision stated Mrs. Elkins's wish that Halliehurst Hall should never be used for dormitory purposes for men, but "shall be maintained as a dormitory for women students, Faculty members . . . and for classrooms, library and other legitimate College purposes." The deed also required the trustees to establish a fifty thousand dollar fund to provide an annual income of approximately three thousand dollars "to be used exclusively . . . in the maintenance of said premises" and to be known as the "Halliehurst Fund." Reserved to the Elkins heirs were all mineral, oil, and gas rights should such later be discovered in the land.[6]

In a resolution of appreciation sent to Mrs. Elkins, the trustees noted that only one member of the board remained who had been identified with the college in 1904, but that "all are aware of the fact that the founding of the College was made possible by the vision and gifts of Senators Davis and Elkins." That "one member" remaining was the beloved Dr. F. H. Barron whose service on the board continued long afterward. The preceding month, death had come to Dr. A. H. Hamilton, also one of the original trustees, and the third of the founders of the college, along with H. G. Davis and S. B. Elkins. D&E had awarded a D.D. degree to Mr. Hamilton in 1916, the third such degree it ever had conferred. Of his death, President James Allen wrote

6. Trustee Minutes, December 31, 1923, pp. 97-115; Trustee Executive Committee Minutes, July 6, August 16, September 4, October 14, 15, December 31, 1923, pp. 109-32.

that "the College has lost a man who, in the founding of the institution, rendered service that was wholly commensurate with the service of others at the time and indispensable." Later, in memory of Dr. Hamilton, the faculty established the Hamilton Honor Society to give "special honor to students of marked scholastic ability." Members of the junior class whose grade average at the end of the year was "not less than A" were eligible.[7]

In the light of her contributions in the 1920s Hallie Davis Elkins surely deserves to be ranked near to her father and husband and Dr. Hamilton among those who nurtured the college in the early years. During 1924, plans were completed to move the college from Sally Mike Hill to Halliehurst Farm. As had been agreed, Mrs. Elkins was consulted in regard to the style of the new buildings to be constructed. The advice of landscape artists and architects was sought in order to avoid doing anything that might mar the existing attractiveness of the property. Described at the time as having "about seventy usable rooms," Halliehurst Hall was designated as "a dormitory for young women." Actually there were about forty rooms and some of the larger rooms were later equipped for classroom use. In addition to the mansion

The Gatehouse and gateway to the Halliehurst grounds.

7. *Ibid.,* December 31, 1923, p. 101; Faculty Minutes, May 26, 1930, p. 55.

and adjacent to it (where the Jennings Randolph Library Building now stands) was a large indoor swimming pool useful both to physical education classes and for recreational purposes. There were also several small houses (such as the present Admissions House) which soon became available for faculty homes or other purposes.

Walter F. Martens, an architect from Charleston, West Virginia, then engaged in building the Governor's Mansion there, was appointed to prepare the plans for necessary alterations in Halliehurst Hall and for the new buildings. He drew up a campus plan showing proposed locations of walks, dormitories, an open air theatre, athletic grounds, a liberal arts hall, a science hall, and a central heating plant. Construction of only the last three was to be undertaken immediately. In September 1924, bids were received from thirteen companies wishing to construct the new buildings. All bids were rejected as being too high—they ranged from $350,000 to $229,000—and the architect was instructed "to take up with the four low bidders the matter of reducing their original bids." The next morning, the board convened and decided to award the contract to the Harrison Construction Company of Richmond which had offered to construct Liberal Arts Hall, the Science Hall, and the Central Heating Plant at a total cost of $228,400. Work was to begin within ten days and be completed by September 1, 1925. The board appointed a building committee consisting of A. Spates Brady, E. A. Bowers, Dr. F. S. Johnston, and Dr. Barron to deal with details. Inevitably, there were many problems, the first of which was that Harrison Construction Company decided not to undertake the project. The contract was then given to the next lowest bidder, Banks and Branneck, Inc., of Charleston, West Virginia, who had submitted a bid of $228,500. They thought the project could be completed in three hundred working days.[8]

The cornerstone of Liberal Arts Hall was put into place in elaborate ceremonies in the afternoon of June 10, 1925, with H. G. Kump as the principal speaker. The *Inter-Mountain* recorded that "the occasion was one of deep importance to those who have worked tirelessly and given their money to make the expansion of Davis and Elkins College possible" and asserted that "it represented a long step forward." E. A. Bowers speaking for the

---

8. Trustee Minutes, July to September, 1924, pp. 118-30.

Liberal Arts Hall and Science Hall.

trustees, stated that all concerned had a great responsibility "to make sure that the program does not falter nor stop short of completion of the present buildings, but goes on to the fulfillment of the needs" of the college in the future.[9] Unfortunately, Mr. Bowers's admonition was not needed. The top floor of the Liberal Arts Hall was left unfinished for more than thirty years and the second floor of the Science Hall was left open for use only as an auditorium for a long time before being divided into classrooms and laboratories. As for the remainder of the buildings plotted on the original campus plan, other than the Heating Plant, none was ever constructed as proposed and none was even started until a quarter of a century after the ceremony just described.

It was anticipated that D&E's share of the proceeds from the "United Crusade" financial campaign would pay for the new buildings and also add significantly to the endowment. The trustees also planned to sell the "Old College" property after the move to the new campus in the mid-twenties. At the outset of the campaign, the board had decided that President Allen would need to devote much of his time to the "United Crusade." Thus, in the

9. Elkins *Inter-Mountain*, June 11, 1925, p. 1.

fall of 1920, Willis H. Wilcox, professor of English and history, was elected to be "Vice-President without additional compensation," thus filling a position which had been vacant since the resignation of Louis Koontz as dean in 1917.[10] Professor Wilcox, trained in English and history at the University of Michigan, Columbia University, and the Johns Hopkins University, was an impressive man physically and intellectually. He helped greatly in rebuilding the faculty after the war, being in 1920 the senior faculty member other than President Allen and Professor Barron, despite having come to the college as recently as 1918.

Among those who joined the faculty and staff in the postwar period were several who would play significant roles in the life of the college for many years. Miss Virgie Harris began work as registrar in 1918 (even before completing her B.A. degree requirements). She was officially appointed to that office in 1922, and she served in that capacity for several years and then as a librarian for much of the remainder of her life. At about the same time (1919), Miss Anna Parmesano became secretary to the president, a position she continued to hold throughout the administration of every D&E College president from James E. Allen to David K. Allen, retiring when the latter did in 1964, after some forty-five years of faithful service. In 1919, Harry E. Whetsell began his long career at D&E, first as instructor in mathematics, director of athletics and basketball coach. Six years later, on July 1, 1925, he became secretary of the board of trustees and assistant treasurer of the college, while continuing to teach mathematics. Subsequently he was appointed the first business manager of the college and then acting president in a period of crisis in 1939-40.

In 1920, Mrs. Harriet B. Baker became associated with the college as an instructor in what had come to be called the "Normal Department" concerned with the training of school teachers in a two-year program leading to a "Normal Certificate." Her service continued into the 1940s. Although not to serve for so long a time, one of the outstanding men to join the faculty in 1920 was Thomas J. Hale, professor of politics, social science and philosophy. An alumnus of Washington and Lee with a M.A. degree from Chicago and a law degree from the University of Alabama, Hale was an especially able and popular instructor, of

---

10. Trustee Minutes, October 14, 1920, p. 79.

The faculty in 1922.

whom alumni said, "you really did not experience a D&E education unless you had a course from Professor Hale."

Charles E. Albert returned to the faculty in 1922 as professor of physics and civil engineering and dean of the men's dormitory. He had, since his first appointment (1911-13) married an Elkins girl, a former D&E student, Jeanne Marstiller, who was most influential in persuading him to return to Elkins when the opportunity to rejoin the faculty was offered to him. In 1925, when W. H. Wilcox resigned, Professor Albert succeeded him as dean, a position he was to hold for a longer period of time than anyone else except Dr. Thomas R. Ross.

In 1923, D&E enticed Cam Henderson, the head coach at Muskingum College since 1920, to accept the position as director of athletics and coach. He quickly began to emphasize intercollegiate competition in football and basketball and soon developed outstanding teams in both sports.

The 1925 appointment of Raymond B. Purdum as professor of chemistry was destined to be of great significance. He had earned three degrees at the University of Virginia where he had held the prestigious DuPont Fellowship, before beginning his career at D&E which was to last more than a quarter of a century, including nearly a decade as president of the college. Irving Miller also came in 1925 as professor of music, remaining until his death in 1950.

In 1926, S. Benton Talbot, an Elkins native and an honor graduate of D&E, joined the faculty as instructor in biology. The only other person teaching in that department then was Benjamin I. Golden, M.D., a part-time lecturer. In a real sense, Benton Talbot was the founder of the Biology Department. Subsequent to his first appointment, he completed his doctorate at the Johns Hopkins University and then continued here as professor of biology. He served for more than thirty years as one of the best loved and most influential faculty members in the history of the college, and in his later years was dean of the college.

Jennings Randolph also came in 1926, being appointed instructor in public speaking and journalism and director of intercollegiate athletics and publicity. Although his service as a faculty member was relatively brief—ending after his election to Congress in 1932—he has for more than fifty years been closely identified with D&E, working tirelessly as faculty member and trustee and using his great influence, both as a member of the House of Representatives and, since 1958, as a United States Senator, to promote the best interests of Davis and Elkins College.

With the appointments of Professors Whetsell, Albert, Purdum, Talbot, I. Miller, Hale, Miss Harris and Mrs. Baker, D&E for the first time had a group of faculty members who were willing to devote much or all of their professional lives to this college. Their predecessors had often been very able men and women, but with the exception of James E. Allen as president and Dr. F. H. Barron (who taught only part time from 1904 to 1924 when he retired from the faculty and became president of the board of trustees and always had another profession as his primary concern), none stayed long enough to develop the loyalty and commitment which are so essential to the success and ultimate survival of a viable faculty. Without the sense of continuity and the *esprit de corps* provided by such a group in the faculty, which is the indispensable element of an educational institution, the whole concept of collegiality soon collapses. Regardless of all else accomplished by those who came in the twenties—and their achievements were significant—perhaps of most importance in the long run was that they persevered. They became the faithful core who would orient the generation of faculty members who would come in the 1940s and 1950s.

In 1920, the custom of naming each graduating class in honor of a faculty sponsor was begun, the class of 1920 being known as "The Wilcox Class." In the same year, the faculty decided to adopt an academic year calendar providing for two eighteen-week semesters. Only the B.A. and B.S. degrees were offered, the Bachelor of Literature having been discontinued. Each degree required 128 semester hours of credit, with 92 hours of work specifically required in designated departments for the B.A. degree and 97 for the B.S. degree. The candidates for the B.A. no longer were required to offer credit in either Latin or Greek, but if they did not do so, they must complete twelve hours in French or German, the same as for the B.S. degree. Otherwise, in the 1920s as before, the only difference between the requirements for the two degrees was that more credit in English, history, and the social sciences was specified for the B.A. and more hours in mathematics and natural science for B.S. Both required eight hours of Bible and twelve of philosophy and the presentation of a Senior Thesis. Later, in 1924, the B.S. in Education degree was authorized, requiring essentially the same courses as the B.A. degree except that no mathematics was specified and that all electives must be taken in the Department of Education.

The Commercial Department added a "Civil Service Course" to the programs offered in the preceding decade. It also advertised that "for the convenience of students who cannot attend the day school, ample rooms and equipment are provided downtown in the night school."

All dormitory residents were required "to attend church services regularly on Sabbath morning" and all students were expected to attend chapel services daily. These requirements remained in effect throughout the decade, but enforcement of them became increasingly difficult and the Faculty Minutes indicated that there was frequent discussion of "What to do about it?" Such expedients as subtracting "one per cent from the monthly grade of any student absent unexcused from Chapel more than once a month" and stating that "persistence in Chapel absence will regularly require the suspension of the student from all College privileges for at least one week" apparently were not effective.[11]

11. Faculty Minutes, 1918-27, *passim.*

Although there were only five graduating seniors in 1920, the college enrollment had increased from the thirty-seven of 1918-19 to seventy, thirty-eight of whom were freshmen and sixty-six of whom were West Virginians—mostly from Elkins.

Recipients of degrees included Stanley Bosworth, who was to serve many years as prosecuting attorney and circuit judge in Randolph County, and Vernon B. Harris, who became a prominent business leader in the state and an ardent supporter of D&E. Bess Johnson (Mrs. S. Paul Perry) received a "Certificate of Proficiency in Public Speaking." She was an Elkins girl who in the 1920s and 1930s became a famous radio personality, first as the commercial voice of "Lady Esther," then as an actress in such programs as "Love Rules the World," "Today's Children," and "Hilltop House."[12]

It is interesting to note that in 1922 every senior receiving the B.A. degree was graduated with honors and six of the seven immediately began teaching, though one of the six, Freeman J. Daniels, studied law and later became a prominent attorney and a D&E trustee. Others in that class included Virgie Harris, already registrar at D&E, Emily Barry, Jackson Stover, and Omar T. Goddin. The valedictorian of the class of 1923 was Felix B. Gear, in later life to be elected moderator of the General Assembly of the Presbyterian Church in the United States. Both Robb Keyser, a future trustee of D&E and his bride-to-be, Edna Hostettler, were graduated in 1924 as was Siegmund Benton Talbot, who spent virtually his entire professional life as a faculty member at his alma mater.

In 1926 at the last commencement at the "Old College," twelve B.A., two B.S. and two B.S. in Education degrees were awarded to "The Hensley Class." Leona Harper (Mrs. Felix Gear) was the valedictorian, and Bayard Green and Edna Warfield (Mrs. Harry McNeish) were among the honor graduates.

Enrollment in 1925-26 totaled 185 college students. The annual cost for a dormitory student had increased to five hundred dollars per year, but tuition for community students was only one hundred dollars and most students were from Randolph County. Twenty years before there had been no graduates, only six students, and total cost for room, board, and tuition had been approximately two hundred dollars per year, with tuition alone only

---

12. *The Senator,* October 23, 1927, p. 1.

fifty dollars. Times and circumstances had changed and the college had outgrown its facilities on Sally Mike Hill. Two things had not changed in twenty years, however—the persistence of an annual operating deficit and the incredibly low salaries paid faculty members. Budget figures indicate in the mid-twenties that the total amount paid in salaries for all faculty members was less than the base salary for one associate professor in 1979—and there were no "fringe benefits" in those days—nor would that situation soon improve.

In 1922, *The Phoenix,* which since 1916 had appeared three or four times a year as a combination news and literary publication, became an annual, the forerunner of the *Senatus,* and the first effort to publish a weekly newspaper was undertaken. Volume I, Number 1, of *The Senator,* a weekly, appeared on December 4, 1922. The editor-in-chief was Benton Talbot, a sophomore, whose brother Richard was a freshman reporter. Printed on 10¾-by-14-inch newsprint, the four-page issue contained a large photograph of the 1922 football team with an accompanying front page article reviewing the "football season," there were several news articles, alumni notes, two columns of jokes, a few poems, and eleven advertisements placed by Elkins business establishments, as well as one boosting a play to be given December 12.

Editor Talbot's interest in biology as well as his sense of humor are revealed in the introductory paragraph of his first *Senator* editorial, entitled "Why the Freshman?"

> The freshman may be spoken of as the "amoeba" of collegiate life. Whatever theories of evolution one may adhere to, the word "freshman" . . . automatically brings to mind a mental picture of the "Garden of Eden" stage in man's search for knowledge. Freshmanhood is surely the Eden which admits no shadow to overcast the sunny sky of his seraphic delight. . . . As Adam, man of clay, must have felt when he first opened his eyes to the strange glories of this place called the world, so the freshman smiles his naive smile and starts on his explorations of an organized college with all the artlessness and trust of the first man.

Among news items in the first *Senator* were these: "We are very glad to have Jeanne Marstiller Albert, Ex-11 . . . back with us again as a professor's wife." "Professor Allen took Mrs. Allen to Baltimore where she underwent a severe operation."[13]

---

13. Mrs. James E. Allen, the president's first wife, died a few months afterwards in 1923.

This verse of one of the "poems" suggests the existence of a campus problem not limited to the decade of the Roaring Twenties nor peculiar to D&E:

> "When the Professors are out of sight
> We look at notes with all our might
> Cheat oh cheat that is our song
> We have to cheat to get along."

The *Senator* has been published, in various formats since 1922, with occasional brief suspensions caused by lack of funds.

The "United Crusade" campaign launched in 1921 had proved to be a great disappointment to the college. Although approximately $1.1 million, the established goals, was pledged, the value of the Halliehurst Farm gift was included in that figure as a part of D&E's promised $500,000 share and, as could have been expected, a significant number of pledges were never paid. As late as January 1927, nearly four years after the "Crusade" solicitation had ended, more than $508,000 in pledges had not been collected and nearly $160,000 had already been written off as "uncollectable."[14] Thus, it was impossible to add $200,000 to the D&E endowment as had been planned—or even to collect enough to pay for the new buildings.

In 1924, the college provided a rent-free house on the Halliehurst estate to the "Crusade" chairman who was attempting to get people to pay their pledges. Also, in that year, the membership of the board of trustees was increased to twenty-four members "to the end that the influence of the College be extended and greater opportunity be created to divide the work of re-building and re-establishing the College." Neither of those actions brought much money to the coffers. The feeling of distress was augmented by the fact that in 1924, the General Education Board informed President Allen that it could not send D&E the usual one thousand dollar contribution for current expenses "as they had not received sufficient funds" from the churches to support higher education.[15]

Nevertheless, with commitments made to proceed with the new buildings and with hopes high that pledges would soon be paid, the trustees continued with the construction on the new

14. Trustee Minutes, January 28, 1927, p. 140.
15. *Ibid.*, July 8, 1924, p. 120.

campus until the summer of 1926. This work included not only the erection of Liberal Arts Hall, the Science Hall, and the Heating Plant, but also extensive repairs in Halliehurst and the installation of a new heating system there; construction of a sewage system, driveways, telephone lines, and power lines; repairs to the swimming pool, a cottage, and the greenhouse; the landscaping of the grounds, and the purchase of new furniture and equipment. The total costs of all this amounted to $283,276.27. The college had received only $206,277.35 in cash contributions from the campaign. Thus the building fund was in the red approximately $77,000. That, in addition to accrued deficits, resulted in a total indebtedness of more than $105,000 when the college was moved to the Halliehurst campus in the summer of 1926, thus confirming President Allen's doubts and fears in regard to moving the college.

Formal, day-long ceremonies to dedicate the new buildings were held on June 4, 1926, with colorful academic processions from the Davis Memorial Presbyterian Church to the auditorium in the Science Hall in both the morning and afternoon. The state superintendent of schools, the president of West Virginia University, the presidents of eleven other colleges in the state, and numerous representatives of the Synods and Presbyteries attended. Dr. William C. Covert, the general secretary of the Board of Christian Education of the Presbyterian Church in the U.S.A., gave the principal address. President James E. Allen, LL.D., presided at the morning convocation. (He had in a recent year been awarded the honorary degree by Hampden-Sydney College on the twenty-fifth anniversary of his graduation there.) Having the year before succeeded Senator Sutherland as president of the board of trustees, Dr. Barron was in charge of the afternoon ceremonies.

In the extensive newspaper coverage given the Dedication Day events, the editor of the Elkins *Inter-Mountain* waxed eloquent about the grace and beauty of the modified Georgian style red brick buildings, trimmed with limestone, and described the "smoke stack" of the Central Heating Plant as "a real work of art—100 feet and 8 inches in height. It is really an ornament to the building and this cannot be said of all smoke stacks." He was also impressed with the provision for a room eighty-five by twenty feet in dimension on the second floor of Liberal Arts Hall for use as a library. His article concluded with these prophetic words: "It is given to no human being to accurately peer into the future, but Davis and Elkins College seems to have laid a foundation to which will be added, from time to time, additional equipment in buildings, laboratories, libraries, and all else that goes with a high grade education."[16]

Harry Whetsell, then business manager, recalls with amusement that when he presented the budget for furnishing the Science Hall to the trustees, one member of the Finance Committee who had had little formal education objected to a two thousand dollar item for "laboratory equipment." Mistaking "laboratory" for lavatory," the trustee avowed that he was "agin spending so much money for commodes!"

Soon after acquiring the Halliehurst estate, the trustees appointed Richard Barry to look after the grounds while construction of the buildings was underway.[17] He lived with his parents in the Gatehouse which still stands at the entrance of the campus and remained in the employee of the college for many years. Remembered by several generations of students for his friendly interest in campus life, Dick Barry was responsible for an early tradition which Dr. Charles Albert described as follows:

> Several weeks before Christmas Dick would drag some logs up between Liberal Arts and Science Halls, and a few days before the Christmas vacation began he would start the fire so the students between classes could enjoy it. Dick said the smoke and fire made the season "smell more like Christmas."
>
> He stretched a rope from the lower entrance to Liberal Arts Hall to a limb on one of the trees near by. To the limb he fastened a cow bell so that a pull on the rope rang the bell. He also hung a string of sleigh bells over the door of the Science Hall so that any student could ring the bells. As Christmas was approached the tinkling of the cow bell and the clashing of the sleigh bells announced often and enthusiastically that "Christmas is a coming."
>
> The entire mid portion of the second floor of Science Hall was as an auditorium at that time. Dick decorated the stage with Christmas trees, Spanish moss, poinsettias, and other materials that he secured from different parts of the country at his own expense. The halls of both buildings he embellished with beautiful and unique decorations which attracted the notice of many towns-

---

16. Elkins *Inter-Mountain*, June 3, 1926, p. 1.
17. Trustee Minutes, July 8, 1924, p. 119; Harry Whetsell interview with Thomas R. Ross, March 27, 1979.

people who came to see them. At the Christmas party Dick presented the Christmas Queen with a bouquet of violets.

The Tradition passed when Dick left the employ of the College.[18]

The first students to attend classes on the new campus were those 240 enrolled in the 1926 Summer School. All but two of them were West Virginians. Most were from Elkins and Randolph County or from neighboring counties within commuting distance. Total enrollment of regular college students for the 1926-27 academic year was indeed encouraging. There were thirty-eight seniors, thirty-three juniors, seventy sophomores, and ninety-five freshmen. In addition, there were various "unclassified students" and fourteen in the academy. Public high schools having become common by the mid-twenties, there was no longer much need for private preparatory schools. Thus D&E discontinued the academy in 1927. Provisional admission of freshmen "lacking proper preparation in Mathematics, Latin, French or German" was permitted and tutors from the senior class, under the supervision of the head of the appropriate department, were available to help the entering student remedy his deficiency.

The growth of the student body in the postwar years from 70 in 1919-20 to 236 in 1926-27 was one factor in reviving D&E's prewar interest in intercollegiate athletics. Another influence, of course, was that in the era of the "Roaring Twenties" pleasure-seeking Americans were giving much more attention than previously to sports. Baseball and prizefighting were being commercialized on a large scale and this soon spread to some extent to intercollegiate football and basketball. The rise of "big-time athletics," designed not primarily for the physical training and enjoyment of students, but to promote "College Spirit," attract alumni gifts, and entertain the public, was generally as characteristic of American higher education in the decade as was the decline of classical curricula and the widespread de-emphasis on the religious and moral purposes of education. More important, however, than such trends of the times, so far as D&E is concerned, was the appointment of E. Camden Henderson as coach in 1923. Also, it was of some significance that many of the

18. Albert, *loc. cit.*, pp. 19-20.

men who had attended D&E and participated in athletics in the prewar years lived in Elkins and vicinity in the twenties and afterward had a natural interest in promoting a strong competitive sports program.

As Kent Kessler phrased it in his history of athletics in West Virginia, "In this year of 1923 an athletic hurricane was born up in Randolph County hills which swept through the country, playing havoc with many great institutions. It was called the Scarlet Hurricane of Davis and Elkins College and the force was generated by Cam Henderson and his famous football and basketball teams."[19] In 1923, D&E's football team was undefeated and untied, winning all eight scheduled games. Such scores as 47-3 (D&E-Salem), 52-0 (D&E-Fairmont), 54-0 (D&E-Morris Harvey), 51-0 (D&E-West Virginia Tech), doubtless explain why the losers felt they had been hit by a hurricane.

Coach Henderson was not merely interested in football. He "shook the weeds" looking for basketball players as well as for promising recruits for his football team. It is said that if he could not find the type of athlete he wanted in the high schools of West Virginia, he would go to "far away places to get his material."[20] His spectacular success the first year gave him considerable leverage with the local fans and some of the trustees. Thus, on September 9, 1924, in what may have been an attempt at an "end run" around President Allen and the faculty, John Brown, C. W. Maxwell and H. P. Mullennex appeared at a meeting of the board of trustees to request that "$4,500 be appropriated for athletics for the coming year." The minutes record that "President Allen objected to the amount asked for, stating that the funds available would not permit such an appropriation in addition to the necessary Faculty and other current expenses." He might well have been outraged at this interference in the management of the college, but on that point the record is silent. The board, however, agreed "to appropriate $3,600 to be paid in twelve installments of $300 each" to be used by the coach and the athletic committee.[21]

In the 1924-25 season, the D&E basketball team had an unusual array of talent. Harry M. ("Red") Crimm and Miles Kochenderfer were outstanding guards. Fred Christy, the center,

---

19. Kessler, *op. cit.*, p. 255.
20. *Ibid.*, p. 256.
21. Trustee Minutes, September 9, 1924, p. 129.

was the leading scorer, and Randall McKinney and Bill Barrett were fast and excellent forwards. This quintet won twenty-two straight games, losing none. This was the first perfect record in basketball in the history of West Virginia. In addition to beating all their state rivals, the D&E team defeated both Catholic University and George Washington University, thus gaining much good publicity for the college in the Washington, D.C., area. The "Senators," as the D&E teams are called, also tied the University of Virginia for the championship of the Old Dominion and beat such strong northern teams as those from Geneva College, and Niagara, Buffalo, and Alfred universities.[22]

The 1923 football and 1924-25 basketball records put D&E "on the map" in the realm of intercollegiate athletics and greatly enhanced Cam Henderson's standing with the trustees. Thus, at its regular meeting on June 9, 1925, "the board instructed the President to provide $2,700 for Coach Henderson's salary for nine months." At that time, the twelve-month salary for President Allen, who had served the college for eighteen years—including fifteen years as president—was $3,600, having recently been raised from $3,000. The salary of Dean Albert for ten months was $3,000; that of Harry Whetsell, the business manager, was $2,400 for twelve months; and Miss Harris, the registrar, $1,800 for twelve months. The highest paid senior professors with doctorates received $2,500 for nine months. In short, Henderson was paid the same monthly salary ($300) as the president and the dean and more than any other faculty member.

In addition, the board directed the president to allow the athletic committee to have "a fee of $6.00 per regular student to come out of the entrance fee of $10.00." As if the trustees' sense of propriety and system of priorities (indicated by the appropriation for Henderson's salary and the distribution of the lion's share of the entrance fees to support athletics) were not enough, two additional actions further irritated the faculty. First, the board gave to Coach Henderson the responsibility for seeing "that each student who seeks to represent the College on any athletic team has reached his scholastic requirements at least 2 days before a game is to be played." Professor Whetsell had the task of explaining this action to the faculty at a later date. Secondly, the board appointed a committee of its own members

---

22. Kessler, *op. cit.*, p. 257.

"to have general oversight of the athletics of the College."[23] Both of those functions were, and always before had been, the responsibility of the faculty and officers of the college. Soon the rules governing eligibility and grants, adopted in 1908 and 1909 (described in chapter 3), were being ignored with impunity.

It is rather ironical that at the same meeting at which it took the above actions, the trustees lamented the "unprecedented financial distress" of the college in a petition to the General Education Board of the Presbyterian Church. They asked the board to increase its annual grant to three thousand dollars and urged its secretary "to write to every pastor in the Synod of West Virginia, requesting him to lay upon the hearts of his people the necessity of larger donations for Christian Education." Not surprisingly, soon after that board meeting, W. H. Wilcox resigned as academic vice-president and professor of English and history, and he and his wife, for several years professor of music, left the college. Professor Charles E. Albert was appointed dean in succession of Wilcox and the use of the title of vice-president was discontinued for the next forty-five years.

In the fall of 1925, D&E had another good football team. Although not as successful in terms of wins as in 1923, the 1925 team scored 244 points to 32 for its opponents. The highlight of the season was that D&E was invited to play Army in Michie Stadium at West Point. There were six All-American players on the Army team that year. The cadets had defeated Notre Dame 27 to 0 before the game with D&E, but when the game with the Scarlet Hurricane ended, the best the great Army team could do resulted in a narrow 14 to 6 victory over the Senators.[24]

In 1926, after the college moved to the Halliehurst campus, Jennings Randolph became director of athletics as well as publicity, while Cam Henderson concentrated on coaching. During the 1926-27 season, with a basketball squad which included veterans Barrett, Christy, Kochenderfer, and McKinney and such newcomers as Max ("Hippo") Poscover (weighing nearly three hundred pounds) and Robert N. "Red" Brown (later a great D&E and West Virginia University coach and director of athletics), D&E won both the State Conference Championship

---

23. Trustee Minutes, June 9, 1925, p. 131; and Faculty Minutes, October 28, 1925, p. 187.
24. Kessler, *op. cit.*, p. 257.

and the West Virginia Collegiate Championship. The Senators defeated every team they played in the state, including a proud victory over West Virginia University by a score of 36 to 27.[25]

During the height of the fame of the Scarlet Hurricane, Geraldine Morgan, a student, wrote the words and music of a song that was militant, snappy, and cheerful, and which promoted zest and enthusiasm among the students.[26]

> Davis-Elkins, fight
> You know we're with you, Scarlet men of might.
> Plunge right through that line
> You'll just leave them all behind.
>
> On to victory, for Davis-Elkins, D and E.
> Senators will win this game.
> Cheer that old team on to fame.
> Come on, Scarlet Hurricane.

During 1924 and 1925, *The Senator* was published monthly instead of weekly as previously. In the spring of 1925, the senior class issued a 112-page yearbook also called *The Senator*. It had an excellent group photograph of the faculty seated out-of-doors and wearing overcoats and hats. There were nine men and nine women faculty members that year—one man and one woman had Ph.D.'s, three other members held master's degrees but the remainder had no degrees above the baccalaureate. The professor of public speaking held a Bachelor of Oratory degree and, to the amusement of many students, her listing in the catalogue was "Margaret L. Dills, B.O." One page was devoted to each member of the graduating class. There was a formal photograph of each senior in cap and gown and also a snapshot and a biographical sketch with emphasis on the characteristics and activities of each. Among the notables were Donald K. ("Damper") Crawford, president of the student body and of X.O.D. (later an Elkins attorney); John A. Cain (also to become an Elkins lawyer); and Bryan Hamilton who would soon become superintendent of the Randolph County schools.

Appropriately, there were several pages depicting the successes of the Scarlet Hurricane in football and basketball in the 1923-25 season. "Crafty Cam" Henderson—that nickname was

---

25. *Ibid.*, p. 258.
26. Albert, *loc. cit.*, p. 18.

to be used frequently by friends and foe in the next ten years—was described as "a tall, easy going, and seemingly good natured chap who had very little to say." However, he was credited with the ability "to instill into the men fighting spirit and the spirit of teamwork."[27]

Note was taken also of the success of D&E's debate teams which had won five of the six state contests in 1924-25. The subject was "Resolved, that Congress should be given power to override decisions of the Supreme Court in which an act of Congress is declared unconstitutional." The Histrionic Club produced W. S. Gilbert's *Pygmalion and Galatea* as the major dramatic presentation of the year.

Since *The Senator* was revived as a newspaper in 1926, the senior class that year called their annual *The Nautilus*. It was edited by Lillian Harris with Bayard Green as business manager. This was a hard cover yearbook, a respectable forebear of the *Senatus*. It was dedicated to Dr. Leighton B. Hensley, professor of Bible and Greek and pastor of the Beverly Presbyterian Church, the sponsor of the class. In addition to excellent individual photographs of the faculty and members of the senior and junior classes and group pictures of the sophomore and freshman classes, there were photographs of the athletic teams and of various student organizations with well-written descriptions of the activities of each. Four of the seventeen faculty members had Ph.D. degrees and one an M.D. Among the organizations in existence at the time of the move from Sally Mike Hill to Halliehurst Campus, the following were deemed quite important: The Zeta Chapter of Chi Beta Phi, the honorary science fraternity, had been established at D&E in January 1925. Fi Batar Cappar, a mock fraternity to promote "pep and school spirit" which was first organized at West Virginia University, formed a chapter at D&E in October 1925. The Chi Phi and Phi Sigma Theta sororities, both local social organizations, were quite active, as were the Chi Omicron Delta, Chi Delta Chi, and T.V.C. fraternities. There were also a Commercial Club, a Debating Society, and a Forensic Association. It is interesting to note that in 1926—twenty years before the Truman Administration established the Department of Defense—the subject for the intercollegiate debates in West Virginia by the Forensic Associa-

---

27. *The Senator*, 1925 Yearbook Edition, p. 51.

tion was "Resolved, the United States should substitute for its departments of Army and Navy one unified department of National Defense."[28]

At the first commencement ceremonies to be held on the new campus, June 8, 1927, the Honorable H. C. Ogden of Wheeling delivered the address. Twenty-six degrees were awarded then and eight more members of the class completed their work and received their diplomas at the end of the summer session. Burlin Barnes, later a member of the faculty, was president of the senior class which included two other future faculty members, Richard H. Talbott and Marvin Lewis Vest, as well as John S. Caplinger, later to be Randolph County Clerk, whose senior thesis was a useful essay on the history of D&E in the early years. Keith Cunningham and Reginald Woodward also were graduated in '27, the former becoming a prominent attorney in Elkins and the latter a public school teacher and coach; both were lifelong boosters of their alma mater.

During Commencement Week, the trustees voted to create the office of business manager, elected D. H. Hill Arnold to succeed E. A. Bowers as college attorney, and authorized the Executive Committee to sell the Old College property, including the President's House. They also renewed their request to the Presbyterian General Education Board and to the Synod and Presbyteries "to make the College a more serious financial obligation and increase their appropriations if at all possible." Mrs. Elkins gave three thousand dollars to help with the deficit, but finances were still in bad shape. Acknowledgment was made of the gift of a fine telescope by Mathew J. Kelly of Elkins. During the following months, the Chi Beta Phi Scientific Fraternity built the Mathew J. Kelly Astronomical Observatory on land given to the college for that purpose by Mrs. Elkins.[29]

In August 1927, Jennings Randolph directed a summer school for coaches, the first of many such summer programs for similar purposes. Cam Henderson, as well as visiting instructors from other institutions, provided instruction in the coaching of basketball, football, and other sports.

An event of interest to the college as well as the community was the October 15, 1927, ceremony to unveil the equestrian

---

28. *The Nautilus,* 1926, p. 70 and *passim.*
29. Trustee Minutes, June, 1927, p. 148.

Equestrian statue of Senator Davis:
"The Iron Horse."

statue of Henry Gassaway Davis at the junction of Sycamore Street and Randolph Avenue. President Allen presided and the principal speakers were John W. Davis, the 1924 Democratic nominee for president, and Howard M. Gore, governor of West Virginia.[30] Popularly known as "The Iron Horse," the Davis monument has been a landmark for over half a century. It has occasionally been a target of "vandals" armed with paint brushes or whitewash—especially if fans of a nearby rival college were dissatisfied at the outcome of an athletic contest at D&E!

Although managing to win the West Virginia Conference Championship in 1927, defeating all state competitors except the university, the Scarlet Hurricane found that their 1927 football schedule was a bit strenuous for a small college team. Overall,

30. Elkins *Inter-Mountain,* October 15, 1927, p. 1.

they won five and lost five games, but their non-conference opponents included Georgetown University, the University of Louisville, the U.S. Military Academy, and the U.S. Naval Academy as well as in-state rivals. It was said that D&E was the only institution other than Notre Dame "ever to have the honor of playing against the Army and Navy elevens in the same season."[31] The D&E star was Mac Bowles, the team captain, from Muskegon, Michigan.

More impressive was the fact that in 1927-28, the Senators, for the second consecutive year, won both the West Virginia Conference basketball championship and the state title during a season in which they defeated West Virginia University three times. Randolph stated that "many sports editors declared the 'Scarlet Hurricane' quite the finest floor combination ever seen." He took the team on a trip to Florida where a victory over Florida University gave the little college much favorable publicity.

Someone has written that 1928, when D&E won the state championship in football, was the year of the "Indian Uprising." The "Scarlet Hurricane" not only defeated all West Virginia rivals, but also beat Navy 2-0 and tied the Quantico Marines 12-12. The phrase "Indian Uprising" had reference to the fact that by the end of the decade, Coach Henderson had recruited several Indian students from the Haskell Institute in Kansas to play football for D&E. Outstanding among these were Albert Hawley from Montana, Ben Fairbanks, Simon Gurneau, and Elijah Smith of Wisconsin. Other great players in the late twenties were Neil Rengle and Alva ("Chief") Wagner from Minnesota, and Claude Warren of Parkersburg.[32]

Commencement Week in 1929 was designated for observance of the twenty-fifth anniversary of the founding of the college. Robert S. Irons, the only living member of the class of 1910, the prosecuting attorney of Randolph County, was the principal speaker at the Alumni Day convocation. There were violin and voice recitals, a dramatic production, a tennis match and a baseball game. Hallie D. Elkins, Grace D. Lee, and John T. Davis, the daughters and son of Henry Gassaway Davis were lauded for their contributions to the college and for helping to finance the twenty-fifth anniversary.[33] United States Senator

---

31. Davis and Elkins College Catalog, April, 1927, p. 71.
32. Kessler, *op. cit.*, pp. 259-60.
33. Trustee Minutes, June 4, 1929, p. 154.

Royal S. Copeland of New York gave the commencement address to the class of 1929 which numbered among its members Henry Hamilton, later to become principal of Elkins High School; Kirkland McKee, also a future Randolph County teacher and longtime Dean of Potomac State College; Margaret L. MacVean, John C. Leonard, and Harold B. Stalnaker—all future Randolph County teachers; and D. Alton Gilmore who became a Presbyterian minister and a trustee of D&E. As of that date, D&E had granted baccalaureate degrees to 215 persons, had conferred twenty-four honorary D.D. degrees, had issued ninety-nine Standard Normal Certificates, and had awarded special diplomas to 133 students in the Business School, fifteen in Dramatic Arts, and three in Music.[34]

At the beginning of the 1929-30 academic year, just before the Wall Street Stock Market crash, 180 regular students enrolled at D&E. There were also fourteen special students and fourteen in the Business School, as well as several part-time music and drama students. Instruction in Saturday and night courses was offered and for the first time there was a "Parsons Extension"— apparently a night course in geography offered in a Parsons, West Virginia, classroom for twelve students.

The "Scarlet Hurricane" won the state championship in football again in 1929 and also defeated Saint Louis University, Quantico Marines, Villanova and others, and tied Fordham 6-6. It was said that "The backfield of Rengle, Warren, Wagner, and Smith was one of the greatest in the state history."[35]

The 1929-30 basketball team won twenty-three of twenty-six games. Fourteen of the contests were with out-of-state teams and D&E did not schedule either WVU or Wesleyan that year. High scoring Senators were Dale Peters, Ellis Vest, and "Red" Brown. In 1930, the football team traveled into various sections of the nation, playing such institutions as North Dakota State and North Dakota University, Oklahoma City, Mount Union, Waynesburg, Furman, John Carroll, Albright, Rider, and Saint Frances in five intersectional contests.[36]

The amazing achievements of the "Scarlet Hurricane" football and basketball teams in the Roaring Twenties were a source of

---

34. Davis and Elkins College Catalog, April, 1930, pp. 14, 101-10.
35. Kessler, *op. cit.*, p. 262.
36. *Ibid.*, p. 262.

great pride to D&E and to the community. They are the stuff of which legends are made. The athletic traditions established then have been influential for half a century, inspiring championship efforts in later decades especially in basketball and soccer. That a very small, desperately poor, recently founded college could have attained such a record is a phenomenon resulting from a combination of factors including the times, the circumstances, and the talents of such unusual personalities as Cam Henderson and Jennings Randolph—a combination unlikely ever to occur anywhere again.

Inevitably there were less pleasing aspects of the situation. In an era when the moral fiber of the nation was flabby and respect for law and ethical conduct low (as demonstrated by the Harding scandals, lynchings, and the flagrant disregard of prohibition at all levels of society), it should not be shocking to discover that a college coach sometimes used ineligible players or that some students plagiarized term papers or cheated on examinations. Something is somewhat out of kilter in *academe,* however, when the Faculty Minutes record that, although President Allen had checked on the academic work of the football players, his checking "does not affect the team as the new ruling of the Board of Trustees required the coach to ascertain the standing of members of the team."[37]

Subsequently, Dean Albert objected, futilely, to students being permitted to remain in college a fifth year in order to participate in athletics.[38] In 1929, the Eligibility Committee of the conference investigated, found that Coach Henderson had allowed a student who "had flunked his courses" to play in a football game against Wesleyan, and ordered that the game be forfeited to Wesleyan.[39] It has been claimed that one of the star members of the 1928-29 basketball team had played on a well-known professional team before coming to D&E and thus was not eligible to participate in intercollegiate competition.[40] That same year, "nearly every opponent" protested Henderson's use of a basketball player who had "used up his eligibility"—i.e., already participated for four years. In December, President Allen in-

37. Faculty Minutes, October 2, 1925, p. 183.
38. *Ibid.,* December 12, 1928, p. 41.
39. Kessler, *op. cit.,* p. 262.
40. *Ibid.,* p. 261; Frank Wimer interview with Thomas R. Ross, August 2, 1979.

formed the trustees of the "serious situation in which the Athletic Committee finds itself by virtue of being disqualified for playing with the University, Wesleyan, and Fairmont" because the D&E coach had used ineligible players.[41]

Of course, the critical financial condition of the college was further burdened by the costs of recruiting athletes and supporting the extensive travel schedules. On some of the longer trips, funds would be exhausted and the athletic director would have to call or telegraph Mrs. Elkins or some other patron to wire enough money to enable him to get the team back to the campus from some faraway place.

The shock which finally awakened the majority of the board of trustees to the evils inherent in permitting the "athletic tail to wag the academic dog," as they had done, came in 1930. As early as 1926, there had been discussion of the need for accreditation by the North Central Association of Colleges and Secondary Schools.[42] In September 1928, President Allen told the faculty that he hoped the college could be accredited within eighteen months because he felt that the lack of accreditation "may account for the loss of an unprecedented number of students this year."[43] With much satisfaction, he informed the faculty in January 1930 that a North Central Association visitation had been scheduled for sometime after February 5 to evaluate the college.[44] After the visit of the officials in March, Dr. Allen received an extensive report from the North Central Association detailing the reasons for denying accreditation to D&E. The president discussed the contents of the evaluation with the faculty in May and with the trustees in June. There were four major areas of weakness: (1) an insufficient number of books in the library, (2) an inadequate endowment, (3) a faculty with too few members holding graduate degrees, and (4) the condition in athletics.[45]

After hearing this report, the board of trustees adopted the following resolutions and sent a copy of the Alumni Athletic Committee, which for several years had dominated college intercollegiate athletic policy, apparently with board acquiescence:

41. *Ibid.*, p. 261; Trustee Executive Committee Minutes, December 10, 1929, p. 254.
42. Trustee Minutes, June 4, 1926, p. 134.
43. Faculty Minutes, September 25, 1928, p. 37.
44. *Ibid.*, January 21, 1930, p. 32.
45. *Ibid.*, May 2, 1930, p. 54.

The Trustees of the College have heard the complete report of the North Central Association made in March. While there are many commendations in this report, there are some serious criticisms, probably justifiable, and among them, the criticism of the management of athletics.

The Board deplores the present tendency toward professionalism among the Colleges of the country, or as practiced by some of the athletic or alumni associations connected with the same. While it appears that possibly some of the things done with reference to football here may be subject to criticism, it is perfectly certain that any such practices indulged in . . . are commonly also practiced by other Colleges in West Virginia and elsewhere, and particularly by those connected with institutions that have broken off athletic relations with Davis and Elkins.

In view of this report and in view of further criticism as submitted by certain members of the Trustees, coming to them from various sources, we advise the athletic committee to look toward a less pretentious schedule in football, both as to the number of games played and to the strength of the opposing teams. We believe it is unwise for Davis and Elkins College to schedule too many large universities which are not natural competitors of a college of this size.

The Board regards it as unfortunate the Davis and Elkins College is not playing next year in football with any West Virginia team.[46]

Of course, by the time the board finally awoke to the situation which it had begun to permit to develop as early as 1924, it was too late to affect the decision relative to accreditation. Indeed, it was too late even to make any immediate change in the schedules for 1930-31. The significance of the North Central Association evaluation was discounted by many who did not understand that accreditation made any difference, but it was not lost sight of by the faculty and the more thoughtful of the trustees and alumni.

Meantime, the Great Depression which had begun in the autumn of 1929 deepened, bringing with it changes to D&E, to intercollegiate athletics, and to much else in the America of the 1930s.

46. Trustee Minutes, June 3, 1930, p. 177.

V

D&E in the Depths of the Depression: 1930-35

Between the stock market crash of October 1929 and the inauguration of Franklin Delano Roosevelt as president of the United States on March 4, 1933, the America of the Roaring Twenties fell apart. Her economy was in unprecedented disarray, her spirit was near breaking, her institutions were deeply shaken. Four million workers were unemployed in 1930, eight million in 1931, nearly thirteen million by 1933. No facet of American life escaped the scars of the Great Depression. The fog of despair hung over the land. To reform that economy, to restore that spirit, to reestablish those institutions, to bring relief to those unemployed, to recover from that depression, to replace despair and fear with hope and faith—those were the aims of President Roosevelt throughout much of the desperate decade of the thirties. That he was determined to preserve capitalism, democracy, individual freedom, and personal security, when much of the rest of the world was turning to communism, fascism, socialism, or militarism, distinguished him from leaders of most other nations devastated by the depression. That he sought the advice and used the talents of college and university professors and other intellectuals—"The Brain Trust," his detractors labeled them—and that he was deeply concerned about education and young people in the era of financial panic and unemployment were characteristics which differentiated the president from most American politicians. Directly or indirectly, Franklin D. Roosevelt's election to the presidency in 1932 proved to be of vital significance to the world and in the history of Davis and Elkins College in subsequent years.

If D&E had barely been able to survive during the 1920s when most of the nation enjoyed prosperity, what would be her fate in the depths of the worst depression America had ever suffered? In 1928, the last year of boom times, the board of trustees was still trying to sell the Old College property and was discussing the feasibility of suing persons who had not paid pledges made in the "United Crusade Campaign." So great was the financial distress that year that the board voted to take $5,100 from designated Scholarship Accounts and put the money in the Plant Fund, and President Allen had to inform the faculty that "there would be some necessary delay in full settlement for salaries in the summer school."[1]

The following year, after electing Thaddeus Pritt to succeed the late N. I. Hall as treasurer of the board, the trustees began to formulate plans to issue "bonds and interest-bearing coupons in the principal sum of $150,000" for the purpose of "providing funds and funding the present floating debt." Three hundred such bonds were to be offered for sale, each having a maturity value of $500 dollars "to be payable, principal and interest, in gold coin of the United States of America" in 1939. As security for the bonds, the college pledged its properties and the as yet uncollected subscriptions of funds promised to the "United Crusade Campaign."[2] The bonds were prepared and, in January 1930, President Allen urged all faculty members to buy one or more of them so that the indebtedness on the college buildings could be liquidated.[3]

During the spring of 1929, Mrs. Elkins offered to give the college $100,000 on condition that an additional $200,000 be raised.[4] Before anything was done in regard to this, the depression began and nothing came of the proposal.

In 1930, the faculty introduced the concept of students' concentrating in a "major" field of interest supplemented by a "minor." This became effective in 1931 for all degree candidates. A departmental major consisted of twenty-eight to forty semester hours and a minor of eighteen to twenty-four semester hours, depending on the departments chosen. There was no essential change from the preceding decade in the general course requirements specified for the B.A. and B.S. degrees.

There was increasing interest in politics, drama, and other activities during the depression. J. Buhl Shahan, a junior and

1. Trustee Minutes, June 5, 1928, p. 150; Faculty Minutes, April 13, 1928, p. 34.
2. Trustee Minutes, June 4, 1929, and October 30, 1929, pp. 154, 156-74.
3. Faculty Minutes, January 21, 1930, p. 52.
4. Trustee Minutes, June 4, 1929, p. 153.

business manager of *The Senator,* was the only West Virginia college student to enter the National Oratorical Contest in 1930. His subject was "American Youth and the Constitution." In later years, he became a political science professor at D&E and elsewhere and a member of the West Virginia Senate. Jennings Randolph first ran for Congress in 1930.[5] He was not successful, but D&E students were proud to boast that "He's the youngest candidate for that office in West Virginia political history."[6]

The popular play, *Rossum's Universal Robots,* by Karel Capek was presented in the spring and was said to be the "climax of the most brilliant season" of D&E drama in the history of the College." The theme of the play had to do with "the discovery of a way to produce chemical life in the form of human beings" and the production of these as "Robots." The art director was Northam Gould who was said to be "especially fitted for his place" since he had worked behind the scenes at the production of the original "R.U.R." in New York several years earlier.[7] His wife, Eleanor Cody Gould, a well-trained actress, directed the play. They were both D&E faculty members from 1928 to 1930.

The first class to be graduated in the 1930s had twenty-eight degree candidates. Among them were Robert ("Red") Brown, Neil Rengel, Alva ("Chief") Wagner, and Claude Warren—all outstanding athletes. Future D&E trustees Samuel R. Hoover and W. R. ("Bill") Cromwell; Louis H. Nefflen, later an Elkins physician; Sallie Hamilton, Elva Harris, Elizabeth Fling, Fred Green, Mary Louise Tallman, and Byron Woods were also prominent seniors in 1930 and their class sponsor was Professor S. Benton Talbot.

It is very interesting, and may be surprising to some, to note that the Great Depression did not cause a decrease in enrollment at D&E during the 1930s. In fact, registration statistics reveal a slight increase in the number of full-time students in the regular sessions during the decade as the following summary indicates:

1929-30	180	1935-36	235
1930-31	182	1936-37	233
1931-32	190	1937-38	209
1932-33	195	1938-39	204
1933-34	183	1939-40	191
1934-35	213		

5. *The Senator,* April 30, 1930, p. 1.
6. *Ibid.,* June 2, 1930, p. 3.
7. *Ibid.,* April 30, 1930, pp. 1, 4.

Likewise, enrollment of part-time students, students in the special six-weeks "spring semester," and in the summer sessions generally remained constant. Although not consistent year by year, there was a gradual increase in the proportion of female to male students attending D&E during the decade until, in 1938-39, the total of women exceeded that of men (103 to 101) so far as full-time regular students were concerned. The next year, however, there were only 70 girls to 121 boys. The widest divergence was in 1933-34 when there were 118 men to 65 women.

Doubtless several factors accounted for the stability and slight increase in the college's enrollment in the thirties. The tuition rate remained low (seventy-five dollars per semester). There were virtually no jobs for young people elsewhere. Most of the D&E students lived within commuting (often walking) distance and could board and room at home. Such New Deal agencies as the Federal Emergency Relief Administration and the National Youth Administration provided financial aid to college students. Also, of course, the Randolph County area, not being highly industrialized, had not been as devastated by the Great Depression as were more urban areas. Never having benefited much by the false prosperity of the stock market boom of the twenties, the people of Elkins and vicinity suffered less shock from the 1929 "Crash." Furthermore, Elkins was a railroad center of some significance and a market town for farmers, lumbermen, and miners of a rather wide area. Being the seat of county government and having a first class post office, a federal courthouse, other government agencies, major hospital facilities, public schools and the college, Elkins included a number of professional people and civil servants among her population. Since, in the depression, the cost of living was low, those with steady incomes in such a community fared reasonably well compared to people in most other areas of the nation. Also various New Deal programs such as the Civil Conservation Corps, the National Youth Administration, the Works Progress Administration, and the Tygart Valley Homestead projects at Dailey and Valley Bend, all brought money into the local economy. Thus, it is evident that even in the depths of depression there were numerous families who could raise the small sums needed to finance a son or daughter at D&E for two to four years (most students who entered seem to have stayed less than three years, as the freshmen and sophomore classes usually were about twice the size of the junior and senior classes).

During Commencement Week of 1930, President Allen announced that $21,000 in gifts had been received during the year. A $1,000 check from Jesse Riddle (B.A., 1912) was said to have been the largest amount ever received from an alumnus. The college library had added 473 volumes during the year and had 5,500 books and "hundreds of bound volumes of periodicals" as of that time.[8] In his annual report to the trustees, Dr. Allen outlined a program to be completed within ten years. His stated goals were "first to relieve the college entirely of debt, to increase the endowment to $1,000,000, to build a physical education building, to complete the Liberal Arts Hall and the Science Building, and to add materially to the number of books in the library." He foresaw the need to develop a good Department of Business Administration, a good course in forestry, and a small Department of Horticulture.[9] Emphasizing that D&E had a good Department of Education, he asserted that the college "is insisting as far as the law will allow, upon the prospective teacher pursuing thorough courses in English, Science, Mathematics, History, and Modern Languages prior to undertaking the more technical work." He also reported that the college would continue its policy of admitting qualified students "to give them a chance to do their best, but to graduate only such as have shown ability to pursue college work successfully."[10]

Later in the summer in an interview with a local news reporter, President Allen stated that "the principal task ahead of the Trustees is to increase the endowment to meet current expenses," and asserted that "under present conditions" he was "unwilling to attempt any expansion until the cost is definitely guaranteed."[11] He also said that lack of endowment and inadequate library facilities had been two of the reasons the North Central Association had for denying accreditation to D&E and that he had applied to the Carnegie Foundation for financial assistance with which to purchase several hundred books.

At the first faculty meeting in the fall semester of 1930, President Allen described plans for the First Annual Forest Festival which was to be held at the end of October. Several of the major

---

8. Elkins *Inter-Mountain,* June 4 and 10, 1930.
9. *Ibid.,* July 5, 1930.
10. *Ibid.*
11. *Ibid.,* August 11, 1930.

events, including the coronation of the Queen of the Forest, were to be held on the campus. The president asked all faculty members to cooperate in every way possible to make the event a success.[12] Originally conceived by George Dornblazer and others as an autumn homecoming observance for former Elkins residents, the Mountain State Forest Festival, since its inception fifty years ago, has become one of the outstanding affairs of its type anywhere in the nation and has grown so much that it usually attracts more than 100,000 visitors each year. From the beginning, the leading citizens of Elkins as well as college personnel have cooperated in the arrangements. A glance at the program for October 30-November 1, 1930, (price twenty-five cents) indicates that Margaret Straley of Ripley was Queen Silvia I. She received her crown from Governor William G. Conley at colorful ceremonies on the D&E campus at the foot of the hill below the Liberal Arts Hall. Professor Irving Miller directed the Queen's Chorus and Professor Mildred Bryant Johnston was the director of a "Historical Pageant of Randolph County." Other D&E personnel or their wives participating in various capacities were President Allen, Dean and Mrs. Charles E. Albert, Professor and Mrs. Harry Whetsell, Professor L. E. Dobbins, and Mrs. T. J. Hale. The first Forest Ball was held in Halliehurst Hall, beginning at 10:00 p.m. on October 31. The following day, the Grand Feature Parade, with A. Spates Brady as grand marshal, started at 10:00 a.m., followed by a football game between D&E's "Scarlet Hurricane" and a team from the University of Oklahoma. Each day, the Curtis Wright Flying Circus performed for the gasping crowds at Davis Field.[13]

The trustees were informed early in 1931 that the Alumni Athletic Committee had "serious financial" problems and owed the college $1800. C. A. Gross and Earl Maxwell promised that that deficit would be paid, but they asked the trustees to provide twenty-five full-tuition grants to athletes for the spring semester. The board's Executive Committee agreed to authorize the grants and then appointed a special committee "to ascertain all facts pertaining to the functioning of the Athletic Committee." At the same time President Allen advised the trustees that the

12. Faculty Minutes, October 13, 1930, p. 61.
13. *Official Program of the Mountain State Forest Festival,* October 30; November 1, 1930, *passim.*

cumulative current expense deficit of the college "was at least $25,000."[14]

In the spring of 1931, the faculty devoted some time to discussion of the problem of grading. Dr. C. W. Gwinn, professor of education, suggested that D&E adopt "the system of letters in grading hereafter" and the president appointed a committee to study the matter. The faculty later voted to accept the committee's recommendations that the college adopt a marking scale of A, B, C, D, and F. A student was required to have at least 136 quality (slightly above a C average) to be eligible for graduation and a minimum of 300 quality points to be considered for graduation honors (*cum laude*), 320 for *magna cum laude* and 360 for *maxima cum laude*.[15]

Near the close of the 1930-31 academic year, the first full year of the depression, the editors of *The Senator* reviewed the state of the college in a long editorial. They observed that "in spite of the economic depression that is being experienced on all college campuses, the enrollment here at Davis and Elkins has not been greatly affected by the so called hard times." Commenting on the continued success of the football and basketball teams, the writers also called attention to the fact that varsity letters were first awarded at D&E in 1931 and that the college had a golf team for the first time that year. Through the generosity of the Lee family who lived in Graceland (Mrs. Arthur Lee was a daughter of Senator Davis), the four-hole golf course adjacent to the back campus had been made available for use by the college players and was being cared for by interested students under the supervision of Professor Talbot. Other highlights of the year mentioned were the organization of a Student Volunteer unit (students planning to be missionaries), the establishment of a chapter of Alpha Sigma Phi, the national forensic fraternity, the publication of a book by Dr. C. W. Gwinn, professor of education, and the fact that the class of 1931 was the largest ever to be graduated at D&E.[16]

---

14. Trustee Executive Committee Minutes, January 31; February 17, 1931, pp. 260-61. Later when the Alumni Trustee Committee was disbanded Messers Gross, Maxwell, and Harper, who had advanced several thousands of dollars to support the athletic program, were to "write off" what they had spent. (C. A. Gross interview with Thomas R. Ross, 1979.)

15. Faculty Minutes, April 10, May 7, May 13, 1931; January 26, 1932, *passim*.

16, *The Senator*, May 22, 1931, p. 2.

More than seventy-five members attended the annual meeting of the alumni association in early June. S. Benton Talbot was elected president and Don Wolfe vice-president. A major topic of discussion was the need for accreditation for the college. Bryan Hamilton of the class of 1925, superintendent of the Randolph County schools, presented a resolution that the alumni association "most cordially approve the efforts being put forth by the Faculty of Davis and Elkins College to secure recognition by the North Central Association." The resolution also expressed concern that D&E graduates who had been certified to teach be permitted to do so "without compelling them to take six hours of additional work in a North Central Association College" because D&E had not attained accreditation.[17] Subsequently, the State Committee of the North Central Association notified President Allen that in the future "the graduates of Davis and Elkins College, including the school year 1930-31, will be approved as teachers in the North Central High Schools of the state, provided they meet state certification laws. Graduates of years previous to 1930-31 must complete six semester hours in an accredited institution."[18]

At its June meeting, the board of trustees authorized the granting of honorary Doctor of Laws and Doctor of Literature degrees in the future "provided, however, that not more than one LL.D., one Litt. D., and two D.D. degrees are to be granted in any one year." It was also agreed that students who had attended D&E for three years could complete their fourth year at another institution, transfer the credit back to D&E and receive their degree with their class.

Because the deficit for the year was approximately $11,000, the board instructed its president and the president of the college, with the assistance of Jennings Randolph, to proceed with a "Financing Program in Elkins and throughout the state in an endeavor to collect annually at least four hundred $25 cash donations to assist in the operation of the College and the payment of the operating deficit."[19] This campaign began in Elkins on June 10 with the goal of raising $2,500 in the community before beginning the statewide canvass. The *Inter-Mountain* printed the

17. Elkins *Inter-Mountain,* June 3, 1931.
18. Letter from Dan H. Perdue to James E. Allen, August 20, 1931. Printed in the *Inter-Mountain,* August 22, 1931.
19. Trustee Minutes, June 2, 1931, p. 180.

list of donors and within a few days more than $2,000 was collected. The last few hundred dollars were not obtained, however, and the effort to get three hundred $25 gifts from residents elsewhere in the state proved to be impossible as the depression worsened in 1931.[20]

Thus, at the end of July, the board's Executive Committee met with the faculty to discuss the necessity of a reduction in salaries for the coming year. By a unanimous vote, a motion was adopted "that all salaries above $2,000 for the year be reduced by 10 percent."[21] Despite the objection of President Allen and Dean Albert, the faculty and trustee members voted that "the 10 percent reduction be announced in the press as a voluntary contribution in this time of depression" and "Mr. Randolph was requested to prepare a brief story which was later read to the joint meeting and approved."

A few weeks later, a group of faculty wives, in cooperation with some of the leading women of the city, organized the College Aid Club. Mrs. W. E. Baker was chosen president and Mrs. Flora Gawthrop was appointed membership chairman. An invitation to join was issued to "every women in Elkins who is interested in the city and its progress" since they "must be vitally concerned with the development of the Davis and Elkins College." President Allen and Glen Watring, president of the student body, both spoke at the meeting expressing appreciation for the interest in and efforts to assist the college.[22] Since 1931, the College Aid has been active in behalf of the college and has accomplished much of benefit to the institution, its members giving generously of their time, talents, and money.

The 1931 football team was one of the best in the history of the college, finishing the season with ten victories and only one defeat. The "Scarlet Hurricane" led the nation in scoring with 344 points. Only Saint Louis University ever scored against D&E, winning over the Senators 20 to 6. Saint Louis University claimed five of the D&E team were ineligible so Coach Henderson played only those who were. This perhaps accounted for the loss. Argus Winters made 13 touchdowns and 78 points.[23] Other

20. Elkins *Inter-Mountain*, June 10-September 16, 1931, *passim.*
21. Faculty Minutes, July 30, 1931, p. 79, and Trustee Executive Committee Minutes, July 28, September 18, 1931, pp. 263-66.
22. Elkins *Inter-Mountain,* September 2, 1931.
23. Kessler, *op. cit.,* p. 263; Harry ("Bud") Shelton interview with Thomas R. Ross, August 14, 1979.

outstanding players included Albert Hawley (one of the great "Indians"), John Whitfield, Lester Ingram, and Robert Markowitz—all seniors—and Harry L. ("Bud") Shelton, a sophomore and one of the all-time athletic stars at D&E, later to be an outstanding coach and faculty member at his alma mater. The basketball team was less successful, but had a respectable season. Dale Peters scored a total of 330 points and was said to be one of the best players in the East.[24]

Harry L. ("Bud") Shelton

Despite the token reduction in salaries and the efforts of Elkins friends to help, the college was unable to meet its payrolls in the fall semester. Thus, in mid-December, the trustees held a special meeting to consider the growing financial crisis. Although agreeing to honor grants already made, the board ordered that no more athletic scholarships were to be awarded. Then, noting that "salaries of members of the Faculty are unpaid for the entire College year" and that the board "does not have funds available to pay such back salary or to secure future salary which may accrue and does not know how such funds may be procured," the trustees adopted the following resolution: "It is resolved therefore, that the Faculty be fully advised of the financial condition of the College, to the end that if the Faculty desire not to remain in the employ of the Board of Trustees, or to close the College at the end of the semester, such privilege is available to them."[25]

This resolution was not to become effective until January 15, 1932, and could be rescinded by the Executive Committee "if donations in encouraging amounts" should be received in the

24. *Ibid.*
25. Trustee Minutes, December 15, 1931, p. 182.

thirty-day interval. That it never had to be implemented was due to the fact that Hallie Davis Elkins gave the college ten thousand dollars and to the willingness of most of the faculty to continue whether paid in full or not.[26]

It is remarkable to note that only two faculty members resigned after the summer meeting when the 10 percent salary reduction was voted. It is not certain that one of those did so because of that action since he voted for it and did not leave until late August. He was Dr. Gwinn who received an appointment to the faculty of a Pennsylvania teachers college. Professor David Kirby, former president of Morris Harvey College, succeeded Dr. Gwinn in September 1931.[27] The other member to resign was a professor of French and German who had served for two years. Professor George E. Kerchner, who had taught Bible and history since 1927, resigned in April to accept a pastorate in a Presbyterian church in New York.[28] All others remained and most accepted reappointment for 1932-33.

Inasmuch as February 22, 1932, marked the two hundredth anniversary of the birth of George Washington, D&E observed Washington's birthday with special ceremonies. A "quart of soil from George Washington's private garden" at Mount Vernon was ordered from the "Mt. Vernon Ladies Association" and was used to plant a "Bicentennial Tree" on the campus (this was done on May 9 since February is no time to plant a tree in Elkins).[29]

At the 1932 commencement, the first diplomas were awarded to students who had completed a three-year course in nursing which had been developed as a cooperative program between the college and the Davis Memorial Hospital. Among those awarded the B.A. degree was President Allen's son, James E. Allen, Jr., at whose birth twenty-one years earlier, the students had raised a diaper on the flagpole on the old campus. Subsequently, he received twenty-seven honorary degrees, including an LL.D. from D&E, became a trustee of his alma mater, commissioner of education and president of the University of State of New York and finally U.S. Commissioner of Education in the Nixon Administration.

26. *Ibid.*, June 7, 1932, p. 184.
27. Elkins *Inter-Mountain*, August-September, 1931, *passim*.
28. Faculty Minutes, April 8, 1932, p. 88.
29. *Ibid.*, January 29, 1932, p. 87; and an official certificate from the Plant Quarantine and Control Administration, dated May 7, and a memo on it is now in possession of Miss Anna Parmesano, p. 44, of her scrapbook.

Jennings Randolph won the Democratic nomination for representative in Congress in 1932 and was elected in the November landslide which sent Franklin D. Roosevelt to the White House and Judge H. G. Kump of Elkins to the Governor's Mansion in Charleston. Jennings Randolph, the senior United States Senator from West Virginia in 1979, is the only member of Congress who served there throughout the era of the New Deal. The beginning of his career in Congress with the Special Session which was called in March 1933 marked the end of Randolph's service as director of athletics and publicity and instructor in public speaking and journalism at the college, but did not diminish his interest in D&E.

Randolph's last months as director of athletics in 1932-33 were interesting. Although the football record of six victories to five losses seemed mediocre, the Senators played against some tough competition. Among the victories was a 27 to 6 win over the Quantico Marines. Outstanding players in 1932 were Ellis Vest, Lester Corzine, Jim Wallace, Howard Fluharty, "Bud" Shelton, and Bill Tinney. The basketball team played twenty-three games in '32-'33 winning sixteen and losing seven. What made the season memorable was a trip to the West Coast which included games with Valparaiso, Kansas State, Denver, Nevada, Loyola of Los Angeles, and others in the West, and winning eight of nine contests after their return to West Virginia. The five regulars on the team were all Elkins High School graduates whose mentor had been Coach Frank Wimer. They were Lester Heavener, Allen Thurman Hodges, Henry Clay Martin, Harry ("Bud") Shelton, and George Ellis Vest. In defeating West Virginia University, the Senators played the entire game without a substitution being made.[30]

Shortly after the November election in 1932, the board of trustees met to consider the college's chronic monetary problems. They instructed President Allen to write to Mrs. Elkins to advise her of the "extreme financial needs at this time." The board also noted Mrs. Elkins's illness and sent her a message expressing hope for her recovery and appreciation for her help.[31] However, in less than four months, on March 1, 1933, Hallie Davis Elkins died in Washington. In a resolution of regret, the trustees reviewed

30. Kessler, *op. cit.,* p. 264.
31. Trustee Minutes, November 15, 1932, p. 185.

Athletic Director Jennings Randolph, *left*, and Coach Cam Henderson with the 1932-33 basketball team.

her long interest in the college that her father and husband had helped to establish, her gift of the Halliehurst estate in 1923, and the fact that "since then she has come to the rescue of the College several times in making substantial donations for the payment of Faculty salaries and as an advisor to the President and in other ways had been the most generous benefactress of the College."[32] Mrs. Elkins bequeathed $25,000 (far less than had been anticipated) to D&E to establish the Hallie Davis Elkins Endowment Fund, but her death meant that a reliable source of money for operating expenses in times of crisis was no longer available. Few people realized what a loss this was to President Allen who had for so long been able to depend on either Senator Davis or Mrs. Elkins for financial aid when all else failed and he was desperate. Many tributes to Mrs. Elkins from local citizens who knew her were printed in the *Inter-Mountain*. All mentioned her generosity and her graciousness. Perhaps the following quotation best represents the characteristics many sought to describe:

> Mrs. Elkins never tired of seeing to it that the old and the young, those prominent in local society and those who were not,

32. *Ibid.*, Executive Committee Resolution, March 3, 1933, p. 191.

had the same attention. She was a hostess of the rarest type. And but a short time in her presence made one feel he was really in the company of a woman who appreciated his visit. She had a host of friends. While her services to the College, the Y. M. C. A., and the hospital were widely known to the community, her personal charities and gifts are remembered by a great many people here ... I personally know of a number of promising students whose general education has been entirely the gift of Mrs. Elkins, and she has made it possible for students giving promise of art, whether in music, sculpture, or painting, to receive training both in this country and abroad.[33]

The class of 1933, known as the Harry E. Whetsell Class, was the first group in more than ten years to have a *maxima cum laude* valedictorian. He was Rowland C. Hansford who received a B.S. degree and who had an average higher than 95 throughout his four years. He had majored in chemistry and obtained a position with the DuPont Corporation shortly after commencement.[34] Later he pursued graduate study and has had a distinguished career in science and business. Other prominent members of the class were James Wallace, an outstanding football player, and Kent Watring, both of whom became successful Elkins businessmen, and Mabel Woodward, long a teacher in Randolph County and for some years a member of the college library staff.

The trustees met as usual during Commencement Week. Ex-Senator Sutherland was elected president of the board, resuming a position he had given up several years earlier. Dr. R. B. Purdum attended the meeting to present several proposals from the faculty for the board to consider. These included a request that a committee of the board meet with the faculty at least once a year, that faculty members be issued written contracts stating their salary and duration of service, that whenever a student holding any scholarship allowed his grade average to fall below C+ (77.5 percent), he must forfeit his scholarship, that no athletic grant should exceed $75 (full tuition) a semester and that no more than fifteen such grants be awarded in any semester, that definite steps be taken to raise funds to pay past-due salaries and to increase the endowment, and that more alumni be elected as trustees. The response of the board was immediate and, in

---

33. James E. Allen quoted in Elkins *Inter-Mountain,* March 2, 1933, p. 1.
34. Elkins *Inter-Mountain,* June 7, and July 18, 1933.

general, affirmative. Motions to direct the Executive Committee to meet with the faculty annually, to restrict scholarships and athletic grants, and to request the Synods and Presbyteries to nominate alumni for membership on the board were passed. The matter of contracts was referred to the Executive Committee. A committee to govern athletic policy was appointed to replace the controversial Alumni Athletic Committee. The new committee was to include a trustee, the president and business manager of the college, a faculty member elected by the faculty, a student from the senior class, and one member of the Alumni Association. Harry F. Whetsell was appointed a "special trustee" to distribute $23,000 in college bonds for payment of faculty salaries in arrears at that time.

The board also established a nine-man committee (three trustees, three faculty members, and three alumni) to plan and carry out a campaign to raise funds for faculty salaries and to balance the 1933-34 budget.[35] This group, soon to be called "The Special Development Committee," immediately began its work under the chairmanship of Dr. R. B. Purdum. In his first report to the board at a special meeting in November, Dr. Purdum stated that the committee thought that prompt action should be taken to provide adequate dormitory facilities for both men and women if enrollment was to be increased. He also urged that the trustees publicize the needs of the college and provide his committee with mailing lists of prospective donors and students and that the college should attempt to acquire the Graceland estate adjacent to the campus. The board responded by voting to ask the college architect to make an estimate of the cost of remodeling the Old College building as a boys' dormitory and making Halliehurst Hall more usable as a girls' dormitory, but postponed any action on acquiring Graceland. It did agree to a "vigorous campaign for students and to undertake a more extensive publicity program" and authorized the Development Committee to prepare a budget for this work for the consideration of the Executive Committee. Dr. Purdum was given leave to be absent from his classes as necessary in November, December, and January to carry forward this program.[36] It was at this board meeting that Harnus P. Mullennex began his long period of service on the board. He and

---

35. *Ibid.*, June 29, 1933; Trustee Minutes, June 5, 1933, pp. 186-88.
36. *Ibid.*, November 7, 1933, pp. 190-91.

Dewey Fleming were alumni elected at this time in accordance with recommendations made in June.

During the winter and spring of 1933-34, Dr. Purdum organized a "Student Goodwill Team" and visited twenty-nine high schools in West Virginia and Maryland to talk about D&E and to show seventy-five colored "lantern slides" of the college. Board member E. D. Wilson gave the money to have the slides made and A. Spates Brady donated $125 and furnished a car to help finance the trip to the high schools as well as to eighteen church and other groups. The Goodwill Team reported that its forty-seven engagements had brought D&E to the attention of 12,900 high school students and 2,350 adults at an average cost of $7.00 per visit. In addition, the Development Committee aided by the student body made an intensive door-to-door fund raising campaign in Elkins and netted $1,050. Altogether the activities of the Development Committee between November and June brought in $3,063 including $417 contributed by faculty members, $425 by trustees, and $332 by alumni. The committee had also prepared and had printed some twenty thousand leaflets to be mailed for publicity purposes.[37]

After receiving Dr. Purdum's report at its June 4, 1934, meeting, the trustees expressed appreciation for the work of those involved and voted to discharge the Development Committee. The board then discussed the idea of employing the Williams Financing Corporation to launch a $500,000 fund-raising campaign.[38] Nothing came of that discussion—which is all that could realistically have been expected in the midst of a depression. For several years thereafter, Dr. Purdum continued to take Student Goodwill teams to visit high schools in efforts to recruit students.

Meanwhile, in the fall of 1933, two additions of significance were made to the faculty. Professor Charles A. Stevenson of Morgantown became head of the Education Department succeeding David Kirby who had resigned to become secretary of the state board of education, and Laura Jean McAdams was appointed professor of French and German. Also, Benton Talbot returned from a leave of absence at the Johns Hopkins University where he had completed his work for and been awarded the Sc.D. degree. Dr. Irl Schoonover, an alumnus who had recently

---

37. *Ibid.*, June 6, 1934, pp. 193-95.
38. *Ibid.*

received a Ph.D. in chemistry at Princeton, was appointed instructor in chemistry and was to be in charge of all classes when Dr. Purdum was absent in connection with his work as chairman of the Development Committee.

In December, the library received the W. S. Tompkins collection of some six hundred books, many related to Appalachian history, as a memorial to Crawford Scott, a pioneer.[39] Several other gifts of books and bound volumes of scientific journals were given by faculty members, alumni and friends during the year as efforts were made to correct the deficiency in the library earlier noted by the North Central Association. By the end of the spring semester, the volumes cataloged totaled more than ten thousand and the librarian reported that "eight years before, the library had seemed to be housed spaciously, but now more room is seriously needed."[40]

The 1933 football team played eleven games, winning nine with one loss and one tie. They won the scoring championship of the nation with 352 points. The game resulting in a 7-7 tie with WVU was one of the best of the season and the Senators did so well that the college declared a holiday to celebrate the "moral victory." "Bud" Shelton, president of the student body, H. D. Fluharty, and Kenneth Talbott were among the D&E stars selected for the first All-Conference team at the season's end.[41]

Although enrollment for 1933-34 was the smallest of any year from 1931 to 1941 and only twenty-three seniors were graduated, the 1934 commencement was notable because of the presence of Mrs. Franklin D. Roosevelt as the principal speaker. She was accompanied to Elkins by Mrs. Harold Ickes, wife of the Secretary of Interior, and to the campus by Governor H. G. Kump and Congressman Jennings Randolph. Mrs. Roosevelt visited Elkins several times in the mid-thirties in connection with the building of Valley Homestead Projects at Dailey and Valley Bend and had become interested in D&E. Inasmuch as there were so many introductions and "remarks" scheduled, the faculty decided to

---

39. College Catalog, 1933-34, p. 23; Elkins *Inter-Mountain*, July 17, December 11, 1933.

40. Virgie Harris, Master's Thesis on West Virginia libraries, 1951, p. 19.

41. Kessler, *op. cit.*, p. 265; Elkins *Inter-Mountain*, October 30, 1933; Harry ("Bud") Shelton interview with Thomas R. Ross, August 14, 1979. Bud Shelton made twelve touchdowns in 1933 and Bill Tinney kicked twenty-seven extra points.

Mrs. Franklin D. Roosevelt speaking at
D&E's commencement in 1934.

omit the valedictory address from the commencement program (with the consent of the valedictorian, Chester Powers). In her brief address, Mrs. Roosevelt advised the graduates to "try to consider what is useful to do and try to devise new ways of service" and, with her typical optimism, she predicted "a new life and better social existence" for Americans in the future.[42] Well-known members of the class, in addition to Powers, were Harry L. Shelton and Eugene E. Hutton (both of whom later became faculty members), and Harry E. McNeish (whose wife, the former Edna Warfield, class of 1926, had taught speech and drama at the college for several years).

Partly as a result of the work of Dr. Purdum and the Goodwill Team, partly because of improved economic conditions, the enrollment of regular students increased by 30 to a total of 213 in the fall of 1934. The college offered full tuition scholarships to one outstanding enrollee in each of the six Civilian Conservation Corps in the eastern West Virginia district. Five CCC boys ac-

---

42. Elkins *Inter-Mountain*, June 7, 1934, p. 1; Faculty Minutes, June 5, 1934, p. 114.

cepted and registered.⁴³ President Allen commented that the college had reached the age that it was "educating the sons and daughters of former students"—though unfortunately he did not identify them. He also observed that D&E had "never had more applicants who want to work their way through College."⁴⁴

In cooperation with the supervisor of the Monongahela National Forest, Arthur A. Wood, and his staff, the college offered a lecture course in forestry during the winter of 1934-35 for the first time. Those who enrolled received college credit if they completed the course and there was talk of developing a forestry school—or at least a pre-forestry program—at D&E.⁴⁵

In December, President Allen discussed with the faculty his intention to attend a meeting with Governor Kump and a committee of private college officers to discuss "plans to get the eight state colleges to make a tuition change that will enable the church colleges to work with fairer competition" in attracting West Virginia students. The governor had agreed to take the matter to the legislature. Apparently nothing came of this since the problem still existed forty-five years later!⁴⁶

The 1934 football team was not successful—having the first losing season since Cam Henderson had become coach in 1923. "Nobody knows why," Dr. Allen told the *Inter-Mountain*.⁴⁷ To help cheer up the campus community, a group of faculty members planned a Christmas party. One who participated has described it in these words:

> Halliehurst Hall was decorated with evergreen and red ribbon bows. The four people who were instigators, promoters and sponsors were: Professor Harry E. Whetsell; Dr. R. B. Purdum; Dr. S. Benton Talbot and Professor Charles Stevenson.
> Students and Faculty were to be at Halliehurst by 8:00 p.m. A surprise was promised. The surprise: the arrival of Santa Claus, himself, in the old Elkins sleigh, pulled by a team of horses driven by Steve Martin. It was a grand entrance that Santa made with his HO! HO! HO's and the distribution of a present for each person

---

43. Elkins *Inter-Mountain*, September 12, 1934, p. 1; *The Senator*, November 28, 1934, p. 1.
44. *Ibid.*, September 4 and 8, 1934, p. 1.
45. *Ibid.*, October 21, 26, 30, 1934, January 16, 1935, *passim;* Faculty Minutes, October 1, 1934, p. 117.
46. Faculty Minutes, December 4, 1934, p. 120.
47. Kessler, *op. cit.*, p. 265; Elkins *Inter-Mountain*, December 14, 1934.

present. Punch and cookies were served by Miss Virgie Harris and Professor Laura Jean McAdams—to me the ride up the serpentine drive was one of the most delightful experiences I have ever had.[48]

The Senator, which had had to suspend publication in 1931 because of a lack of funds, began again with the issue of November 28, 1934. The major news was that the trustees had selected the Reverend Herman Jones as "Financial Secretary" as of November 1. He had helped in the preceding decade with the famous "Million Dollar Campaign" and was now returning to the newly created position on a temporary basis to try to raise "more funds for the paying of current expenses," something which President Allen asserted was "absolutely necessary to maintain the present status of the College."[49] Although of short duration then, the office of "Financial Secretary" was a predecessor of the Development Office of a later era.

As noted in chapter one, in addition to the annual gifts of Senators Davis and Elkins, it was because of the low salaries of faculty members that D&E could boast of keeping tuition and fees at a "merely nominal level." For thirty years the trustees and the Presbyterian constituencies to whom they were responsible had utterly failed to undergird the college with an endowment. The tendency to rely on the old senators and then on Hallie Elkins for gifts and on underpaying (and belatedly paying) faculty and staff had become traditional. Thus, in the crisis of the Great Depression—with the senators and Mrs. Elkins dead, virtually no endowment, low tuition (often uncollected), and an expensive athletic program—the college could survive only at the expense of the faculty and through the efforts of a few Elkins businessmen who were willing to give aid and extend credit. Faculty salaries were drastically slashed as a few examples vividly illustrate. In 1929-30, President Allen's salary was $4,200. In 1933 he voluntarily reduced it to $3,000 and for 1936-37 his successor's salary was $2,400. In 1929-30, the salary of Dr. R. B. Purdum, the senior professor with a Ph.D. was $3,000; by 1936-37 it was $1,500 and at that level it remained through 1941. Indeed, by 1940 no one (except the new president) received more

48. Letter from Professor Charles A. Stevenson, Morgantown, W.Va., to Thomas R. Ross, Elkins, W.Va., January 24, 1979.
49. *The Senator,* November 28, 1934, p. 4.

than $1,500 and only three senior faculty members received that much.[50]

Not only was morale somewhat low and the chronic lack of funds producing another crisis in the winter of 1934-35, but the faculty was concerned about excessive class absences, "tardiness among the faculty and students," and the fact that Miss Harris, who had been registrar since 1922, reported that the grades "are the poorest group of grades ever recorded."[51] The committee appointed to consider "the advisability of discontinuing the senior essay requirement" recommended after a four-month study that that time-hallowed, but much abused, degree requirement be abolished, and the faculty voted unanimously to do so.[52] One reason was that, as Dean Albert had often pointed out, too many seniors seemed to "get help on" their essays—or, in some cases, simply bought them. The editors of *The Senator,* in an editorial on the need for an honor system, asserted that "one of the most crying needs of Davis and Elkins College today is some program to combat the dishonesty among its students. A conservative estimate of the number of students who, under the proper conditions, resort to dishonesty to acquire a grade at our College is between eighty-five and ninety per cent."[53] Doubtless, that was a gross exaggeration. Professor Charles A. Stevenson, commenting on the problem, has written of an episode which happened in his class that year which moved him greatly:

> One experience that I recall was one which impressed me as much as any thing I ever experienced. It was examination time at the end of the second semester. Before the examination started, 3 football boys appeared in my office and in most sincere and solemn manner, said: "Professor, several of us were reviewing for your examination, one of our team members said—I'm going to shoot pool—you people study—I'm going to sit on the back row and copy what I need! Then they concluded—"You have always been so fair and considerate with us that we think you deserve to know that this team member is going to cheat." Without mention of any names, they departed. So when time came for the examination, most of the students sat in their regular seats but one member of

---

50. Trustee Executive Committee Minutes, June 27, 1929, August 23, 1933, August 1, 1940, *passim.*
51. Faculty Minutes, November 4, 1934-April 9, 1935, pp. 119-24.
52. *Ibid.,* March 5-June 27, 1935, pp. 123-34.
53. *The Senator,* May 11, 1935, p. 2.

the class sat in the rear row. After the blue books and typed examination questions were distributed, I took a batch of ungraded tests and sat down to the left of the class member and began grading papers. After a short time, the would-be cheater handed in his blue-book without writing a word. No one ever mentioned this again. But what ever else they may have been, they were men of integrity and honor. The Alumni list of the class of 1935 attests to the success of this fine group of young men and women. "The salt of the earth!"[54]

In December, *The Senator* editorially attacked the rule requiring chapel attendance three times a week. "Is the administration blind that it cannot see the present system of compulsory chapel breaking down upon their heads? . . . Eliminate entirely the compulsory attendance of chapel, and in its place offer an optional chapel on Tuesday and Thursday, at the same hour, devoted entirely to religious worship," the editor suggested. In a companion editorial entitled "We Want Action!" the faculty was blasted for maintaining a curriculum "sadly lacking in upper division courses." The solution suggested for the admittedly overloaded professors was to "alternate the upper division courses. Whether or not this solution is used, the students are asking in no uncertain terms that the faculty wake up to the fact that Davis and Elkins is a four-year institution."[55] Complaints about chapel and curriculum remained favorite topics for student editorials for each successive generation throughout the next four decades!

D&E had an unusually fine debate squad in the spring of 1935. Paul Snedegar, William Overholt, Arthur Wolfe, and Roy Delauder represented the college in the statewide meet at Huntington. The subject was one which is still timely: "Resolved: That nations should agree to prevent the international shipment of arms and munitions."[56] Snedegar later earned his M.D. degree and for years headed the D&E Health Service while maintaining a busy ENT practice in Elkins.

Louise Sleeman had the highest grade average at the end of the first semester, outranking Carl Devine, *The Senator* editor,

54. Letter from Professor Charles A. Stevenson, Morgantown, W.Va., to Thomas R. Ross, Elkins, W.Va., January 24, 1979.
55. *The Senator,* December 12, 1934, p. 2.
56. *Ibid.*, February 27, 1935, p. 1.

by one point.⁵⁷ Many years later, after her marriage to A. Lee Linhart, Louise served as a member of the faculty in physical education and then as the first director of social activities in Benedum Hall.

Although no yearbook had been published for several years, the senior class revived the tradition of sponsoring an annual in 1935. They christened it *The Senatus,* a title used ever since for the D&E yearbook. The 1934-35 basketball team, revived with some "new blood" after a rather poor record the preceding year, won the conference tournament.⁵⁸ Ed Gutowski, a sophomore, was the captain of "one of the youngest teams ever to represent any college," according to *The Senator,* and had "the distinction of being the only sophomore ever to hold the position of captain of an athletic team" coached by Cam Henderson at D&E. "Buck" Jamison and Charles Watson, both freshmen, and Forest Kendall, a junior, were also outstanding players and all four were named to the All-Tournament and the All-State teams.⁵⁹

In February the trustees accepted a gift of twenty-five acres of land adjacent to the campus from the Elkins heirs. At the same time, the board was informed that the Alumni Athletic Committee "had decided to resign from further participation and direction of the College athletics." The trustees agreed "with the understanding that the financial obligations of the Committee will be discharged by the Committee."⁶⁰

At the final faculty meeting of the year, Harry Whetsell, on behalf of the faculty, presented Dr. James E. Allen a traveling bag saying "We express our esteem to the President who has served so faithfully for twenty-five years, and present this bag as our token of esteem."⁶¹ A testimonial dinner in observance of Dr. Allen's quarter of a century as president of D&E was held at the Davis Memorial Presbyterian Church. Various business and professional men and alumni spoke of his service to the community and of how his influence had "enhanced and enriched the lives of many young men and women." "You have inoculated into them character," Judge John F. Brown said. Another asserted: "There

57. *Ibid.,* December 12, 1934, p. 1.
58. Kessler, *op. cit.,* p. 265.
59. *Ibid.,* and *The Senator,* February 27, 1935, p. 3.
60. Trustee Executive Committee Minutes, February 5, 1935, p. 280.
61. Faculty Minutes, June 3, 1935, p. 129.

is no man who ever lived in this community who more richly deserves this honor." Boyd Wees, born in the county before the city of Elkins was founded, paid high tribute to Dr. Allen's integrity . . . as well as his influence in the field of education."[62]

At the 1935 commencement, the highest scholastic rank was changed from *maxima cum laude* to *summa cum laude*. Two students attained that honor, Carl Devine, the valedictorian, and Leola M. Wills. Other honor graduates include Louise Sleeman, Kathryn Isner, and James W. Green, Jr. Among the more prominent members of the class were Mary Brady, Winifred Neale, Edgar Baker, Paul S. Hart, Carl Moore, Ralph H. Quick, and I. D. Talbott.

Even before Commencement Week, there were rumors that James E. Allen was being considered by the state board of education for appointment as president of Marshall College. Inasmuch as H. G. Kump of Elkins was governor, W. W. Trent, formerly of Elkins, was state superintendent, and David Kirby, recently a D&E faculty member, was secretary of the board of education, the newspapers suggested from the beginning of the speculation that Dr. Allen was the "favorite candidate" of the state board. Thus, when the appointment was announced in Charleston by W. W. Trent on June 21, Elkins people were not taken by surprise. President Allen immediately resigned from the D&E faculty, accepted the Marshall presidency and arranged the appointment of Cam Henderson as director of athletics and coach at Marshall.[63]

Although he had spent twenty-eight years of his life at D&E and had seen much accomplished since he had joined the faculty as a young man in 1906 at the beginning of the third academic year, it is clear that James E. Allen was not altogether reluctant to leave in 1935. The death of Mrs. Elkins two years earlier had deprived him of the one dependable financial "angel" who had enabled the college to struggle through the crises of the preceding years since Senator Davis had died. He had been bitterly disappointed that she did not bequeath a substantial sum to endow the college. He had become increasingly frustrated that in the five years since he had outlined his "Ten Year Program" in 1930, the trustees had made no progress in achieving the goals of relieving the college entirely of debt, increasing the endowment, or im-

---

62. Elkins *Inter-Mountain*, June 14, 1935, p. 1.
63. *Ibid.*, June 7, 14, 22, 1935, *passim*.

proving the physical facilities. By the mid-thirties, he had come to feel that "he no longer had the full support of the Trustees and of several of his Faculty members."⁶⁴ The failure to achieve accreditation had been a grave disappointment to him and he saw little hope of accomplishing that essential goal in the foreseeable future.

Also, as one of his sons has written, Dr. Allen's decision to leave D&E was in part prompted by "the failure of the people of means within the Presbyterian Church to share their wealth through substantial gifts and bequests in financial support of the College despite his tireless and ceaseless efforts in the church pulpits and business offices throughout the Synods of West Virginia and surrounding areas." Too, the president had come to believe that "the College needed a younger man with the capacity and desire to devote full time to the development of financial support—particularly endowment monies."⁶⁵

Furthermore, of course, President Allen had never been paid an adequate salary and he refused to accept special perquisites (such as the gift of an automobile offered by the trustees) when his faculty was underpaid. He had five sons, one of whom was in high school, one in college, and one in Harvard Medical School in 1935. In the late twenties, Dr. Allen had married a widow with a daughter. With D&E frequently unable to pay faculty salaries on time and he being without a private fortune, the necessity of providing adequately for his family was an ever-present problem. Thus, the chance to go to Marshall College came at an opportune time in the life of James E. Allen, offering him a solution to his existing problems as well as a position in which he could play a larger role in the educational life of the state.⁶⁶

In retrospect, one can see that few men have had as great an impact on the development of Davis and Elkins College as did James E. Allen. As his longtime colleague, Dr. Charles E. Albert, wrote years later, "Dr. Allen led the College through the most depressing period in its history. . . . A man of less courage and faith would have given up, but he, always strong and optimistic, held on in the belief that a better day would come."

64. Letter from Robert A. Allen, St. Albans, W.Va., to Thomas R. Ross, Elkins, W.Va., March 21, 1979.
65. *Ibid.*
66. *Ibid.*, and interviews of Thomas R. Ross with Harry E. Whetsell, March 27, 1979, and Anna Parmesano, June 5, 1979.

Unquestionably, President Allen's resignation marked the end of an era at D&E. The "better day would come," but it was still a long way off in June of 1935.

VI

Struggling for Survival: 1935-43

A sudden change in the leadership of an institution, whether it be in the presidency of a nation, a great corporation, or a small college, inevitably creates tensions and unrest even in the best of circumstances. This is especially true in a situation where the outgoing president has been in office a long time as had been the case with President James E. Allen at D&E. Because of the timing of his appointment at Marshall, there was no opportunity for advance planning in regard to Dr. Allen's resignation or the choice of his successor. Having met as usual during Commencement Week in 1935, some two weeks prior to Dr. Allen's appointment as president of Marshall, the D&E trustees, for some strange reason, did not deem it necessary to reassemble that summer to consider the selection of a new president. Instead, the board's Executive Committee met on June 27 and accepted with "deep regrets" Dr. Allen's decision which resulted in "the severance of his relations to the College." The committee decided that "no steps should be taken toward the selection of a permanent president of the College" until the Presbyteries and Synods concerned could be consulted for suggestions as to a suitable man to appoint.[1] Then, the committee considered a letter from a trustee recommending the appointment of Dr. R. B. Purdum because "he possesses youth, enormous energy, enthusiasm, superb educational training, good practical common sense and business ability, faith in the future of the College, and confidence of the Faculty and students."[2]

1. Trustee Executive Committee Minutes, 1935-41, June 27, 1935, pp. 1-4.
2. *Ibid.*, p. 9; Letter from George E. Bevans, Fairmont, W.Va., to Frederick H. Barron, Elkins, W.Va., June 26, 1935.

President Charles E. Albert and Miss Anna Parmesano
who served as secretary for six presidents.

After general discussion, the committee voted unanimously to appoint Dean Charles E. Albert to be acting president "subject to confirmation by the Board of Trustees of the College."[3] The board did not meet either to give "confirmation" or to make any arrangements or plans for the appointment of a president until June 2, 1936, almost one year after the vacancy occurred.

While in session the Executive Committee passed a motion stating that "the College Trustees assume no liability whatsoever for any indebtedness heretofore existing or incurred" by Coach Henderson and the Alumni Athletic Committee. Another resolution passed requested Henderson to present to the trustees "a letter stating officially that there had been no engagements or commitments made with students to participate in college athletics for the fall of 1935, and explaining what were the athletic arrangements with players for the years 1934-35 and 1935-36, if any."[4]

Bayard Green, president of the Alumni Association, then met with the committee to discuss the appointment of Henderson's

3. *Ibid.,* p. 5.
4. *Ibid.,* pp. 2-3.

successor. The consensus was that an effort should be made to get Coach Frank Wimer to accept the position as director of athletics and athletic coach, but after conferring with the committee on July 5, Coach Wimer stated that he could not accept.[5]

Meanwhile, shortly after taking office, President Albert called a faculty meeting to discuss a proposal from the board regarding the budget for 1935-36. The plan suggested was that the salary rates be continued at the level of the preceding year, but "that all current revenues from operating the College activities" be used to pay necessary expenses *other than salaries* and that whatever money was left would be "applied pro rata upon current 1935-1936 salaries as they mature" but that no payments would be made "on arrears of salary to anyone until such current salaries are first paid in full." Furthermore, if current salaries were not met in full at the end of the year, the faculty was asked "to waive such balances as are owing to them."[6]

The faculty was not willing to agree to this proposal. Approximately thirty thousand dollars in unpaid salaries had already accrued. Thus, in the first place, the members with longer service to whom much was owed were being asked to do without any immediate payments on salary in arrears. Secondly, everything else was to be paid before anything was to be available for current salaries. Thirdly, everyone was requested to agree in advance that if current salaries were not met in 1935-36, the unpaid balance for that year would be waived with the mere "understanding" that if "revenues of the College in succeeding years produce a surplus, such surplus shall be applied pro rata upon any deficiency occurring in 1935-1936."[7] Therefore, the faculty in a series of meetings in July and early August discussed this matter and finally replied by voting unanimously to request the board's Executive Committee to maintain the salary schedule as of 1934-35 and to authorize the payment of 10 percent of funds available for payroll distribution to former employees, "now creditors of the College," and 90 percent to current faculty, and that they share pro rata according to the salary scale, regardless of their tenure of service.[8] This was agreed upon and the academic

5. *Ibid.*, June 27 and July 5, 1935, pp. 6-10.
6. *Ibid.*, July 18, 1935, p. 13; and Faculty Minutes, July 18, 1935, p. 137.
7. Faculty Minutes, July 23, 1935, p. 140.
8. *Ibid.*, July 23, August 1, 1935, pp. 140-41; and Trustee Executive Committee Minutes, August 6, September 5, 1935, pp. 21, 23.

year began with only two new faculty members. Lewis Vest was appointed to teach the courses in physics and mathematics formerly offered by President Albert, and Harry L. ("Bud") Shelton succeeded Cam Henderson as director of athletics and coach of football and basketball.

In February, the faculty was informed that the board's Executive Committee was working on a plan for 1936-37 which included efforts to make income meet expenditures, to secure at least five thousand dollars in cash donations, to start paying indebtedness to faculty, to campaign for more students, and to begin meeting standards required for accreditation.[9] Later in the spring, Dr. Henry H. Sweets, executive secretary of the Presbyterian Board of Christian Education, Richmond, and Dr. C. C. McCracken, general secretary of the Board of Christian Education, Philadelphia, came to the college to discuss financial conditions with the Trustee Executive Committee, but nothing tangible resulted from the conferences.[10]

The 1935 football season was a disappointment to Coach Shelton. He lacked reserves and had to face a difficult schedule. Two of the best players from the previous year had transferred to Marshall with Coach Henderson, and Shelton had to put freshmen in several positions. The '35-'36 basketball team had a fine conference record (12-2) but lost several outside games and finished the season with a 19-10 standing. The 1936 *Senatus* recorded that "Coach Shelton's activities have resulted in a high standard of athletics, clean and respectful, all of which goes to make a recognizable representation in athletic circles. 'Bud', as he is familiarly known, has won the support and respect of the students and friends of the College, and each is giving him their whole-hearted support in his future campaigns which we are certain will meet with the highest success."[11]

Thirty-one students received bachelor's degrees at the 1936 commencement, making that the largest class graduated so far. Among the better known seniors were Robert A. Allen, a son of the former president; Jo Ellen Bowers, the editor of *The Senatus* and May Queen; Alan and Thomas Green, Keith Heltzel, president of the student body and subsequently a faculty member;

9. *Ibid.*, February 4, 1936, p. 147.
10. *Ibid.*, March 3, 1936, p. 149.
11. *The Senatus*, 1936, p. 60.

George Goldberg, Brandon Harper, Thurman Hodges, and Forest Kendall, outstanding athletes; Paul Snedegar, and Lindsey J. Phares, later to be a D&E trustee and the recipient of an honorary Sc.D. degree at the 1979 commencement in recognition of his outstanding achievements as an inventor and as vice-president of Raymond International, Inc.

During Commencement Week, on June 2, 1936, the board of trustees finally took up the matter of selecting a president of the college. However, it could not act since the quorum of two-thirds of the membership which the constitution required be present to elect a president was lacking. In view of subsequent events, it is interesting to note that at the June 2 meeting, a committee of alumni and a group representing the student body appeared before the board to urge the appointment of Dr. R. B. Purdum as president. Both groups were allowed to speak and were requested to file "the petitions, recommendations and poll they referred to in their discussion."[12] Before adjourning until July 6, the board instructed the Executive Committee (which a year earlier had appointed Dean Albert to be acting president) to confer with three members to be selected by the Alumni Association and with the Elkins Businessmen's Association in regard to a choice of a president. Apparently no effort had been made during the preceding year to solicit applications for the presidency, and, even at this belated date, the board made no effort to involve the faculty in the selection process. Inasmuch as probably the single most important function of college or university trustees is to choose a president, the failure of the D&E board to consider seriously beginning a search for a successor to James E. Allen immediately after his resignation in 1935 and their failure to have a quorum present when finally meeting to act on the matter in June of 1936 is incredible!

When the board met on July 6, fifteen of the twenty-two members were in attendance—the bare minimum for the two-thirds required for a quorum when electing a college president. The Executive Committee's report (giving no evidence that the committee had consulted either alumni or Elkins businessmen as directed, much less faculty or students) was presented and the committee nominated Dean Albert and advocated "his imme-

12. Trustee Minutes, June 2, 1936, p. 199.

diate election."[13] A motion to permit the reading of a pro-Purdum report "embodying the opinions of Faculty members, students, alumni, and citizens on the election of the president" was tabled. Subsequently, with inexplicable inconsistency, the trustees voted to permit the reading of a letter from the four students who had appeared at the June 2 meeting to support the appointment of Dr. Purdum. A trustee then placed the name of R. B. Purdum in nomination. The members voted by ballot three times without reaching a decision. Finally, "on the fourth ballot, C. E. Albert was elected President of Davis and Elkins College for the year ending June 30, 1937."[14] Before adjourning, the board voted to order its president and four other trustees "to make a thorough investigation of candidates for the Presidency of the College and report at least two names of available men outside the Faculty" at the June 1937 meeting.[15]

President Albert, having already labored for a year as acting president, thus began his term with a kind of second "probationary" year. His board was divided and apathetic, he had a faculty faction which was disappointed, and there were students, alumni, and citizens of the community with strong feelings of dissatisfaction either with the board's decision or with its procedure or with both.

The board's failure in the 1920s and early 1930s to act responsibly in connection with financial, athletic, and other issues had often dismayed many faculty members and friends of the college and had ultimately frustrated President James E. Allen. In retrospect one can see that, unfortunately, the trustees' negligence in giving immediate and proper attention in 1935 to procedures for selecting his successor, their ineptness in dealing with faculty, students, and alumni, and their utter insensitivity to the awkward position in which they placed President Albert in 1936 were symptomatic of the weaknesses of the board then and for several years thereafter.

There were no significant changes in the characteristics of the college or in the curriculum during the last half of the decade of the 1930s. The Student Christian Association, known as "The

---

13. Trustee Minutes, July 6, 1936, p. 203. The committee report is included in full.
14. *Ibid.*, p. 202.
15. *Ibid.*, p. 203.

S.C.A.," was organized in 1936 and remained an important campus institution for more than thirty years. Its first officers were Alan Green, William Overholt, Don Erwin, and Martha Barnard.[16]

Undoubtedly the most interesting and exciting event occurring on the D&E campus in 1936 was the visit of President Franklin D. Roosevelt. He talked about conservation to a huge crowd on the front campus prior to the crowning of the queen of the Forest Festival on Thursday afternoon, October 1, a month before his landslide reelection victory in November when he carried forty-six of the forty-eight states. Following the coronation, a pageant entitled "Legend of Peace," written by Mrs. Lewis Vest and directed by Claire Fiorentino, later a D&E faculty member, was presented.[17] President Roosevelt's visit established a precedent which has been followed by several of his successors including Presidents Truman, Nixon, Ford, and Carter as well as by presidential candidates such as Governor Adlai Stevenson and Vice-President Hubert Humphrey.

At its meeting on June 1, 1937, the board of trustees decided to open Halliehurst Hall as a "dormitory for girls the following September under the auspices and direction of the College Aid." Halliehurst had been used for a time beginning in 1925-26 as a residence for out-of-town women students, and a few girls continued to live there after it became the residence of President Allen and his second wife (the "Lady Principal of Halliehurst Hall"), but the building had not been used as a dormitory since the early thirties. The board also ordered that the accrued salaries of the faculty should be paid with Davis and Elkins College bonds. The president of the board was instructed to appoint a special Finance Committee of board members, alumni, church pastors and businessmen to raise funds to redeem the college bonds which were to mature October 30, 1939. Also, a renewed effort was to be made to sell the Old College property by dividing it into lots for residences. The committee which had been directed the preceding June to bring in two nominees for president did not report, and no action was taken relative to the appointment of a president, the trustees apparently having forgotten that they had

---

16. Faculty Minutes, May 18, 1937, p. 163 and insert.
17. Official Forest Festival Program, 1936; Elkins *Inter-Mountain,* October 1, 2, 1936, p. 1.

appointed President Albert for only a one-year term! However, his name was included in the list of members of the board's Buildings and Grounds Committee so the assumption is that he was expected to continue in office.[18]

The 1937 graduating class was smaller than usual and more seniors received the B.A. in Education degree than either the B.A. or B.S. degrees. Honorary D.D. degrees were awarded to Felix B. Gear of the class of 1920, then a professor of Bible at Southwestern and later dean of Columbia Seminary and moderator of the General Assembly of the Presbyterian Church in the United States, and to Glen O. Yount, pastor of the Huttonsville Presbyterian Church and a trustee of D&E. Dr. Charles J. Turck, soon to become president of Macalester College, delivered the commencement address.

A week later, President Albert was awarded an honorary LL.D. degree at Southwestern College. Subsequently, in 1939, his alma mater, Lafayette College, also conferred the LL.D. degree on Dr. Albert.[19]

Several faculty members resigned at the end of the 1936-37 academic year. The venerable Thomas J. Hale, who had served as professor of social science and philosophy since 1920, had to retire because of illness. The heads of the English Department and the Commerce Department both left to accept positions in other colleges outside the state, as did the professor of French and German and an instructor in public speaking and drama. Their replacements remained only one or two years, thus beginning a trend towards a high percentage of faculty "turnover" annually which continued throughout the next two decades.

In the fall of 1937, a short-wave radio station was constructed in the Science Hall and was assigned call letters W8RGJ. D&E students were selected for listing in *Who's Who in American Universities and Colleges* in December, apparently for the first time. *The Senator* joined the Associated Collegiate Press in the same month. A Commerce Club was organized in 1937 and two years later was developed into the Beta Alpha Beta fraternity which became one of the most active campus organizations.

Despite the splendid efforts and skillful coaching of "Bud" Shelton, the athletic teams of the late 1930s did not match the

18. Trustee Minutes, June 1, 1937, pp. 204-6.
19. Elkins *Inter-Mountain*, June 8, 1937; November 4, 1939.

records of those of the twenties. There were some outstanding players such as Ed Gutowski, John Shelton, Labe Gregory, Basil Sharp, Art Tebor, John Suba, Jim Smith, "Ace" Federovitch, Dick Hockenberry, Jud Hudson, and Vic Celio in football and Huck Miers, Ed Gutowski, "Press" Maravich, Martin Allman, Don Green, Mike Winne, Charles Weese, and Art Tebor in basketball, but no conference or tournament titles for D&E. One memorable triumph was D&E's 7-0 victory over West Virginia Wesleyan on October 16, 1937. To celebrate, the following Monday was declared a holiday at D&E.[20]

Coach Shelton was hindered by lack of funds and inadequate facilities. In 1937, he led a drive to raise money to build an athletic field near the campus. He appeared before the board of trustees in June of 1938 and got approval for a limited number of tuition grants for athletes with the understanding that he would collect all income from athletics, use the money to pay expenses and, if any were left, use it to help to pay board and room costs for the athletes he selected for such benefits.[21] The truth is that in those years (1936-39), Coach Shelton fed a good many of his players a lot of free meals in his own home, meals prepared by his gracious wife, Kathryn, who also often washed and repaired the teams' uniforms to save the college money. In 1938-39, the Sheltons lived in the old presidential house with twenty-seven athletes who were quartered there.[22]

Senator Davis Elkins donated $694 to pay for athletic equipment requested by Coach Shelton for the 1938-39 season. The board instructed the Executive Committee "to appoint an Athletic Committee to work with and advise" Coach Shelton. At the same time, H. P. Mullennex pointed out "that the special Finance Committee ordered at the June, 1937, meeting had never been appointed, and as a result no action had been taken on a campaign to raise funds to reduce the bonded indebtedness."[23]

As early as March of 1938, President Albert informed the faculty that due to lack of funds, the College Catalog would "be abbreviated," that the financial picture was "not good, and that

20. Kessler, *op. cit.*, pp. 266-67; *The Senator*, 1936-39, *passim*.
21. Trustee Minutes, June 7, 1938, p. 207.
22. Trustee Executive Committee Minutes, December 18, 1936, p. 36, and Elkins *Inter-Mountain*, April 9, 1937, p. 7; Shelton-Ross interview, August 14, 1979.
23. *Ibid.*, p. 207.

there is no assurance of salaries for next year."²⁴ A brief campaign for funds was undertaken by friends of the college in Elkins and vicinity, and by May, Dr. Albert informed the *Inter-Mountain* that the "prospects are that no deficit in the College Fund will appear at the end of the year, if the campaign continues with vigor." That that statement was largely for "public relations" purposes is suggested by the fact that the trustees stipulated in June that "salaries be reduced for the second semester" of 1938-39 if necessary to balance the budget.²⁵ The faculty discussed the financial situation and considered at length the possibility of "dropping athletics altogether."²⁶

On June 5, the Chi Beta Phi Sigma honorary sorority presented to the college the stone archway at the entrance to the Nature Walk and conducted ceremonies dedicating it as "The S. Benton Talbot Nature Walk." The arch was a model of the entrance into the Monongahela National Forest. It was Dr. Talbot who first conceived the idea of the Nature Walk in 1928 when the first botany course was offered at D&E.²⁷

The revived dramatic society known as "The Playcrafters" presented the popular comedy, *Brother Rat,* during the last week of May. Among the cast were Penrod Clower, Elwin Roberts, and Don Erwin, all later to become Presbyterian ministers in West Virginia; and Thaddeus Pritt, Jr., who later served as Randolph County Sheriff and as postmaster of Beverly.²⁸

President James E. Allen returned to the campus to deliver the Commencement Address for the class of 1938. Among the seniors graduated was Albert G. D. Levy, eighteen years old, an exile from Hitler's Germany, said to be the youngest student ever graduated from D&E up to that time. Also among the graduates were Carl J. Antolini who became an Elkins dentist and a loyal D&E booster; Sadavioe Goddin, Bonnie Marsh, and Charles McCollam, all of whom became teachers in the county, and Margaret Trickett (Mrs. George McLaughlin) who has long been an active supporter of D&E.²⁹

24. Faculty Minutes, March 1, 1938, p. 174.
25. *Ibid.,* June 7, 1938, p. 209.
26. *Ibid.,* June 6, 1938, p. 176.
27. *The Senator,* May 20, 1938, p. 1.
28. *Ibid.,* p. 1.
29. Elkins *Inter-Mountain,* June 8, 1938, p. 1.

In the summer of 1938, at the suggestion of Professor Harry Whetsell, the faculty decided to have one chapel service a week, on Wednesdays at 11:10 a.m., instead of three times a week at an earlier hour as had been customary for more than thirty years. Through the cooperation of the minister, Dr. J. M. Lacy, and the Session of the Davis Memorial Presbyterian Church, arrangements were made for chapel to be held in the sanctuary of that church. Students were dismissed from classes at eleven o'clock and walked down Sycamore Street to assemble at eleven-ten for a forty-five to fifty-minute service.[30]

A *Senator* writer, noting the increased use of Sycamore Street and the fact that the Graceland estate had recently been sold by the Kennedys (Davis heirs who then owned it), wrote an interesting article on the sycamore trees which by 1938 had grown to form a long archway over the street between the campus and the City Park. He observed that:

> At the turn of the century, about 1902, these trees were moved from their habitats along near-by streams and from urban nurseries, and were planted in their present positions by a Mr. Doyle, who was head gardener of the Elkins estate, brought from Baltimore. "Immense holes were dug and filled with rich soil," Richard Barry, who lives in the Gatehouse, told a *Senator* reporter. "The trees had great balls of earth around them, and were planted with great care." They were planted by Senator Elkins along the rock-and-cinder road, considered a fine one in those days, which he and Senator Davis maintained. At one time or another, every student who has passed along Sycamore Street has marveled at the stately beauty and the loveliness of the tall sycamore trees that flank the street.[31]

The Senator boasted of a circulation of one thousand in the fall of 1938, and it frequently was issued in six-page editions carrying national and world as well as campus news. On the editorial page under the list of staff was printed "Our Platform" which urged completion of the upper floors of the Liberal Arts and Science buildings, the opening of a "Boys' dormitory," the establishment of a Department of Journalism, and "setting up a full, rounded intra-mural athletic program." Betty Marstiller (Mrs. R. Gordon

---

30. Faculty Minutes, August 8, 1938, p. 179; *The Senator*, September 23, 1938, p. 1.
31. *The Senator*, November 18, 1938, p. 1.

Barrick) wrote a weekly "gossip column" entitled "Betty Co-Ed." The librarian announced in December that circulation figures indicated that A. J. Cronin's *The Citadel*, was the most read book at D&E that year and that the *Reader's Digest, Time, American Mercury, Harpers,* and *Scribners* were the favorite magazines of the students. Several editorials in the course of the year pointedly discussed the need for repairing and painting Halliehurst Hall—a subject for *Senator* editors in every decade since. Events in Europe—the Munich agreement and Hitler's subsequent destruction of Czechoslovakia—were noted with some alarm in *Senator* columns. One writer asked, "Will Hitler continue to change the map of Europe in the face of the Democracies of the world?"[32]

During the fall of 1938, President Albert attempted to improve relations between the college and the Presbyterian Synods of West Virginia. He began discussions with representatives of the Southern Synod relative to having recommendations for membership on the board of trustees come directly from the Synod rather than from the various Presbyteries. Such a plan was finally approved in 1943. The Southern Synod also granted D&E the income of $25,000 received from the sale of Greenbrier College in Lewisburg in 1938.[33]

In February of 1939, the college launched another financial campaign in the hope of raising six thousand dollars "urgently needed" to meet current expenses, but like so many efforts of a similar nature previously attempted, this drive failed to achieve its goal.[34] At the same time, the Trustee Executive Committee authorized Coach Shelton to borrow nine hundred dollars in order to carry on the athletic program for the remainder of the year.[35]

During the same month, the Student Council petitioned the faculty to have a "compulsory assembly on Friday of each week" in addition to the Wednesday chapel. Unbelievable? Almost half of the faculty voted against it, but the motion carried. The officers of the student body wanted some means of getting the students together for business meetings, pep rallies, and enter-

32. *The Senator*, September, 1938-May, 1939, *passim;* March 24, 1939, p. 1.
33. *The Senator*, September 15, October 21, November 14, 1938, *passim;* Trustee Minutes, June 6, 1939; May 31, 1943, pp. 213, 234.
34. Elkins *Inter-Mountain*, February 3, 28, 1939, p. 1.
35. Trustee Executive Minutes, February 3, 1939, p. 45.

tainment.³⁶ At the first assembly held thereafter, the students voted to amend the Student Body Constitution to provide that class presidents be included as members of the Student Council and for the election of two "Senators" and cheerleaders prior to the opening of football season.³⁷

At a special meeting in April, the trustees approved final plans to subdivide the Old College campus into 109 lots to be sold as quickly as possible. There was hope that a Works Progress Administration (WPA) project could be arranged in order to install a public sewer system if the land could be annexed to the city.³⁸

Thirty-seven seniors received degrees at the 1939 commencement. An honorary LL.D. degree was awarded to Congressman Jennings Randolph. This was the first LL.D. degree conferred by D&E and Mr. Randolph was the first person who was not an ordained minister to receive an honorary degree from this college. The commencement speaker was Dr. James Shera Montgomery, the chaplain of the National House of Representatives.

During the summer of 1939, arrangements were made to establish a Civil Pilots "Flying Training School" at D&E. The aim of the program, which Congress had recently authorized in view of German and Japanese aggression, was to provide "airmen thoroughly schooled in the basic principles of flight theory and flying who in time of national emergency would serve as a body from which the military and naval forces could draw material for accelerated training." Congressman Randolph was instrumental in getting D&E approved as one of the 166 colleges and universities initially participating in this program under the auspices of the Civil Aeronautics Authority. More than twenty D&E students, including one co-ed, Miss Thelma Clark, registered for the instruction.³⁹

On August 10, the Executive Committee of the board of trustees, ordered "that due to the financial conditions facing the College, and in order to avoid further indebtedness" Professors Edward C. Keefe (English), Wiley E. Hodges (political science and economics), and Allen B. Cunningham (mathematics and

---

36. Faculty Minutes, January 10, February 13, 1939, pp. 186-88.
37. *The Senator,* February 21, 1939, p. 1.
38. Trustee Minutes, April 13, 1939, p. 210.
39. Elkins *Inter-Mountain,* August 28, September 11, 15, November 8, 1939, *passim.*

physics) "be relieved of further duties at the College and that the courses taught by these professors be distributed among other members of the College Faculty."[40] Coming only a month before the beginning of the fall semester, this action was not only a blow to the men concerned but very upsetting to President Albert and other faculty members. The three professors appealed to the board, but to no avail.[41] The end of the Albert administration was fast approaching.

From the time in 1936 when the board of trustees had appointed Charles E. Albert to the presidency for one year until June of 1939, there is no record of any action having been taken relative to his continuing to serve as president of the college. On June 6, 1939, however, the board had appointed a committee of trustees "to make a survey of the needs of the College and to nominate a man for the presidency who will best serve the interests of the school. This selection will be presented to a full meeting of the Board of Trustees for their approval and as soon as feasible."[42]

It is not clear whether Dr. Albert was aware of this action at the time, and there is no evidence that any effort was made to involve the faculty in the search for a new president. What is certain is that during the first week of the fall semester, on September 19, 1939, Dr. Albert suddenly announced his resignation as president of the college "to become effective on the appointment of a successor." On the same day, Harry E. Whetsell announced his resignation, effective October 15.[43]

Two days later, the Trustee Executive Committee met, with Dr. Albert present as its secretary, and resolved "that this Committee take cognizance of the resignation of President Charles E. Albert and reports to the Board that the Committee has no recommendations save that the Board speedily and definitely determine upon a man for the presidency and, as early as practicable, convene, elect, and install such new president." Harry Whetsell's resignation as business manager, associate professor, and secretary and assistant treasurer of the board was referred to

40. Trustee Executive Committee Minutes, August 10, 1939, p. 51.
41. Trustee Minutes, October 16, 1939, p. 217. (Keefe did return in 1940 for two years.)
42. Trustee Minutes, June 6, 1939, p. 213.
43. Elkins *Inter-Mountain*, September 19, 1939, p. 1.

the board without action or recommendation by the committee. The committee scheduled a board meeting for October 3 and called a joint meeting of the Executive Committee and the entire faculty for 3:00 p.m. the next day.[44]

At that meeting, the financial situation was discussed at length. Dr. Barron, chairman of the Trustee Executive Committee, finally asked: "Are we willing to carry on as at present?" There was no response from the faculty except that Professors Purdum and Stevenson requested that a decision be withheld until after a meeting of the Synod on September 25 and the meeting of the full board on October 3. Dr. Barron suggested that it be "understood that we carry on the work at Davis and Elkins College at least for the first semester, and probably for the year, as at present." He advised Mr. Whetsell to "go ahead, order books, buy coal, etc. for this semester and probably for the year."[45]

The board could not muster a quorum for October 3 and postponed its meeting until October 16. Meanwhile, Dr. Barron, then president of the Tygarts Valley Bank (having retired from the ministry), was quoted in the press as stating that "the names of more than one proposed president will be presented to the Board" by the Special Committee to select a college president.[46] Apparently, Dr. Barron, chairman of the Executive Committee, was not well informed as to the plans of the Special Committee.

Finally, on October 16, the trustees met. Without any expression of appreciation for Dr. Albert's services, the board voted to accept his resignation "to take effect when a president is elected and officially takes charge of the presidential duties." Then the Special Committee reported and presented the name of only one man, Dr. Francis J. Brooke, pastor of the Ruffner Memorial Presbyterian Church of Charleston, for the presidency. Sometime between 2:00 p.m. and 5:00 p.m., after much discussion, the trustees voted to elect Dr. Brooke. Meanwhile, Dr. Albert, unwell and very upset, sent word that he was unwilling to remain in office any longer. The board, having taken no action to accept Harry Whetsell's resignation as business manager, decided to

44. Trustee Executive Committee Minutes, September 21, 1939, p. 53.
45. *Ibid.*, September 22, 1939, p. 54.
46. Elkins *Inter-Mountain*, October 10, 1939, p. 1.

make him chairman of an "Administrative Committee," consisting of himself and two local trustees, George Wilson and G. A. Yount, to "administer the affairs of the College until the formal installation of a new President." Dr. Albert was appointed professor of mathematics and physics "at a salary of $200 per month."⁴⁷

Acting President Harry E. Whetsell

Immediately following the board meeting, it was announced that Dr. F. H. Barron and Attorney E. A. Bowers had resigned as trustees.⁴⁸ In less than a week, the *Inter-Mountain*, headlined the announcement that the "Davis-Elkins Presidency is Declined by Dr. Brooke." The news article revealed that previous to appointing him, the board had had no opportunity to offer Dr. Brooke the position but "had hoped that he would accept." The Reverend A. L. Currie, chairman of the Special Committee to select a president, expressed regret at Dr. Brooke's decision. He was quoted as saying that there would not be another meeting of the committee "for several weeks," but that it would "be the duty of the Special Committee to continue to seek a president."⁴⁹ Indeed, "several weeks" proved to be an understatement.

The faculty met on October 30 and Mr. Whetsell explained the administrative situation and asked for faculty cooperation. He informed the faculty that a committee of the board was to begin "a campaign for the College for funds for operating expenses in the Northern and Southern Synods, one-third of the goal to be collected in this vicinity and two-thirds in the state."⁵⁰ Inasmuch as no one had been appointed dean after Dean Albert had been

---

47. Trustee Minutes, October 16, 1939, pp. 216-17; interviews of Thomas R. Ross with Mrs. Charles E. Albert, Harry E. Whetsell, and Anna Parmesano.
48. Elkins *Inter-Mountain*, October 17, 20, 1939, p. 1.
49. *Ibid.*, October 23, 1939, p. 1.
50. Faculty Minutes, October 30, 1939, p. 192.

named acting president in 1935, the duties of that office, as well as duties of the president and of the business manager, were among the burdens borne by Harry Whetsell in 1939-40. Obviously, neither Colonel Wilson nor Dr. Yount had the time, the interest, or the experience to be of much help in "administering the affairs of the College." Consequently, Mr. Whetsell got approval to add several faculty members to the "Administrative Committee." In addition to their regular duties, Miss Virgie Harris, the registrar, was placed in charge of publicity; Dr. Purdum of promotion and development; Dr. Talbot of student personnel work; Dr. Marshall of Christian education and chapel; and Professor Stevenson of curriculum matters.[51]

In a front page editorial entitled "Our Gratitude to Whetsell," *The Senator* stated that:

> Professor Harry E. Whetsell, treasurer of the College (and about a million other things which require him to act in an executive capacity), deserves more than a bouquet of orchids for the fine way in which he is managing the College, despite his other responsibilities. Many students do not realize the strain under which he is laboring when they continually make demands of him, or they would not do so so often ... There is a general demand for more instructors. Little time can be given to the individual needs of those majoring in certain fields when a professor is as crowded as some D & E instructors are. However, there is a general feeling that things will work out in the very near future to the satisfaction of everyone. Until that time, it is absolutely necessary that everyone co-operate to his or her fullest extent to make D&E a worthy school—a place of which one may be proud.[52]

Coach Shelton's "Scarlet Hurricane" football team did much to boost morale that fall. A 19 to 0 victory over arch-rival Wesleyan was especially sweet and even though the season's record was 5-1-4, D&E's "Ace" Federovitch, Jud Hudson, Jim Smith, and Vic Celio were selected for All-Conference honors. The 1939-40 basketball team finished with a 14-12 record and "Press" Maravich was an All-Conference selection.[53]

In January 1940, A. Spates Brady loaned the business

---

51. *Ibid.*, December 12, 1940; Trustee Executive Committee Minutes, December 11, 1940, p. 58.
52. *The Senator*, November 14, 1939, p. 1.
53. *Ibid.;* Kessler, *op. cit.*, pp. 266-67.

manager enough money to pay the faculty salaries. In the same month, the Trustee Executive Committee appointed Dr. R. B. Purdum to take over the work of "raising cash for operating expenses and selling bond receipts."[54]

On March 11, 1940, the Trustees' Executive Committee appointed Harry Whetsell acting president of the college "until a permanent president is appointed." This ended the service of the two trustees on the Administrative Committee. There was speculation that a president might be elected at, or before, the regular June meeting of the board, and the Trustee Executive Committee announced that it was "considering plans for a financial campaign for the College which will be launched in the near future."[55] This fund drive began with a dinner in Elkins attended by some fifty persons, Dr. R. B. Purdum, presided as chairman of the Development Subcommittee of the College Administrative Committee. The speakers were local trustees and President Whetsell, and it was indicated that the campaign was being sponsored by the Executive Committee of the board of trustees and the Elkins Chamber of Commerce. Funds obtained were to be used "for current expenses, to add new departments to meet the present economic and cultural trends in education" and to add "social programs, concerts, and an intramural program of sports."[56] Contributions received were helpful, but totally inadequate to meet even the first objective.

In May, the students elected "Press" Maravich to be president of the student body. He was an outstanding athlete and more than a decade later he would return to D&E as basketball coach.[57] The academic year, 1939-40, surely one of the most difficult the college had seen, ended with commencement on June 5. The speaker was Ruth Bryan Owen Rohde, former United States Minister to Denmark and daughter of William Jennings Bryan. She spoke of the war in Europe which Hitler had launched the preceding fall and of the threat to democracy posed by a Nazi victory. She concluded by stating "I believe that democracy has done too much for mankind to be lightly tossed away. I believe

---

54. Trustee Executive Committee Minutes, January 8, 1940, p. 58.
55. Elkins *Inter-Mountain,* March 12, 1940, p. 1; Trustee Minutes, June 1, 1940, p. 219.
56. Elkins *Inter-Mountain,* March 18, 19, 22, 1940, *passim.*
57. *Ibid.,* May 6, 1940, p. 1.

that the American people will rise again, as they have in the past, to the defense of the American way and having risen, will fight if necessary to the last drop of blood." Mrs. Rohde was introduced by Congressman Jennings Randolph, her famous father's namesake. She had been a member of Congress when Randolph was first elected and had introduced him on the floor of the House of Representatives when he began his service there.[58]

President Robert Todd Lapsley Liston

At their annual meeting on June 4, without any consultation with faculty representatives (or anyone else so far as the records show), the board of trustees appointed Dr. Robert Todd Lapsley Liston to be president of the college, at a salary of $4,200, effective September 1, 1940. Dr. Liston, then forty-two years of age, was a native of Alabama and had a wife and two young sons. A graduate of Davidson College, he had earned B.D. and Th.M. degrees at Union Theological Seminary in Richmond, and a Ph.D. at the University of Edinburgh in Scotland. Ordained a Presbyterian minister by the Greenbrier Presbytery in 1925, he began his career as Associate Pastor of the Beckley Presbyterian Church and Supply Pastor of the Old Stone Church in Lewisburg. He later served churches in Virginia and was assistant professor of Greek and Hebrew at Union Theological Seminary for two years. At the time of his appointment as president of D&E, he was professor of Bible at Southwestern College in Tennessee.[59]

At the same meeting at which they elected Dr. Liston, the trustees approved a plan which allowed the Synod of West Virginia of the Presbyterian Church, U.S., to nominate a professor of Bible who was also "to have oversight of the religious

58. *Ibid.*, June 5, 1940, p. 1.
59. *Ibid.*, June 17, 1940, p. 1.

life of the College student body." The Synod agreed to provide the financial support for that professor.[60] Final approval was also given to the legal documents necessary to modify the college bonds, extending maturity date from 1939 to October 30, 1949. The bonded indebtedness was stated as being $114,000 as the new decade began.[61]

For various reasons there was a general reorganization of the board at that meeting. Eldon D. Wilson, a Richmond insurance executive, who had been president of the board for several years, resigned as a member and as president. Dr. Nelson H. Thorne, pastor of the First Presbyterian Church in Clarksburg, was elected president. Colonel George W. Wilson replaced H. P. Mullennex as vice-president, and A. Spates Brady, who had been chosen to fill the vacancy created by the resignation of E. A. Bowers, was appointed chairman of the Executive Committee which also included Elkins residents Thaddeus Pritt, Sr., Frank E. Wilson, and G. H. Neale.[62] Later in the summer, when Harry E. Whetsell resigned from the faculty, the board chose President Liston to serve as secretary of the board, a position Whetsell had filled since 1925. At its meeting on August 1, the Trustee Executive Committee adopted a resolution recognizing "the fact that Mr. Harry Whetsell's resignation takes effect today. The Committee wishes officially, in the name of the College, to express its gratitude for his long, unselfish, and effective service to the Institution." The committee also authorized the continuance of the college's athletic program with Judson Hudson and Jesse Kniley as coaches and with "Colonel George W. Wilson to supervise finances and Dr. S. Benton Talbot to supervise personnel.[63]

Dr. Liston recalls that he arrived at D&E in July "with a carbuncle on my neck and with my wife sick in Memphis. When I first saw the College account books we had $24, no income expected till September 15, and we owed salaries of $700. The instructions given me by the Chairman of the Executive Committee were to get together the Trustees, Faculty, students and church constituency. He said they were divided among themselves, and suggested drastic methods to get unity, chiefly

60. Trustee Minutes, June 4, 1940, p. 218.
61. *Ibid.*, p. 219.
62. *Ibid.*, pp. 220-21.
63. Trustee Executive Committee Minutes, August 1, 1940, p. 64.

by subtraction. I soon felt that I had succeeded in getting many of them together on one thing: they were united on the idea that D&E needed a successor for me!"[64]

Dr. Liston's memory in regard to "subtraction" is certainly accurate so far as the faculty is concerned. In addition to Professor Whetsell, several other veteran faculty members resigned in the summer of 1940. These included Dr. Charles E. Albert (who was offered a salary of $1,350 if he cared to continue to serve as professor of mathematics and physics), Coach Harry L. Shelton, and Professor Charles E. Stevenson, as well as some with briefer terms of service.[65] Within the next year, Miss Virgie Harris, who had been registrar since 1922, also resigned, as did seven others, some of whom had stayed only one year. By 1942, with the departure of Mildred B. Johnston, who had served since 1929, Dr. Thomas F. Marshall, longtime professor of Bible and History, and two professors with brief service in English and in languages, only four of the faculty who were here in 1940 remained—Professors R. B. Purdum, S. B. Talbot, Irving Miller, and Mrs. Gilbert Overholt, a part-time music instructor. In later years, Professors Albert, Harris, Harriet Baker, and Shelton would return, but as the new decade began, the faculty was rapidly falling apart.

Although inexperienced in administrative work and somewhat tactless in some relationships, Dr. Liston should not be regarded as solely to blame for this disruption of the faculty. The trustees had repeatedly mismanaged the matter of selecting a president for five years. In so doing, they had shamefully humiliated Dr. Albert both in the beginning and the ending of his brief presidency, and had used, offended, and cast aside Mr. Whetsell who, like Dr. Albert, had served the college long and faithfully. They had not only ignored the faculty in selecting Dr. Liston, they had offered him a beginning salary completely out of proportion to that of other faculty members and in flagrant violation of the time-honored tradition that a president's salary per month should not greatly exceed that of a senior professor (except, of course, that the former received a twelve-month income plus housing and an expense account). Furthermore, the faculty and

64. Letter from R. T. L. Liston, Davidson, N.C., to Thomas R. Ross, February 19, 1979.
65. Trustee Executive Committee Minutes, August 1, 1940, p. 64.

other groups had been divided long before Dr. Liston came, as has been noted already in this history. There were several factors which help explain Dr. Liston's difficulties. First, as he has said: "The liberal arts tradition was what I thought a college like D&E should represent."⁶⁶ Thus, he was not in harmony with the tendency, apparent from the earliest years, for the college to provide a lot of vocational courses and to overemphasize athletics. Secondly, Dr. Liston believed "that being a good Christian and a good church-member was the most important duty and the most important public relations activity for Faculty, students, or anybody else interested in the College."⁶⁷ Dr. Liston's very conservative religious viewpoints and his implication that "being a good church member" was more important than scholarship and good teaching were bound to offend numerous elements in the college's constituency. Thirdly, Dr. Liston soon realized "that the Trustees really expected the fees of students to carry the costs, looking to that rather than the acquisition of endowment for the future. I was sure that I could not really fit that picture."⁶⁸ Obviously, the new president was not long in detecting the basic weakness of this college at the beginning of the 1940s. Finally, it was naive for Dr. Liston and the trustees to assume that he could bring in new faculty members to replace those who resigned and pay them as much as or more than was being paid to those who had served for years (and had taken a 50 percent reduction in salary during the preceding five years) without the latter resenting such injustice.⁶⁹

At the beginning of his first year in September, Dr. Liston asked the faculty to reorganize the committee structure and requested each faculty member to submit the names of the committees on which he or she preferred to serve. Eight committees were formed: Administrative, Educational Policies, Finance, Library, Athletic, Religious Work, Social Life, and Summer School. The new Administrative Committee, chaired by Dr. R. B. Purdum, replaced the venerable Rules and Regulations Committee. Since

---

66. Letter from R. T. L. Liston, Davidson, N.C., to Thomas R. Ross, February 19, 1979.

67. *Ibid.*

68. *Ibid.*

69. Trustee Executive Committee Minutes, August 1, September 12, November 13, 1940, pp. 64, 65, 70.

there was no dean, the chairman of the Administrative Committee was given the authority "to act in the absence of the President."[70]

New "House Rules" for co-eds living in Halliehurst in 1940-41, included provisions for "Study Hours" from 7:30 to 10:30 every evening with "lights out" at 11:00 p.m. and that "no girl is allowed to go downtown at night alone." Rooms were inspected each Wednesday and Saturday before noon. Senior women having a general academic average of 85 percent could stay out each night until 10:30—juniors were permitted three "nights out," sophomores, two, and freshmen, one—if their scholastic averages were at least 85 percent. All girls "must attend at least one religious service on Sunday at the church of her choice."[71]

At the opening chapel service in the fall semester, President Liston made his first appearance before the student body. He stated that the enrollment of freshmen was 25 percent higher than in 1939 and announced the appointment of five faculty members to replace some of those who had resigned. Congressman Jennings Randolph, a member of the board of trustees, gave a talk on "National Defense." Alluding to the wars in Europe and Asia, he observed that "American youth abhors war, but the young men and women today are as patriotic as in any past generation and will stand ready to join in the defense of our country."[72]

On September 6, 1940, President Franklin D. Roosevelt signed the Selective Service Act, the first peacetime draft in American history. Early in the semester, thirty-eight D&E students and four professors had to register for military service. A campus poll indicated that 123 students favored the conscription law with thirty-nine opposed to it.[73]

The 1940 football team broke even in conference games, but lost all six games played out-of-state. "Ace" Federovitch was the outstanding D&E player that year and was named both to the All-Conference and the Small College All-American team. The basketball record was mediocre and D&E did not enter the 1941

---

70. Faculty Minutes: 1945-1955, October 11 and 16, November 14, 1940, pp. 2, 3, 4.
71. *The Senator,* September 27, 1940, p. 3.
72. *Ibid.,* September 27, 1940, p. 1
73. *Ibid.,* November 1, 1940, p. 1.

conference tournament. "Press" Maravich was named to the All-Conference team.[74]

The West Virginia Intercollegiate Press Association held its nineteenth annual convention at D&E in December 1940 with Congressman Jennings Randolph as the principal speaker. He had been the first president of the WVIPA nearly two decades earlier. Other speakers included Calvin Price, the famous editor of the *Pocahontas Times* and James Weir, editor of the *Randolph Enterprise* and secretary of the State Publishers Association. *The Senator* editor, Lawrence Day, was elected vice-president of the WVIPA.[75]

In January 1941, four D&E students were called into military service, the first of many who would be inducted during the next five years. During the next month Dr. Robert E. Speer, one of the most influential preachers and foreign mission leaders in the nation, was on the campus as the Religious Emphasis Week speaker.[76]

President Liston was formally inaugurated on March 7, 1941. Dr. William Lindsay Young, president of Park College in Missouri and moderator of the General Assembly of the Presbyterian Church, U.S.A., delivered the major address.[77]

Shortly thereafter, the community was saddened by the death of Dr. Frederick H. Barron, the last survivor of the original board of trustees and first faculty. He served for thirty-six years as a trustee, longer than anyone else has ever served, and was pastor of the Davis Memorial Presbyterian Church for almost twenty-five years.[78] One of his sons later served as attorney-general and governor of West Virginia.

A significant event in the history of the college in the early forties was the acquisition of the Graceland Mansion and twelve acres of land on the hill west of Halliehurst in June 1941. Unfortunately, the land in front, from the hillside to Sycamore Street and Randolph Avenue, had already been sold for residential and commercial properties, thus forever marring the once spacious

---

74. Kessler, *op. cit.*, p. 267.
75. *The Senator,* December 6, 1940, p. 1, and December 13, 1940, p. 1.
76. *Ibid.,* January 17, 1941, p. 1.
77. *Ibid.,* March 7 and 14, 1941, p. 1; Elkins *Inter-Mountain,* March 4 and 7, 1941, p. 1.
78. Elkins *Inter-Mountain,* April 28, 1941, p. 1.

grounds of the Davis estate which swept down from Graceland to the stone wall opposite the Presbyterian church and around northwest toward Maplewood Cemetery. The remainder, including the mansion and its service buildings—ice house, caretaker's house, greenhouse, carriage house, and bowling alley—were included in this addition to the college properties purchased by the Southern Synod's West Virginia Presbyterian Educational Fund and given to D&E. The money used was the $25,000 previously mentioned which had been received from the Synod's earlier sale of Greenbrier College.

At the time of its acquisition for the college, Graceland was owned by a syndicate composed of E. W. Channell, B. F. Groves, A. E. Fiorentino, and Joseph Polino. They had purchased it at a public auction on October 24, 1939, when the whole Graceland estate was broken up and sold. Erected in 1893 at a cost in excess of $200,000, Graceland was described as having "19 bedrooms, 11 baths, and other facilities essential to the palatial residence which Senator Davis maintained."[79] Later in the summer, the Elkins heirs gave the college ten acres of land lying to the north of Halliehurst and Graceland, land which separated a part of the original Halliehurst farm from the northern portion of the Graceland acres.[80] This gift was important because it enabled the college to unify into a single tract the hilltop campus and because the timber on the property added materially to the beauty of the setting.

During the summer, the old Davis bowling alley (located where Allen Hall was later erected) and the swimming pool near Halliehurst were repaired and both were ready for use by the college students at the beginning of the fall semester of 1941.[81] The opening of Graceland Hall as a residence for "approximately forty men students, including members of the football team, and four professors" was hailed by *The Senator* as the realization of one of *"The Senator's* platform objectives."[82] A few weeks later a fire which started in a bedroom on the second floor, "presumably from an open fireplace, spread and damaged two other rooms" as well as the dining room below, doing in all some four thousand

79. *Ibid.,* June 4, 1941, p. 1.
80. *Ibid.,* August 28, 1941, p. 1.
81. *Ibid.,* September 18, 1941, p. 1.
82. *The Senator,* September 19, 1941, p. 2.

dollars in damage before being extinguished by the Elkins Fire Department.[83]

A *Handbook for Freshmen* was published at D&E for the first time in 1941. Dr. S. Benton Talbot, serving as director of student personnel, initiated this publication which has been reissued in various revisions ever since.[84]

Shortly after classes began in September, the college pastor, Dr. J. M. Lacy, minister of the Davis Memorial Church, died of a stroke. He had been associated with the college on an informal basis as part-time chaplain for nearly ten years.[85] His successor was the Reverend William Ward who also served for a time as chaplain.

The following week, the twelfth Forest Festival was held in Elkins. It was notable because of the appearance of the U.S. Navy Band to present a concert and since it was to be the last festival for several years because of the coming of World War II. Pan-American Day was a special feature of that festival and the pageant, directed by Claire Fiorentino, had as its theme what one writer called "The Pan-Americanism now sweeping the Country" —a result of President Roosevelt's "Good Neighbor Policy" and of the threat to the Western Hemisphere posed by Nazi aggression in Europe at that time.[86]

The imminence of America's involvement in World War II was recognized by some of the D&E community before the attack on Pearl Harbor on December 7, 1941. The D&E Civilian Pilot Course had more applicants than it could accommodate. Following the announcement of a German submarine attack on an American-owned tanker in the South Atlantic in early October, *The Senator's* lead editorial asserted that "now is the time for action. . . . It did not need the sinking of another American ship to make the American people see that something should be done. That the Nazis are embarked upon a scheme of world mastery is quite clear . . . the Neutrality Act has proved a mistake."[87] In an interview with a student reporter, Steve Martin, who for nearly a

83. *Ibid.*, November 7, 1941, p. 1. The fire occurred on Saturday night, October 25, 1941.
84. *Ibid.*, September 19, 1941, p. 1.
85. *Ibid.*, October 10, 1941, p. 1.
86. *Ibid.*, October 2, 1941, p. 1.
87. *Ibid.*, October 17, 1941, p. 2.

decade had been superintendent of buildings and grounds at the college and was the father of eight children, said that "the United States should enter the war now, instead of waiting and talking so much about it."[88]

Of course, when they came, the Japanese sneak attack on Pearl Harbor on December 7 and the subsequent declaration of war on the United States by Nazi Germany made a tremendous impression on D&E. With the nation's entry into the war, with her people furious at the Japanese and united as Americans have been in no other war, the D&E students and faculty were "moved to render on the home front all possible assistance to the nation's fighting forces." In an editorial entitled "Our Crisis," *The Senator* quoted Thomas Paine's famous 1776 pamphlet *The Crisis:* "These are the times that try men's souls. The summer soldier and the sunshine patriot will, in this crisis, shrink from the service of their country, but he that stands it now, deserves the love and thanks of man and woman."[89]

In 1941-42, at the outbreak of the war, there were 180 students, including 57 residing in Graceland and Halliehurst. Of this total, 99 were male. The next year, there were 110 students, of whom 46 were men who were either too young for service or who had not yet been drafted. In 1943-44, the enrollment dropped to a total of 56 students, all but ten of whom were women. In the last year of the war, there were 61 students, but no senior nor sophomore men, only two junior men and 21 freshmen. *The Senator* led a drive to collect scrap paper and metal as a part of the National Defense Program and urged all faculty and students to buy Defense Stamps and Bonds to support the war effort. In February 1942, the college began to offer elementary and advanced courses in First Aid both for students and for townspeople. On April 10, following a disastrous season in which the D&E football team had won only one game and the basketball team had lost 28 of 29 contests, the trustees voted to abandon intercollegiate athletics "for the duration of the war." These records were due in part to the loss of numerous players during the year to military service. Coach Fred Dickerson entered the navy as a lieutenant and there was little hope of having either players or coaches while the war continued.[90]

88. *Ibid.,* October 10, 1941, p. 1.
89. *Ibid.,* December 19, 1941, pp. 1-2.
90. *Ibid.,* December, 1941-May, 1942, *passim;* Kessler, *op. cit.,* p. 267; Trustee Executive Minutes, April 10, 1942, p. 6.

In May 1942, Gloria Marquette was elected May Queen. Later in the month, President Liston announced that representatives of the North Central Association would visit the campus to examine the possibility of D&E qualifying for accreditation. A few days later, Dr. James E. Allen returned to the campus to deliver the commencement address to a graduating class of thirty-three including future Elkins teachers Margaret L. MacVean, Kathleen D. Fidler, and Alton Pritt. During the same month, the college arranged to participate in the Navy's V-1 Program and in the Army's Enlisted Reserve Program.[91]

At its annual meeting that year, the board of trustees elected Dr. David K. Allen to membership, thus beginning his long association with the college. The board also approved a recommendation that a gymnasium be erected as soon as possible and a recommendation that consideration be given to "the great importance" of construction of a library building.[92] Although neither of these much-needed facilities would be constructed in the decade of the forties, the college did receive a gift of eleven hundred acres of coal lands and a valuable collection of antiques and artifacts from Mr. and Mrs. H. M. Darby in the summer of 1942 and the Darby residence on the corner of Randolph Avenue and Locust Street in August 1943.[93] The latter was used as the college president's home from 1944 to 1978.

During the 1942-43 academic year, the Civil Aeronautics Administration's War Training Service Program was expanded and more than 150 cadets, ranging in age from eighteen to thirty-six, in units of forty, attended eight-week sessions at D&E. Dr. R. B. Purdum served as coordinator of this program and several members of the faculty participated in the Ground School Instruction. The trainees were housed in Graceland Hall and took their meals in Halliehurst Hall. They were transported to the airport for flight instruction. In March 1943, D&E was designated by the Army Air Force as the headquarters for the 334th Army Air Force College Training Detachment. Between March 1943 and June 1944, when the program was terminated, 772 aircrew students were trained at D&E in addition to the CAAWTS cadets mentioned above. From the point of view of the War

91. *The Senator,* May 1, 8, 15, 26, 1942, *passim.*
92. Trustee Minutes, May 25, 1942, p. 228.
93. Trustee Executive Committee Minutes, July 10, 1942, pp. 10-12; *The Senator,* September 14, 1942, p. 1.

The "Darby House": presidents' residence, 1944-79.

Department, D&E's efforts were successful and appreciated, and the Eastern Flying Training Command awarded the college a rating of *excellent*.[94] The income from these government training contracts enabled the college to survive during the war years when there were few civilian students. Furthermore, of course, one cannot measure the ultimate significance of the fact that nearly one thousand men from various states of the East became acquainted with D&E. Numbers of them returned after the war to go to college here and how many others may have advised young people to come here or later sent their own children here is unknown.

The decision to bring the Air Force College Training Detachment to D&E was the major immediate factor which precipitated the resignation of President Liston in late March 1943, almost exactly two years after his inauguration. He recalls that it had "seemed good to bring in a unit of the Army Air Corps. And it seemed to me that I was somewhat out of my element with that (and in other ways)." From the perspective of thirty-four years later, Dr. Liston stated with good humor: "I think that perhaps

---

94. *The Senator,* September 14, 1942 and April 9, 1943, p. 1; The College Catalog, 1943-45, *passim.*

my best service to D&E was my resignation."⁹⁵ At the time, the board of trustees voted to accept his resignation "with reluctance" as of May 1, instead of April 1, in order to give him a month's terminal leave with pay.⁹⁶ *The Senator,* in announcing the president's resignation, observed that during Dr. Liston's administration "the library has been materially increased. Halliehurst Hall has been repaired and its furnishings greatly augmented and the Graceland estate acquired and put into operation as a men's dormitory." The president was quoted as stating that he was leaving D&E "with confidence in the future of the institution. The college can continue forever and ever and ever."⁹⁷ "Forever" is a long time—but so far his prediction has proved to be true.

95. Letter from R. T. L. Liston, Davidson, N.C., to Thomas R. Ross, February 19, 1979, and telephone conversation between Liston and Ross, February 23, 1979.
96. Trustee Exccutive Committee Minutes, March 31, 1943, p. 23.
97. *The Senator,* April 9, 1943, p. 1.

President Raymond B. Purdum and
Dean S. Benton Talbot.

VII

Years of Achievement and Frustration: 1943-53

The Second World War—the first "total war"—involved the American people far more than had the Great War of 1914-18. Its course and its consequences (including incredible examples both of heroism and of man's inhumanity to man, the development of air power and of atomic weapons, the destruction of the great Old World empires, and the evolving of two postwar superpowers) drastically changed conditions of human life on this planet.

On a more minute scale, that war and the postwar era also proved to be a turning point in the history of Davis and Elkins College. The resignation of President Liston in March 1943 and the immediate appointment of Dr. R. B. Purdum as acting president by the Trustee Executive Committee, together with the subsequent expansion of the Army Air Force College Training Program on the campus, ended for several years both the dissatisfaction over leadership and the financial crises which had characterized the preceding decade.

One of the first things Dr. Purdum was able to get the Executive Committee to do was to restore faculty salaries to the approximate levels at which they had been immediately before the depression. This meant virtually doubling most salaries and became effective as of April 1, 1943.[1]

At its annual meeting on May 31, the board of trustees accepted the resignation of Dr. Nelson Thorne as a member and as president of the board and elected Harnus P. Mullennex as president. Mullennex, an alumnus, former faculty member and a brother-in-law of Professor S. Benton Talbot, had long been eager

---

1. Trustee Executive Committee Minutes, April 5, 1943, p. 26.

for Dr. Purdum to become president of the college, as had several other board members, some of whom had supported Dr. Purdum for the position in 1935, 1936, and 1939. Thus, in 1943 the trustees voted unanimously to approve the action of the Executive Committee appointing him acting president and a year later voted similarly to elect him president.[2]

In his eighteenth year as professor of chemistry at D&E, Raymond Brandenburg Purdum was, at the time of his elevation to the presidency, the senior member of the faculty. He had been serving as acting dean of the faculty for several months and was a member of the Elkins City Council, the Rotary Club, and a ruling elder in the Davis Memorial Presbyterian Church. He and his wife had two sons and two daughters and had been active in community, church, and college life for many years. As has been noted already, Dr. Purdum was an excellent teacher and had played a significant role in efforts to recruit students and raise money for the college in the various emergencies of the 1930s. Aided by Congressman Randolph and other trustees, Dr. Purdum had taken the lead in getting the CAA Pilot Training Program, the Army and Navy Reserve programs and the Army Air Force College Training Unit established at D&E in the years from 1939 to 1943.

Affable, intelligent, professional, extremely hard-working, and sincerely devoted to Davis and Elkins College, Dr. Purdum at the outset of his administration determined to rebuild the faculty, improve the physical plant, achieve accreditation, and prepare for an increase of student enrollment as soon as the war ended. His longtime friend and colleague, Dr. S. Benton Talbot, who had been acting dean of students since the preceding summer, was assigned the title of "Acting Dean," combining the duties of dean of the faculty and dean of students in one office. He was later elected by the trustees to be dean of the college and served in that office, and as professor of biology, throughout the Purdum presidency.

Aside from these two chief officers of administration and Professor Irving Miller in music, there were in 1943 no other faculty members who had served before 1941. Stuart Noblin, who had joined the faculty in September 1942 as associate professor of

2. Trustee Minutes, May 31, 1943, p. 233; June 2, July 6, 1926, pp. 199-203; May 29, 1944, p. 239; Trustee Executive Committee Minutes, June 27, 1935, pp. 5-8.

history, was named registrar in April. In 1941, Dr. Joseph Durfee had become associate professor of English, and G. Douglas McNeill, a former lawyer and high school administrator, had been appointed associate professor of social science. Burlin Barnes, a D&E alumnus, had come as assistant professor of physics in 1942, as had Frank Bell Lewis, associate professor of Bible and philosophy, who was subsequently to become president of Mary Baldwin College. Miss Carrie Lanier Brittain also had been appointed that year as Librarian, a position she retained for more than fifteen years.

Succeeding Dr. Purdum as professor of chemistry was Dr. Frank M. Stubblefield who arrived in the summer of 1943. Richard H. Talbott, a brother of the dean, began an eleven-year period of service that fall—first as instructor of physics, then in mathematics, and later also as director of publicity and alumni affairs. Undoubtedly, the most significant of the 1943 appointments was that of Fred A. Miller as assistant professor of mathematics. He served for more than thirty years as one of the ablest classroom instructors ever to teach at D&E. He was subsequently promoted to associate professor, then professor, and was for years chairman of the department of mathematics. He was also registrar, as well as adviser to veterans for a long time; he was the first faculty marshal, and was for a brief period director of the Student Placement Office and of athletics—always teaching full time regardless of his administrative assignments. Within the next two years, three pre-Liston veterans, Dr. Charles E. Albert, Virgie Harris, and Mrs. Harriet Baker, returned to the fold, and Dr. Georgiana Stary and Mrs. Claire Fiorentino (Mrs. "F") joined the faculty, the former as professor of education and psychology, the latter as instructor in physical education and drama. Mrs. "F", a talented actress and accomplished director, influenced generations of students interested in acting, and her productions brought joy to hundreds of theater audiences during

Professor Fred A. Miller

the nearly thirty-five years she was in charge of drama at D&E. Dr. Stary did not stay so long, but she contributed significantly to the development of various programs of the era.

Although assembling a good faculty was a primary concern in the early part of the new administration, the need to provide adequate classroom space for the Army Air Force trainees demanded immediate attention in the spring of 1943. Thus, the board of trustees approved a recommendation authorizing the completion of the second floor of the Science Hall. This project was also viewed as being "of importance in attracting students to the college at the conclusion of the present war."[3] The board at this same time requested Dr. Purdum, Arthur Dayton, and E. A. Bowers to prepare "a suitable charter, constitution and by-laws for the Board of Trustees." A plan proposed by the Southern Synod of West Virginia for nominations of trustees by the Synod instead of by the Presbyteries was adopted.[4]

Congressman Jennings Randolph delivered the 1943 Commencement Address to a senior class composed largely of women. Among them were Kathryn C. Earle and Gloria J. Marquette (now Dr. Gloria M. Payne), the latter soon (1945) to return to begin her long and distinguished career as a member of the faculty in the Department of Business, and both women subsequently to be very active in church and community affairs in Elkins.

During November 1943, the faculty was informed that the Presbyterian Synods had voted to cooperate with the college in a financial campaign. Inasmuch as the trustees were scheduling a special meeting to consider the matter, President Purdum requested the faculty to prepare a written report "on the most pressing needs of the College at this time" to be presented to the board. Subsequently the faculty submitted a paper entitled "The Needs of the College Within the Next Two Years" which, in summary, was taken to the board recommending: "$100,000 for the liquidation of indebtedness, $85,000 for a library, $50,000 for a small gymnasium, and $15,000 for the completion and furnishings of existing buildings."[5]

At its special meeting, the board voted to launch a drive to raise $250,000 and appointed a special committee headed by H.

---

3. Trustee Minutes, May 31, 1943, p. 235.
4. *Ibid.*, pp. 234-35.
5. Faculty Minutes, November 9, 1943, p. 47, and December 7, 1943, p. 48.

P. Mullennex to work with both Synods in meeting the goal.[6] At the same meeting the board adopted the "Set of Standards for Colleges affiliated with the Presbyterian Church, U.S.A." These included the requirements that the college must "adopt a statement of purpose defining its status as a Christian College," must "employ as regular members of the Faculty only men and women who are active members in good standing of some evangelical Christian Church," "shall provide courses in biblical studies and require at least one such course for graduation," and "shall be officially and fully accredited by the regional accrediting agency."[7]

While in session, the trustees considered an offer from George M. Curtis to purchase the Darby residence. The board voted to reject the offer and expressed as its policy that "it will not now or perhaps for many years to come consider disposal of the property, as the Board realizes the intention of Mr. and Mrs. Darby that the College should take and retain this property as a home for the College President or for some other exclusive active College function." However, the trustees did vote at that meeting to sell the former home of the college president on the old campus and four lots for $12,000.[8] After necessary cleaning and renovation of the Darby House was completed during the spring of 1944, President Purdum and his family moved into it in midsummer and the trustees voted that the president should have the use of the property "without the payment of rent."[9]

The financial campaign, launched during D&E's fortieth anniversary in 1944 as the "Forward-at-Forty Fund," focused on the "unparalleled opportunity ahead" in the postwar period. Noting that the United States government proposed to provide "financial aid to all capable ex-service men and women who wish to attend a college" (later implemented in the so-called "G.I. Bill of Rights" which subsidized education for some twelve million veterans), the Forward-at-Forty brochure asserted that "Education under Christian influence is of cardinal importance in this period of readjustment." Thus, it was urged that D&E's supporters must provide the facilities and financial undergirding "to maintain the modern and complete program necessary to attract

6. Trustee Minutes, November 15, 1943, p. 236.
7. *Ibid.*, pp. 236-37.
8. *Ibid.*, p. 236.
9. Trustee Executive Committee Minutes, July 22, 1944, p. 40.

and serve this new group of purposeful, serious-minded students." Four specific objectives of the campaign were described as being: the elimination of the $100,000 bonded debt remaining from the creation of the new campus in 1925-26; the completion of the construction of the Liberal Arts and Science halls, which would "nearly double library and classroom space"; the purchase of some 17,000 volumes for the library to make it "the real center of the cultural life of the college," and the building of a $50,000 gymnasium. If these goals could be achieved, they would make possible the "one more step necessary to place the College in an impregnable academic position—the acquirement of regional accreditation by the North Central Association of Colleges."[10]

Although more successful than major financial campaigns in the past, the Forward-at-Forty goal of raising $250,000 was not achieved. However, enough money was contributed to significantly reduce the bonded debt, to finance some improvements in the Liberal Arts and Science buildings, and to add several thousand books to the library collection.[11] The campaign, directed by professional fund raisers from Ketchum, Inc., actively aided by Dr. Purdum and a committee representing both Synods, was the first statewide and synod-wide drive for D&E in seventeen years. Aside from the funds received, an important spin-off was that the college was brought to the attention of many who were unaware of it or had neglected it. Several of the larger churches made substantial contributions and the Island Creek Coal Company gave $5,000, this being the first instance of what became a continuing interest of that corporation in D&E.[12] Also, out-of-town trustees began to show a greater concern for the college as they participated in the campaign in their own churches and cities.

Of the twenty-three trustees serving in 1944, six were from Elkins (A. Spates Brady, F. S. Johnson, G. H. Neale, Thaddeus Pritt, Frank E. Wilson, and George W. Wilson), most of whom had been active in support of the college for several years. Four of the Northern Synod representatives (the venerable Howard

10. "Forward toward Victory," an eight-page brochure published in 1944 in connection with the "Forward-at-Forty Fund" Campaign, *passim*.
11. Trustee Executive Committee Minutes, July 22, 1944, pp. 39-40.
12. Elkins *Inter-Mountain*, July 10, 1944, p. 1.

Sutherland and Davis Elkins, both former United States Senators; Congressman Jennings Randolph and alumnus Dewey L. Fleming, both longtime and very active trustees) were from Washington, D.C. In addition to President Mullennex, a Pittsburgh businessman, other trustees included David K. Allen of Fairmont, Andrew R. Bird, Jr., of Huntington, George F. Bauer of Sistersville, M. R. Atkinson of Logan, Lloyd M. Courtney of Lewisburg, S. R. Diehl of Martinsburg, W. E. Hudson of Staunton, Virginia, Gordon G. Kibler of Clarksburg, and John A. Visser of Wheeling—all Presbyterian ministers—and Thomas Bloch of Wheeling, Arthur Dayton and George Ward of Charleston, and J. R. Moreland of Morgantown. Most of these men, as well as James R. Henry of Wellsburg, James W. Witherspoon of Beckley, George H. Vick of Charleston, and William M. Ferry of Parkersburg (all ministers) and E. M. Starr of Huntington, Dr. J. Howard Anderson of Welch, Robert S. Flint of Holden, and Robb Keyser of Parkersburg, all of whom joined the board later in the decade, played an active role in support of D&E during the late forties and most of the 1950s. Allen, Bird, Ferry, and Witherspoon in succession served as president (or chairman) of the board, each for several years.

In April 1944, Dr. E. Fay Campbell and Dr. Harry M. Gage of the Presbyterian Board of Christian Education in Philadelphia visited the campus to examine the college and meet with faculty. The purpose was to determine whether the college merited additional financial support from that source. Dr. Campbell asserted that the board would increase its contribution from one thousand to two thousand dollars.[13]

Only thirteen degrees were awarded to seniors in 1944. An honorary LL.D. was conferred *in absentia* on Lieutenant General Richard K. Sutherland, a former student, who was chief of staff to General Douglas MacArthur in the Far East. Mary Margaret Carroll, (now Associate Professor Woodward of the library staff) was a member of that graduating class. The academic year 1943-44 had seen the campus dominated by the military trainees, there being two hundred on the campus most of the time and only fifty-six civilian students. Even in wartime few students lost their zest for fun or their sense of humor. One D&E co-ed wrote the following note to the dean of women who thought it was worth publishing in *The Senator*:

13. Faculty Minutes, March 9, 29, and April 6, 1944, pp. 50-52.

I am writing to ask if you would kindly consider my application for late permission Thursday night, January 28, 1943. I have been invited by a very conventional young man to attend the President's Birthday Ball to be held in the Legion Hall. The ball is given in honor of Mr. Franklin Delano Roosevelt, who has just returned from Africa. I shall try to conduct myself in a highly dignified manner, that is, in a manner befitting a young lady attending a Christian institution and one who lives in close proximity with one of your caliber and that of your respected colleague, Miss Four by Four.

P.S. I promise I shall not become inebriated but—I sure will wing a mean hip, Babe.

Unfortunately for posterity, *The Senator* did not print the name of the writer or reveal whether the permission requested was granted.

For various reasons, *The Senator* was not published during the period from April 1943 until September 1946. Publication of the *Senatus* was also suspended during the war years and was not resumed until the 1947 edition was issued.[14] Although student publications and intercollegiate athletics were suspended and the enrollment of regular students was small, there were some club, class, and fraternity social activities. Student government continued on a limited scale and in 1944, Alma Crosier was elected president of the student body—probably the first co-ed to achieve that position at D&E.

The Army Air Force College Training Program was terminated at D&E at the end of June 1944. By that time the United States had all of the pilots, bombardiers, and navigators needed from such training units and intended to emphasize replacement training for the remainder of the war. The detachment at D&E had trained 772 aircrew members in the preceding fifteen months. Speaking at the D&E Commencement a month earlier, Major Starr M. King, director of the training program of the Army Air Force, had commented that D&E "had never had an inspection that was anything but excellent. . . . It is a grand small school." In a farewell statement, Captain R. L. McCauley, the commanding officer of the D&E detachment, expressed "deep regret" at having to leave and "sincere appreciation" to the college and to Mayor Clay Whetsell and the citizens of Elkins for

---

14. *The Senator,* September 19, 1946, p. 2; *The Senatus,* 1947, p. 41.

the cooperation and kindnesses extended to the personnel and students."[15]

College officials immediately set about preparing for the fall semester. Graceland and Halliehurst were returned to use as residences for civilian students. Although there could have been little hope for an increase in enrollment by September great enough to compensate for the loss of the 204 aircrew trainees who left in June, it was too late to reduce the size of the faculty. Fortunately, two wanted to go on leave of absence for the year, and Fred Miller taught at Bethany College for both semesters, returning in 1945 as an associate professor and becoming registrar in 1946. Nevertheless, there were twelve full-time and two part-time members of the teaching faculty for a student body which numbered eighty-six regular and twelve special students—a faculty-student ratio of approximately one to seven. Good, but terribly expensive! An expanded program of extension classes and Saturday and evening courses attracted approximately one hundred part-time students, but at a tuition rate of $7.50 per credit hour not a great deal of revenue was generated. The trustees did increase tuition to $85 per semester (from the $75 rate which had stood the test of time since 1927). They also decided to charge the president's salary and expenses to the budget of the "Forward-at-Forty" Campaign during the months he was engaged in activities for that effort. In addition to his travels within the state in that campaign, Dr. Purdum also began to venture into New York and New Jersey to make contacts in churches and with schools relative to interesting students in attending D&E.[16]

The faculty spent much time that fall and winter in studying the types of courses which might be developed to meet the needs of veterans who might enroll after the war. A committee under the leadership of Dr. Stary, developed a Community Forum in cooperation with the First Presbyterian Church in Clarksburg. Several outstanding speakers were brought to Elkins under the auspices of this program. Also, a statewide "Friends of the Library" association was organized for the purpose of developing an interest in the D&E library and of obtaining gifts of books and

15. Elkins *Inter-Mountain,* May 29, 1944, p. 1, and June 24, 1944, p. 1.
16. Trustee Executive Committee Minutes, July 22, 1944, p. 39; and Faculty Minutes, March 6, 1945, p. 68.

money in order that in another year "the library will meet accreditation standards."[17]

In March 1945, the faculty voted to begin participation in the North Central Association's Liberal Arts Study Program, an endeavor dedicated to "institutional self-study" for the purposes of improving higher education in the states of the North Central region. Dr. Stary and Dr. Durfee were the first D&E faculty members to attend one of the workshops in connection with that program, a program with which the college was affiliated for many years thereafter.[18]

During the fall of 1944, Dr. Purdum arranged to acquire for the college all of the supplies left on the campus by the Army Air Force Training Unit. These included numerous maps, globes, and charts useful in teaching history and geography, much valuable apparatus for laboratories in the Physics Department, equipment for physical education, and desks, chairs, and dormitory and kitchen equipment adequate to enable the college to accommodate more than two hundred additional students.[19] In May 1945, the college was given an Aeronca Champion Training Plane by Jennings Randolph to whom it was presented at the Elkins Airport by the Vice-President of Aeronca Aircraft Corporation "in recognition of the important contribution which he has made to aviation in America." The congressman immediately donated the plane to the college trustees who were assembled at the airport for the ceremonies.[20]

The college lands were significantly enlarged in this period by the gift of approximately fifty-four acres by the heirs of Senator and Mrs. Elkins. This property, adjacent to the northeast edge of the campus up to the site of the Observatory, included the ridge (where Presidential and International halls stand) around the Lee estate to the Harpertown Road. This grant, which increased the size of the campus by 70 percent was arranged by "two members of the Board of Trustees, Davis Elkins and Thaddeus Pritt, work-

17. Faculty Minutes, November 29, 1944, pp. 62-63, and March 6, 1945, p. 68.
18. *Ibid.,* March 6, November 6, 1945, pp. 68, 73.
19. Trustee Executive Committee Minutes, September 6, 1944, p. 41; Elkins *Inter-Mountain,* November 3, 1944, p. 1.
20. Trustee Minutes, May 28, 1945, p. 243.

ing in close co-operation with President Purdum."[21] Shortly thereafter, in 1945, the trustees sold for twenty thousand dollars the Palace Filling Station on Randolph Avenue which had been a part of the Darby estate. This money was used for retirement of a substantial proportion of the college bonds. The next year the remainder of the Old College was sold to Robert E. Hedrick and the stone from the old administration building was hauled to the campus for future use.[22]

During 1945 plans were discussed for expanding college facilities to meet the needs of an anticipated increase in enrollment in the postwar years. The end of the war in Europe that spring was one factor which led to a registration of 303 for 1945-46 (including 205 freshmen of whom 115 were male) as compared to the total of 98 in 1944-45. The surrender of Japan following the atomic bombing in August led to the war's termination more quickly than anyone had anticipated and meant that vast numbers of veterans and other young people would be free to enter colleges in 1946. Thus, in late 1945 and in the first nine months of 1946, D&E officials hastened to make provision for the classroom space and living facilities which would be necessary for the 1946-47 academic year.

The two unfinished upper floors of the Science Hall were completed to provide laboratories and classrooms. Four large classrooms and several offices for faculty were provided on the previously unfinished top floor of Liberal Arts Hall and a College Book Store was established in heretofore unused space in the basement of that building. A Snack Shop, including the Campus Post Office, was built in an area between Halliehurst Hall and the swimming pool. A residence hall for women, later named Greenbrier Hall, of cement block and frame construction, was erected on the eastern edge of the campus along the drive between the heating plant (Boiler House Theater) and what later became the Admissions House. With assistance from the Federal Housing Authority, a sixty-two-unit building, T-shaped in design, was erected on the western edge of the front campus to provide quarters for 124 veteran students. Known as the "T-House," this building was furnished with double-deck beds, chests of drawers

---

21. Elkins *Inter-Mountain*, December 27, 1944, p. 1; Trustee Minutes, May 28, 1945, p. 245.

22. Trustee Minutes, May 28, 1945, p. 244; May 14, 1946, p. 250.

The campus in 1949.

and chairs, provided by the FHA. Eight additional one-story, barracks-like buildings were located above, below, and in front of the T-House in the area below the evergreen trees along the edge of the campus from Grandview Avenue toward Sycamore Street and behind the Forest Festival pavilion. Several of these were for single veterans, one was for "Pre-Med" students, and others were designed as one-story apartment buildings for married veterans. A large Quonset hut was erected on the top of the hill between Halliehurst and Graceland for use as a Dining Hall. Another Quonset hut was located on the back campus to be used as a "Recreation Center" (and then later as the workshop for the campus maintenance crew). A small unit, erected on what became the site of the parking lot in front of the gymnasium, was known as the "Engineering Shack." These three buildings were obtained from the Federal Works Agency to meet the needs of the college for the purposes indicated in serving veterans. Senator Davis's old carriage house, behind Graceland Hall, was remodeled for dormitory purposes and was used for a time as quarters for the football team after the resumption of intercollegiate athletics following the war's end.[23]

Aside from the work done in Liberal Arts and Science halls, most of the construction was of a temporary nature designed to meet the needs of the immediate future, and thus within a decade most of the buildings (except for the Quonset huts and Greenbrier Hall) would be removed. Enrollment figures for the years 1946 to 1950 suggest how essential it was that such facilities be available if D&E was to be able to serve the needs of that era. As noted above there were 98 students in 1944-45 and 303 in 1945-46. However, in 1946-47 enrollment leaped to 744 (including the largest freshman class before or since—447, a majority of whom were veterans). The next year total enrollment reached 844. Many of them stayed for summer school which in 1948 had an enrollment of 415. In 1948-49, D&E had the largest full-time enrollment in its history—878 regular students, 63 part-time students, and a summer school registration of 501. Because many veterans pursued accelerated programs by attending summer sessions and completing degree requirements in three or three and one-half years, the 1949-50 enrollment declined to 788 in the

---

23. *Ibid.,* May 28, November 12, 1945; May 14, November 22, 1946, *passim; The Senator,* September 19, 1946, p. 1; Faculty Minutes, November 6, 1946, p. 86.

regular terms and 404 in the summer school. Aside from veterans there was also an increase in the number of younger students and in foreign students. D&E was approved in 1946 by the U.S. Immigration and Naturalization Service as an "institution of higher learning for non-quota immigration students."[24]

Another factor related to increased numbers of students coming from the New York-New Jersey areas was the college's affiliation with three "student recruiting agencies" beginning in January 1945. In this connection the question arose as to whether D&E should "open its doors to students of the Jewish faith." The faculty sentiment expressed was in favor, but one wonders why the matter ever came up at all since D&E had from its founding *always* been open to students of all faiths.[25]

During the postwar years, the trustees slowly began to increase tuition and fees. Following the initial action of raising tuition to $85 per semester in 1944 (plus a $25 per semester "Sustainer Fee" covering registration, health, laboratory, library, and student activity fees), the board increased tuition annually until the tuition and fees reached $200 per semester in 1948-49, remaining at that figure for some years until being established at $250 per semester in the mid-fifties.

Relations between the faculty and trustees improved substantially in the mid-1940s. President Purdum initiated the practice of inviting the faculty and trustees to attend dinner together during annual meetings of the trustees. He also occasionally invited trustees to attend a luncheon meeting of the Elkins Rotary Club in order that out-of-town trustees might become acquainted with some of the townspeople. Following the intensive efforts to prepare the campus for the influx of students in 1946, the trustees adopted a motion expressing "gratitude to the President of the College and to members of the Faculty for their devoted and self-sacrificing service in enriching the work of the College."[26]

One of the "services" to which the trustees' resolution referred was the tremendous effort made to prepare for and participate in the process of an evaluation by representatives of the North Central Association. As early as January 1945, less than two years

24. *The Senator,* September 19, 1946, p. 1.
25. Faculty Minutes, January 16, 1945, p. 67.
26. Trustee Minutes, November 22, 1946, p. 251.

after taking office, President Purdum told the faculty that he hoped the college could attain accreditation within another year. The following November, he filed a preliminary application and appointed a special committee consisting of Dr. Stary, chairman; Dean Talbot, Dr. Durfee, and Dr. Stubblefield, to assist him in collecting the data and completing the forms, questionnaires, and schedules demanded by the North Central Association. The examiners, President W. W. Whitehouse of Albion College and Dean C. W. Kieger of Miami University (Ohio), made their inspection of the college during the week of January 14, 1946, and in late March, President Purdum went to Chicago for the final phase of the process, a meeting with the board of review. He was successful and he attributed the attainment of this milestone largely to the faculty. Certainly the work of Dean Talbot and of the committee headed by Dr. Stary had been of the greatest significance. The Survey Report presented by the North Central examiners stated that "the members of the Faculty of Davis and Elkins College have demonstrated an alertness to educational problems seldom found in a college of this size."[27]

Unquestionably, the most significant achievement of D&E in this era—one of crucial importance for the future—was the accreditation of the college by the North Central Association. This had been a cherished goal since the 1920s, and failure to achieve it had been one of the disappointments and frustrations of the presidents and faculty for nearly two decades prior to 1946. That accreditation was possible in the mid-forties was due to a combination of factors which in a large measure had eliminated or modified conditions which had been obstacles to North Central approval in the past. For example, in the late twenties accreditation had been denied because of unsatisfactory athletic policies, too few library books, lack of faculty with advanced degrees, limited plant facilities, and financial instability. In 1946 the full-time teaching faculty numbered thirty-one, of whom approximately 30 percent held doctorates—a fairly satisfactory proportion for that period. The college had not yet resumed an intercollegiate athletic program and thus, athletic policy was not a factor. Plant facilities were infinitely better than ever before and most of the equipment, apparatus, and furnishings were rela-

27. Faculty Minutes, January 16, November 6, 1945; January 8, February 19, March 26, November 6, 1946, pp. 67-86.

tively new. The library, while minimal, had added more than five thousand volumes to the basic book collection within the preceding two years and had adequate space for the time being, as well as having two professionally trained librarians. So far as the financial picture was concerned, lack of endowment remained the major weakness. However, the bonded indebtedness had been virtually eliminated, faculty salaries had been increased to a reasonably respectable level for the times and in comparison to those offered in similar institutions in the area, and financial support from the constituencies was improving. Student enrollment was the largest ever up to that time and appeared likely to increase in the immediate future.

There were weaknesses, of course, including: lack of effort by trustees to get adequate endowment, very heavy teaching loads for faculty, too much reliance on temporary and "make-do" buildings and equipment, absence of any facilities for the fine arts and not many for physical education, lack of any well-defined tenure, sabbatical leave, retirement or other fringe benefit programs for faculty.

In retrospect, the weaknesses loom large and D&E in 1946 appeared stronger than in reality she was. However, in comparison with her past or with many other similar colleges in the region she looked very good, indeed! The success of President Purdum, Dean Talbot, and the faculty in gaining the long-coveted accreditation by and membership in the North Central Association of Colleges is a landmark in the history of D&E.

Certainly some, if not all, of the shortcomings of the college were generally recognized at the time. As early as January 1946, the faculty elected three members to confer with a trustee committee in regard to retirement insurance which would provide an annuity for faculty upon retirement. (Such a plan was subsequently developed with the Columbus Mutual Insurance Company and was in effect until replaced by the present TIAA retirement program.)[28] Later that year, President Purdum in an address to the faculty stressed his desire for adequate financial support; for better salaries, twelve-month contracts, and a retirement plan for the faculty; for maintaining high academic standards; and for "an adequate enrollment of desirable students."[29]

28. *Ibid.*, January 8, 1946, p. 77; Trustee Minutes, May 14, 1946, p. 249.
29. Faculty Minutes II, October 22, 1946, p. 83.

At the time of accreditation, D&E offered the B.A. and B.S. degrees and the Bachelor of Arts in Elementary Education degree. The curriculum was essentially the same as has been previously described herein for the preceding twenty years. However, beginning approximately at the end of the war there was sporadic discussion in faculty meetings of the advisibility of offering courses "for specialized training such as Commerce, Science, Engineering, etc., which veterans may take in one or two years." During 1945-46 decisions were made which resulted by 1947 in the college's offering programs leading to specialized degrees such as Bachelor of Science in Nursing, Bachelor of Science in Business Administration, Bachelor of Science in Physical Education, and Bachelor of Science in Engineering. The B.S. in Nursing was soon dropped, but with the B.A. in Elementary Education, the college from 1947 on offered six degrees, only two of which were traditionally considered appropriate for a liberal arts institution. Soon more students were working for the vocationally-oriented degrees than for the B.A. or B.S. degrees, thus avoiding foreign language study and some of the other liberal arts requirements.[30] It must be noted that this development came *after* the accreditation by the North Central Association in 1946 and that within a decade it seriously jeopardized the continuation of that accreditation.

At the first postwar commencement, in May 1946, twenty of the twenty-five students awarded degrees were women, most of whom received the B.A. in Elementary Education degree. Honorary D.D. degrees were awarded to Andrew R. Bird, Jr., and Gordon G. Kibler, both members of the board of trustees. At its regular meeting during graduation week, the board voted to resume intercollegiate football and to allocate 20 percent of the student sustainer fees collected to support athletics.[31]

The following November at a special meeting, the trustees voted to increase tuition, fees, board and room and to raise faculty salaries for the next year. Made aware of the "heavy teaching loads of the Faculty" resulting from the large enrollment, the board authorized the addition of five full-time faculty members to the staff. It also agreed "to seek the services of a

---

30. *Ibid.*, November 29, 1944, January 16, 1945-December 10, 1946, *passim;* and College Catalogs, 1947-57, *passim.*
31. Trustee Minutes, May 14, 1946, p. 249.

competent Business Manager and Treasurer of the College"[32]
Three new faculty members were appointed by the beginning of the spring semester, only one of whom, Lydia Driggs in Spanish, remained any significant length of time.

In fact, far more than five additional professors were found to be necessary as enrollment continued to swell in the late forties. Among those who joined the faculty in that period were several destined to remain at D&E for many years, as well as some who, while staying only a few years, played significant roles while here. Of those who served for less than a dozen years during the late forties and the fifties, the following will be remembered by many surviving colleagues and alumni. Jeanne M. Albert, a former student and the wife of Dr. Charles E. Albert, became instructor in English in 1947 and remained until her retirement, being especially beloved as the advisor of the Chi Omega Sorority. In the same year Norene Holiday was added to the Language Department. A Georgia lady of the old school, she was especially remembered for storming out of a concert when the ROTC band began to play "Marching Through Georgia" one Sunday afternoon at Halliehurst. Later, Bill Leist, a student M.C., brought down the house at the old "Rec. Hall" when after a skit at the annual "Faculty Take-Off" another student, having finished sweeping the stage with a broom, threw it down. Bill, quick as a flash, shouted: "Be careful, don't damage that broom, Miss Holiday might need it for transportation."

Two distinguished professors, retired from other institutions, joined the D&E faculty in 1947. Dr. David L. Haught, former dean and president of Glenville State College, was named professor of education and psychology and was a valuable member of the Administrative Committee here for several years, as well as being one of the founders of the D&E Student National Education Association Chapter which is named in his honor. Dr. Friend Ebenezer Clark, longtime professor of chemistry and dean of the graduate school at West Virginia University, a distinguished scholar and a unique character, served here for seven years before retiring for the second time in 1953. Another colorful professor of

---

32. *Ibid.*, December 10, 1946, p. 87; Trustee Minutes, November 22, 1946, p. 251. During the years 1945 to 1948 and again in the early 1950s, Ruth Chabut rendered significant service in the management of the treasurer's office, but she was never given the title of business manager.

chemistry who served for a briefer period was Stanley White, a Yale man, who often remarked that he doubted that D&E would long survive because "neither the people of Elkins nor the Presbyterians elsewhere would give a nickel to see the twelve apostles run a foot-race across Cheat Mountain, so they sure won't give anything to the College."

Gasper A. Loughridge, a middle-aged bachelor with a delightful lisp and much artistic talent, also came in 1947 to help Dean Talbot in the Biology Department. He taught huge classes of D&E students about botany for more than a decade. Service here began the same year for J. T. Oldknow, a brilliant young mathematician; Raymond W. Kiser, a chemistry instructor who subsequently became D&E's first director of admissions; and Daniel D. Rhodes, head of the Department of Bible and Philosophy and a popular preacher and teacher. Rhodes later became dean of students, a post he held for three years before accepting a professorship at Southwestern in 1953.

Dean Daniel Rhodes and Dean S. Benton Talbot.

Intercollegiate athletics were resumed following the war in 1946-47 and both the athletic and physical education programs were rapidly expanded thereafter. David E. Warner, a talented swimming coach, joined the faculty in 1947 as head of the department of physical education. He produced winning swimming teams, but more importantly he was largely responsible for developing a curriculum and establishing standards which helped to bring academic respectability to physical education as a major degree program at D&E. Robert N. ("Red") Brown served as instructor in physical education, head coach and director of athletics (1947-50) and was soon able to produce a championship basketball team. Aided by two other famous D&E alumni, Peter ("Press") Maravich (1947-52) in basketball and John ("Ace") Federovitch (1949-54) in football, Coach Brown had begun to put D&E "on the map" again in athletics, when he was offered the head basketball coaching position at West Virginia University where he met with great success both as coach and later as director of athletics.

Of all those appointed in 1947, the two who stayed the longest were Dr. S. Wilds DuBose and Dr. Knox Wilson. Wilds DuBose, educated at Davidson College, Union Theological Seminary, and Duke University, served D&E as professor of religion and philosophy, adviser to the Student Christian Association and department chairman, before becoming dean of the college in a very difficult period. A fine southern gentleman of French Huguenot ancestry, a careful scholar, and devout churchman, he was often in demand as a guest preacher in various churches of the old Greenbrier Presbytery. During his final years before retirement he served as college chaplain. A New Yorker who was never completely comfortable in rural West Virginia, Knox Wilson headed the D&E Department of English for many years and was active in support of *The Senator* and other publications. His wife, Bodil, known to everyone as "Boots," served on the library staff and later as director of publicity.

Not so many faculty were added in 1948. Probably the ablest of that group was Stephen P. Toadvine II, a Cornell graduate, who was an excellent lecturer and a popular professor of economics and business. He was in large measure responsible for bringing a chapter of Alpha Sigma Phi to the campus and was a valuable adviser to *The Senator* staff. Milan D. Stoller in engineering, Floyd DeNicola in history and part-time manager of the book store, and Lee Carl Underwood in business administration, each stayed only five years.

The next year Richard Grant Long, Mrs. Richard Talbott, and Thomas R. Ross were among those added to the full-time faculty. Long, whose graduate work in political science was done at Princeton and McGill, lived only nine years after coming to D&E as associate professor of political science. Endowed with the gift of teaching, a love of mankind, a reverence for truth, and a wonderful sense of humor, Professor Long was certainly one of the best loved and most respected members of the faculty in the decade of the 1950s, and his untimely death in 1957 was a profound loss to the college. He taught European History as well as his courses in political science and he constantly reminded his students (as well as his colleagues and presidents and deans) of Lord Acton's famous dictum: "All power tends to corrupt and absolute power corrupts absolutely." Institutionally, Professor Long's most lasting service was to establish the Office of Student Placement here in 1950.

Mrs. Talbott served for several years in the Department of Education and was especially helpful in developing a good working relationship with the State Department of Education and the Randolph County public schools, the latter being widely used by college students for observation and student teaching experiences required for certification.

The author of this history, in 1979 the senior full professor in terms of years in rank and tenure, joined the D&E faculty in 1949 as associate professor of history, and in 1951 became head of the Department of History. He and Professor Long shared an office and were often seen together—one tall and slender, the other short and heavyset. Thus, in due time, and to their great amusement, students nicknamed them "Mutt and Jeff," after two popular comic strip characters of that day. Readers will realize, it is hoped, that the writer, having participated actively in the life of the college for the last thirty years covered in this book has sought for objectivity by relying on documentary sources as much as possible when it is necessary to describe events or mention roles in which he has been involved.

In November 1949, while still an undergraduate majoring in history at D&E, Jesse F. Reed began teaching art on Thursday nights as a part-time instructor. He was a war veteran and had already completed more than five years of professional art training. In the three decades of his service as a faculty member, he was promoted through the ranks to professor, became the first chairman of the Department of Art, and developed a major in art. Professor Reed attained state and national recognition for his paintings and etchings and was selected for listing in *Who's Who in Art*. Since earning an M.A. in history, he for many years offered courses in Latin American and West Virginia History as well as in art.

In 1950, Tatiana Jardetzky was appointed associate professor in the Department of Modern Languages where she taught French, Russian, and German. A member of a noble family in pre-revolutionary Russia, she had received a thorough liberal education with emphasis on languages, literature, and music in some of the great universities of Europe and became both an accomplished musician and a gifted linguist. Prior to coming to America after thrice escaping Communist and Nazi tyranny, she had taught in Yugoslavia and Austria and had married a distinguished Russian scientist and author. In many respects, she was the most uniquely interesting personality and talented member of the D&E faculty, and following her retirement here she was appointed to the faculty of Harvard University to teach Russian to graduate students.

By the beginning of the decade of the 1950s, Dr. Purdum's four goals of rebuilding the faculty, improving the physical plant, achieving North Central accreditation, and accommodating a great postwar increase in enrollment had been achieved to a remarkable degree. Beyond that, the college had developed a Student Health Service with a dispensary staffed with a full-time nurse and served by three local physicians, Dr. Paul Snedegar, Dr. Charles Leonard and Dr. Louis Nefflen. In addition to Miss Anna Parmesano, whose long service as secretary to college presidents continued, several other administrative assistants who were to give long and faithful service joined the staff for the first time in those years. Elizabeth Guye Kittle, Joyce Teter, Virginia Earle Isner, Florence Lytle, Sally Petit, Louise Girard, Margaret Isner Meadows, and Rita Kyle all began as secretaries in various administrative offices. Mrs. Leonard Zickefoose came as supervisor of the College Commons and dietitian, jobs she managed with great dispatch for many years. Several college generations were nurtured by such unforgettable characters as Russie Hazeltine, Mary Price, and Lena Webb, hostesses (so the catalog titled them—everyone called them "Housemothers") in the various "dormitories."

With the rapid increase in enrollment in the postwar years, student organizations and activities flourished. Campus groups of the prewar era which had been dormant during the war years came to life again in 1945-46. These included Beta Alpha Beta (with Gloria Marquette as faculty adviser), Chi Beta Phi (which in 1946 combined its all-male Zeta Chapter and its Delta Sigma Chapter for women into the present Zeta Chapter), the Student Christian Association, the Playcrafters (revitalized by Mrs. "F"). The orchestra, chorus, and choir (all directed by Irving Miller), the Varsity Club, and the Women's Athletic Association (which revived the annual May Fete with Elizabeth Guye Kittle as Queen of the May in 1946 and James McGee as her escort).

New organizations founded in this era were a Veterans Club, an International Relations Club, Phi Alpha Theta, the Golden Circle, the Golden Chain, Sigma Tau Delta, and the Book Club. By 1951, there were chapters of three national (and one local) social fraternities—Alpha Sigma Phi, Sigma Phi Epsilon, Tau Kappa Epsilon, and Zeta Sigma—and of three national social sororities—Chi Omega, Phi Mu, and Pi Beta Phi—all very active in campus affairs.

Beginning in the late forties when Mrs. Fiorentino left the Physical Education Department to devote her full time to teaching speech and drama, there was a revival in interest in theater at D&E. *Our Town*, presented in 1948, starred Ellis MacDougall (in future years to be a trustee of the college) and Okey Chenoweth, who became a teacher and director of drama. Later that year, *Taming of the Shrew,* under Mrs. F's direction, became the first Shakespeare play to be performed in Elkins since 1922. The next season Violet Snedegar joined Chenoweth and MacDougall in leading parts in *The Silver Cord.* In 1950, *All My Sons* proved to be a popular production, featuring the talents of Leni Felstiner, John Cummings, and Delma Lighty. The comedy, *Kiss and Tell,* was a hit in 1951 with such actors as Bob Bender, Wally Pennington, Elio Mesa, and a newcomer, Patricia Ann ("Tish") Davis, who was just beginning her acting career at D&E. The 1952-53 productions included *The Glass Menagerie, The Philadelphia Story,* and *Candida.* Geoffrey Horne, who became a professional actor on both stage and screen, starred in all three plays. Other talented thespians who participated in leading roles that year included "Tish" Davis, Frances Villee, Elio Mesa, Bob Bender, Gene Penn, Harry Houser, Jim Lonquest, John Halloran, and Dorene Clawson (who years later returned to D&E as the wife of Professor Russell Crouse).

When one recalls that then D&E had no theater—not even a stage—it is remarkable that Mrs. "F" and her students could successfully undertake these presentations. Also she often took casts to perform in high schools and at the Huttonsville Prison.

Publication of *The Senator* on a bi-weekly basis was attempted during the 1946-47 year, with a return the following year to the traditional weekly issues. The first postwar *Senatus*, issued in 1947, was edited by Earl K. Lyons, who was to be a D&E trustee in the 1970s. Thomas Mero, an Elkins veteran, was business manager. The yearbook was dedicated to the memory of the sixteen former D&E students who lost their lives in military service during World War II.[33]

Intercollegiate athletics was resumed at D&E beginning with basketball in 1945-46 and football in 1946-47 under the direction of Harvey Rooker, following his return to the faculty after service in the wartime navy. The records in both sports were mediocre during the first two postwar seasons despite some spectacular victories and some outstanding performances by such athletes as Robert Irwin (later to be a successful Elkins High School coach), Robert Phillips (who would one day return to D&E to coach football), Harold Varner, Ernest Bazzle, Wilson Witten, Stan Moore, and William Holstein. However, with the appointment of Robert N. ("Red") Brown as head coach and director of athletics in the fall of 1947, the situation improved significantly, especially in basketball. The 1947-48 basketball team, coached by Brown (assisted by "Press" Maravich) won 16 of 24 games and ranked third in the conference at the season's end. Then, for the second time in history, D&E won the tournament championship that year (including an 81-54 victory over Wesleyan). The team included some unusually talented players. Carl Payne and James H. ("Hap") Huey received All-Conference honors and Payne and Joe Ceravola were named to the All-Tournament team. Other notable players were Joe Pukach, Ted Chizmar, Jim Clark, Bill Supak, Jim Scott, John Whitman, and Dick Walden. Speaking at a testimonial dinner in honor of Coach Brown and the basketball team, alumnus Denver Watring acclaimed this "the greatest team ever to wear the maroon and white of Davis and Elkins."[34]

---

33. These men were Charles E. Albert, Jr. (son of Dr. and Mrs. Charles E. Albert of the faculty), Clyde Brooks, James Carroll, Ben Fairbanks, Ray Hupp, Jr., Owen Kerns, Edward King, James Maxwell, Jacob Phares, Basil Sharp, William Siebert, John Simpson, Estin Teter, Jr., Phil Williams, Jr., Robert Wolverton, and James Wood (1947 *Senatus*), p. 5.

34. *The Senator*, March 8, 15; April 14, 1948, *passim*.

The following fall, the football team showed some of the old "Scarlet Hurricane" power by winning seven out of nine games against conference opponents. Among the memorable players were Bob Irwin, "Duppy" Anderson, William ("Whitey") Holstein, Myron ("Monk") Miller, and Denver Close—all of whom made the All-Conference teams—and "Hap" Varner, Paul ("Babe") LeRoy, Ken Crane, Jimmy Creaturo, Bill Lunoe, Norman Hoffman, Jim Fugate, Don DeGiovanni, Nat Underwood, Dick Walden, and Frank Zagar. A 13-7 win over Wesleyan in the final game of the season was especially sweet for the Senators' fans! The 1949 season was a big disappointment with six losses in a row and only two victories toward the end of the season. In 1950, with "Ace" Federovitch as coach, the record was reasonably satisfactory and in 1951 D&E won four conference games, losing only two, to finish in second place. Captain Jack Orrison and Bernie Marcinkowey were named to the second All-Conference team. The next year the Senators only broke even in state games, but both Ed Kuchar and Ray Kelley landed berths on the All-Conference team. Other notable players in those years included Ed Baran, Charles Heck, Chet Riffle, Dana McKinney, Joe Orrison, Andy Gussie, Lloyd Hughes, Ivan Daniels, Richard Hill, Charles ("Wapo") Repaci, Robert White, Ed Gardella, James Coffman, and Frank Cavrak.[35]

In 1948-49, the basketball team finished third in the conference but lost out in the tournament. Ceravola, Huey, and Payne were named All-Conference players and, in retrospect, it appears that the season was valuable preparation for 1949-50. That year Coach Brown's "Fabulous Five" (Ceravola, Chizmar, Huey, Payne, and Pukach) aided by Lycurgus ("Skip") Hill, Bill White, Neil Gutshall, and Ray Stepaniak won the West Virginia State Intercollegiate Conference title for the first time since 1934. Shortly thereafter they won the State Intercollegiate Tournament, becoming the sixth team in state history to win both the tournament and the conference championships in the same season. Huey and Payne were named to the All-Conference team for the third straight year as well as to the All-Tournament quintet.[36] On the strength of their season's performance, the D&E team was invited to participate in the National Inter-

---

35. *Ibid.*, 1948-52, *passim;* Kessler, *op. cit.*, pp. 268-70.
36. *The Senator*, March 3, 11, 1950, p. 1.

Coach Robert N. ("Red") Brown, *left*, with Assistant Coach John ("Ace") Federovitch and the 1949-50 championship basketball team: "The Iron Men."

collegiate (NAIB) Basketball Tournament in Kansas City, Missouri. There they won their first two contests, but were defeated by Tampa University in the third. That defeat may have resulted in part from the fact that Ceravola suffered a foot injury and had to leave the game when D&E was ten points ahead. Nevertheless, the team had done exceedingly well in Kansas City. Joe Pukach, only 5 feet four inches, had quickly become the favorite of the tournament crowds. He was named to the All-NAIB second team. Welcomed home from the Missouri trip as heroes, the coaches and "The Iron Men"—as the players were called—were given a testimonial dinner by the city of Elkins at the American Legion Hall on March 20. Mayor Wallace Barron, later governor of West Virginia, presented the players gold penknives and praised them "for the acclaim they have brought to Davis and Elkins College and the City of Elkins."[37]

37. *Ibid.*, March 25, 1950, p. 1.

Seldom has a small college had such a great combination as the "Fabulous Five." "Hap" Huey broke all D&E records for points scored. In his third year, before the end of the season, he broke the previous four-year record of 1,250 points set by "Press" Maravich (1937-41), having scored 1,275 points by February of 1949—with another season yet to play. His total at the end of his four-year career at D&E was 2,104 points. Of Carl Payne, already known as "Mr. Basketball" in Elkins, Dave Reemsnyder of Wesleyan said: "I've been here since 1926 and I can say that Carl Payne is the best basketball player I've ever seen."[38]

Coach Brown left D&E in 1950 to begin his spectacularly successful career as basketball coach (and later as director of athletics) at West Virginia University. "Press" Maravich succeeded him at D&E as coach of basketball and his 1950-51 team had a fine record throughout most of the season and ranked third in the conference with a 15-7 record. "Skippy" Hill was named to the first All-Conference team and Neil Gutshall to the second. The 1951-52 basketball team, the last coached by Maravich at D&E, finished fourth in the conference. That season "Skippy" Hill made both the All-Conference and the All-Tournament teams.[39] The 1952-53 season was a disaster and D&E dropped to twelfth position in the conference, winning only two of sixteen games. Maravich had left and Federovitch coached basketball that year.

In addition to the resumption of football and basketball, several other sports were added to the D&E intercollegiate program in the postwar years. The first of these was swimming which was successfully coached by Professor David ("Seaweed") Warner, head of the Department of Physical Education. The D&E golf team, composed of Henry Collett, "Hap" Huey, Lloyd Hughes and Jack Bennett, won the West Virginia Intercollegiate Championship in 1949. Baseball, tennis, cross-country and track were also developed as "minor sports" in this period. It is interesting to note that D&E was host for the first West Virginia Intercollegiate Track and Field Meet on May 12, 1950. Women's basketball was revived and in 1949 the D&E team, Helen ("Rusty") Weiner, captain, with Lucy Hott as high scorer, won four of their five contests. Field hockey was introduced in 1949

---

38. Kessler, *op. cit.*, p. 268; The 1950 *Senatus*, p. 116.
39. Kessler, *op. cit.*, p. 270.

by Betsy Crothers, instructor in physical education, and later became an important intercollegiate sport for D&E women.⁴⁰

Intramural athletics became an increasingly important aspect of student activities beginning with a softball league in 1948. The competition was often fierce, involving fraternity teams as well as "independents."

The postwar revival of athletics and the spectacular success of the basketball teams in the 1948-50 period, aroused new enthusiasm for the building of a college gymnasium, a major need much discussed and often planned since the 1920s. As early as the fall of 1947, the board of trustees voted to authorize construction of a gymnasium "of sufficient size to properly handle indoor sports and to provide facilities for the Physical Education of all students." Tentative plans for the building were approved as were arrangements which Dr. Purdum had already made to get structural steel from the Federal Works Agency in Danville, Virginia. Also, of course, the inevitable resolution for "a campaign to secure funds" for the project was adopted.⁴¹

The drive to raise $100,000 began in March 1948 and there was much local enthusiasm for its support, partly because of the fact that the basketball team had just won the 1948 Tournament Championship. Radio station WDNE (named in honor of the college) had just been established in Elkins the preceding month and the station gave valuable support and publicity to the campaign, as did the local newspaper.⁴² As usual, however, the goal was not achieved in the time originally estimated and solicitation was continued even after the long delayed construction started with "groundbreaking" on March 21, 1949. The faculty members pledged the money to pay for the flooring, student groups contributed funds, and the local Elks Club gave $5,000. Sam Polino, an Elkins contractor and coal operator, donated the use of excavating machinery and much labor, and President Purdum personally gave oversight to much of the construction. Dr. David K. Allen was the principal speaker at the ceremony of laying the cornerstone in the spring of 1951. Jennings Randolph spoke at

40. *The Senator,* April 4, 1949; April 29, 1950, pp. 3, 7; The 1950 *Senatus,* p. 110.
41. Trustee Minutes, September 29, 1947, p. 255.
42. *The Senator,* February 16, March 22, April 12, 1948, p. 1.

President R. B. Purdum laying the cornerstone
of the Memorial Gymnasium.

the dedication of the building after it was finally in use in February 1952.[43]

The construction of the Memorial Gymnasium was a major achievement, it being the first permanent-type building erected since 1926. Although because of inadequate funds the "Gym" was not the facility that Dr. Purdum and others had hoped for, it was far better than anything of its kind the college had ever had and, at the time, was comparable to or better than what most other West Virginia colleges had. Used for chapel services, convocations, student body meetings, dances, both college and high school basketball games, Forest Festival activities, etc., as well as for physical education classes and offices, the gymnasium has served the institution and the community well for more than a quarter of a century. It is in a sense a monument to the persistence and the tireless efforts of R. B. Purdum. It was during the period of the construction of this building, that some per-

43. *Ibid.*, November 29, 1948-February 8, 1952, *passim.*

ceptive students, observing the president at the site night and day, week after week, determined to overcome all obstacles, gave him the nickname "Bulldog Purdum." In an editorial published at the time of the dedication in 1952, *The Senator* editor saluted "Dr. R. B. Purdum for the construction of the Memorial Gymnasium" and asserted that "without the driving spirit and stick-to-it-iveness of the President of the College, the construction of the gym would have been an impossibility."[44] There can be no question but that the gymnasium project took much of Dr. Purdum's time and energy and that his preoccupation with it diverted his attention from matters of importance with which he otherwise should have been intimately concerned in the period 1949-52.

In those years, the decade of the fateful forties ended and the frustrating fifties began. By a strange coincidence on January 6, 1950, both James E. Allen and Irving Miller died. The former had been president of the college for a quarter of a century before resigning. The latter, who had joined the faculty the same year as had Dr. Purdum when Dr. Allen was president, had served as professor of music for twenty-five years.[45] Each in his own way had contributed the best years of his life to D&E and had touched the lives of many students and colleagues.

In 1947, at the suggestion of Dr. Georgiana Stary, a Summer Workshop in Art was established. This was continued for several years. At the same time, the Summer Language School was started under the direction of John Grant Thompson, head of the Language Department, and this was promoted each summer well into the decade of the 1950s. Beginning with an enrollment of more than 150 the first summer, the Language School subsequently attracted more than 260 students for some of the summer sessions.[46] In 1951, at the invitation of Tatiana Jardetzky, former Premier Alexander Kerensky of Russia visited D&E as a guest speaker for the Summer Language School. Although many statesmen and government officials had visited the college, Kerensky was the only former head of a foreign nation to have done so until President Omano of Kenya came in 1965.

Student interest in campus politics was high in these years—

44. *Ibid.*, February 8, 1952, p. 2.
45. *Ibid.*, January 12, 1950, p. 1.
46. *Ibid.*, September 20, 1948-September, 1951, *passim.*

apparently more so than before or than in recent times. For the first time in 1947-48, the Student Council, under the leadership of President J. Floyd Strader, Vice-Presidents James Rector and Mary Lou Laing, and Secretary-Treasurer Lorrayne Marquette, prepared a budget and was granted the finances with which to sponsor student activities. In March 1949, the student body voted to authorize the Student Council to become a member of the National Student Association and the next fall D&E's Russell Burns was elected president of the West Virginia Federation of College Students.[47] In 1949, under a new plan for governance, Student Council began to meet regularly with the Faculty Administrative Committee to discuss campus issues and problems, to make policies in regard to campus life, and to handle disciplinary problems.[48]

President and Mrs. R. B. Purdum and the Student Council at a dinner honoring the May Queen in the Old Dining Hall.

Beginning with the appointment of Dr. Dan Rhodes as dean of students in 1950 and the election of James L. Wilson as president

47. *Ibid.*, March 7, November 3, 1949, p. 1.
48. Trustee Minutes, May 9, 1949, p. 261.

of the student body in 1951, the influence of the Student Council grew significantly. Wilson's experience as president of the West Virginia Federation of College Students and his rapport with faculty members supplemented his talents as a natural leader. The student government became more concerned with problems of campus-wide importance and less dominated by fraternity interests. In fact, Wilson and the other officers (Leonard Whiting, Peggy Talbott, and Helen Cutright) were fraternity and sorority members, but they had run on a platform promising to end the domination of student affairs by a fraternity clique. They promised "to represent the entire student body without deference to faction, to advance the course of good government, to revitalize school spirit, and to co-operate with the Faculty in enhancing the welfare of the College." By and large they made good on their promises. The council revived such traditions as Loyalty Day, the display of college trophies, and sponsoring pep rallies. It also began to supervise student elections, providing voting booths and definite regulations in regard to campaigns. Major achievements were getting student representation on certain faculty committees, the adoption of a traffic code for the campus, and the revision of the student body constitution. The Student Council also brought a "big name" band (Woody Herman's) for the first all-college dance, "The Senators' Ball," held in the new gymnasium in the spring of 1952.[49]

The standards and goals set by the Student Council in 1951-52 gave impetus to student government as well as to other campus activities for several years thereafter. Jim Wilson's immediate successors as student body president, Scott McCormick, Jim Steen, and Gene Penn all sought to carry forward the policies he initiated. Such *Senator* editors as John T. ("Rusty") Cummings, Donald McGaffin, and Jim Lonquest, aided by staff members and columnists of the caliber of Robert Caplinger, Richard Thomas, Charles Marsh, Charles Angell, Merlin Withrow, Helen Painter, Helen Weiner, Marion Ingram, Paul Hammelman, James Harper, and others, developed the newspaper into an interesting and informative six-to-eight-page weekly. Ardent in support of "student rights," *The Senator* in those years sought both to assist student government and "to keep the campus politicians honest."

49. The 1952 *Senatus,* p. 18.

Dr. S. Wilds DuBose with leaders of the Student Christian Association.

Another prominent organization was the Student Christian Association, then very large and active under the leadership of Professor DuBose and such students as Forest Sheets, Cecil Layman, Young Coo Lee, DeWitt Furrow, Bill Leist, Glenn A. Shackelford, and Jim Parsons. Of the academic groups, Beta Alpha Beta and Chi Beta Phi remained active, and Phi Alpha Theta sponsored a lecture series and published a history magazine throughout these years. The D&E Chapter of the West Virginia Society of Professional Engineers was installed in January 1949. It was in that year, too, that Margaret A. Purdum was a princess in the court of the queen of the Forest Festival.

The graduating class of 1949 dwarfed in size any of its predecessors, having 182 members, including future D&E faculty members Ralph R. Booth (magna cum laude), John ("Ace") Federovitch (who had completed his work the preceding summer), Robert Scott, and Lorrayne Marquette (cum laude). Robert Craig, later to be a member of the Wesleyan faculty for many years, was the valedictorian. Others who remained closely associated with the college receiving degrees that year were Claire Fiorentino, Mabel V. Phares, George McLaughlin, Robert Irwin, Grady F. Guye, and James McGee.

The class of 1950 was even larger—209, the largest ever to be graduated from Davis and Elkins College. Eight honorary degrees were awarded that year also—the greatest number ever. Apparently the trustees had forgotten their 1931 rule limiting honorary degrees to not more than four, no more than one of which should be an LL.D., nor more than two D.D.'s. Former Governor H. G. Kump of Elkins and two trustees, David K. Allen and George Vick, were awarded LL.D. degrees and four D.D.'s were conferred, as well as a Doctor of Music. Margaret Purdum (Dean Goddin) was graduated *magna cum laude* with the class of 1950. Other notable members were Ellis MacDougall (a trustee in 1979), Carl Payne (who was soon to marry Gloria Marquette and become a "Faculty husband"), Woodrow Bodkin, popular manager of the College Book Store, Ralph Wilmoth, later president of the Davis Trust Company, and Frances Weese, later a faculty member in the Nursing Department.

The next year the graduating class was somewhat smaller and only seven honorary degrees were awarded. These included a D.D. to Claude King Davis, soon to become a faculty member, and to Walter W. White, a trustee; as well as LL.D.'s to Esther S. Allen (Mrs. David K.); James R. Moreland, a trustee; and to Professor G. Douglas McNeill, a highly respected faculty member. In 1952, William M. Ferry, a trustee, was awarded a D.D. degree and Jesse F. Reed, instructor in art, received his B.A. degree.

Classes continued to decline in size in this era and in 1953 only one honorary degree was awarded. Scott McCormick, Jr., who became a college professor, was the valedictorian that year and a bachelor's degree was conferred on Colonel Joseph F. Bangham, then a faculty member.

U.S. Senator Harley Kilgore had been the speaker at D&E's fortieth annual commencement in 1950 and his address had dealt with postwar problems and his hopes for peace. Tragically, however, on June 25, 1950, barely three weeks after Senator Kilgore's appearance at D&E, North Korean troops launched a full-scale attack on South Korea. Two days later the Security Council of the United Nations called on member nations to repel aggression in Korea and on the same day President Harry Truman ordered American air and naval forces to go to the aid of South Korea. For the next three and one-half years the fighting in Korea continued and thousands of college-age youth were called into service.

Because most of the World War II veterans who entered college had finished by 1950, enrollment at D&E had began to decline even before the outbreak of war in Korea. From an all-time high of 941 in 1948-49, enrollment had dropped to 788 in the next year, and to 625 in September 1950. Many of the young men were in Reserve Units of the various services or in the National Guard and virtually all others were subject to the draft. By January 1951, eight students who had entered D&E in September were called into service, the first of many soon to go. Thus, on December 12, the faculty adopted a motion which permitted a student who had to leave college after the middle of a semester for military duty to be given a special examination in each course in order to receive credit and a grade.[50]

Anticipating that the war might have a devastating effect on enrollment, Dr. Purdum began in the summer of 1950 to investigate the possibilities of again obtaining some type of military training facility for D&E. As a matter of fact, an effort to get an Army ROTC Unit had been made in 1947, but that had not been possible.[51] By February 1951, President Purdum reported progress on negotiations for an Air Force ROTC Unit. On motion of Professor Long, the faculty voted, with only one dissenting vote, in favor of the establishment of an Air Force ROTC program "on a permanent basis" at D&E. The board of trustees, also with one member in opposition, had voted approval.[52] The D&E ROTC Unit was activated on July 1, 1951, and the Department of Air Science was developed, offering college credit for four years of work, the first two years being compulsory for all eligible males. Students who successfully completed the fourth year and also earned their college degree were commissioned as officers in the Air Force. Lt. Col. Joseph F. Bangham, Jr., was the first detachment commander and professor of Air Science, serving ably for a four-year term. He and his staff received faculty rank and participated actively in the affairs of the campus, establishing a splendid relationship both with the college and the community as well as precedents to be

50. *The Senator,* January 21, 1951, p. 1; and Faculty Minutes II, December 12, 1950, p. 132.
51. *The Senator,* November 24, 1947, p. 1.
52. Faculty Minutes II, February 5, 1951, p. 136; Trustee Minutes, May 9, 1949, p. 262.

Lt. Col. Joseph F. Bangham, Jr., with one of the first Air Force ROTC classes.

followed by their successors throughout the next decade. (After his retirement, Colonel Bangham and his wife returned to Elkins to live and he later became a member of the City Council. His immediate successor, Major L. E. Spears, and his wife, Jae, also became Elkins residents after his retirement from the Air Force with the rank of lieutenant colonel, and she was elected to the House of Delegates in the 1970s.)

In the year following the activation of the ROTC Detachment, a cinder block building was constructed across the road below Liberal Arts Hall to provide office space, a rifle range, and supply room. Long known as "The R.O.T.C. Building," it was later used as a center for speech and drama activities.

The establishment of the Air Force ROTC Detachment, the initiation of participation in the Social Security System, the making of provisions for Group Health and Accident Insurance and Group Life Insurance Plans, and the construction of the ROTC Building were the last significant achievements of the Purdum administration.⁵³ The final years were filled with frustrations for President Purdum and Dean Talbot who had worked so long and hard and had accomplished so much. A small, but troublesome, faculty faction sought to belittle the administration, scoffed at the religious and liberal arts traditions, and spread pessimism regarding the chances of the college to survive. Some trustees were apathetic on the one hand while on the other, two or three maintained the time-honored custom of their predecessors in seeking to meddle in administrative and faculty affairs. Certain fair-weather friends in the town, who were supportive when times were good and so long as they had profited from the expanding business generated by the postwar influx of veterans which enlarged the college population, were not backward about downgrading both faculty and students when times changed.

By 1952, the increased costs of operation due to rising prices resulting from the Korean conflict and the decline in enrollment coincided in adversely affecting D&E. Still largely dependent on tuition and fees because of the lack of endowment and the chronic failure of the Presbyterian synods to provide adequate support, the college again—as so often in the past—faced a serious financial picture.

No one should have been unaware of the problems. Indeed, as early as December 1950, the Executive Committee of the trustees had met with President Purdum, Deans Talbot and Rhodes, and Rudolph Sippola (business manager from 1947 to 1951) to discuss "particularly the financial situation which has resulted from the decline in enrollment attributable to the international political crisis."⁵⁴ Meanwhile, faculty committees had begun to study the grants-in-aid policies (particularly the cost of athletic grants), the student work program costs, scholarships, and the operation of the College Book Store. Recommendations that the various grants be strictly limited and supervised by a Faculty Committee were approved by both the faculty and the board. Professor DeNicola was appointed to manage the College Book Store in addition to teaching in the History Department.⁵⁵

53. Faculty Minutes II, December 1, 1950, p. 129; Trustee Minutes, December 7, 1950, May 14, 1951, May 6, 1952, pp. 271, 273, 280.
54. *Ibid.*, December 6, 7, 1950, p. 270.
55. *Ibid.*, p. 271; Faculty Minutes II, December 4, 1950, p. 129, and May 26, 1951, p. 142.

In 1951, Dr. C. L. Winters, Jr., conducted a survey of Presbyterian colleges affiliated with the Presbyterian Church, U.S.A. His report on D&E, sent to all trustees and faculty members by President Purdum, stated in regard to the management of business affairs, that:

> The Business Manager ... is generally responsible for accounting, safekeeping, and disbursing all College funds. He acts as the budget control officer and purchasing is centralized in his office. ... Business administration leaves much to be desired, primarily because of insufficient assistance. Improvements could be made in:
> a) Drawing off monthly comparative statements of income and expense.
> b) Preparing annual reports on time.
> c) Provision for tightening control on collection of student accounts.
> d) Tightening of requirements for scholarships, grants-in-aid, and tuition rebates.[56]

Dr. Winters observed that the total endowment of $250,774 "is of course inadequate" and that "the major financial need is for increased endowment." Furthermore, he pointed out that the college awarded $37,316 in scholarships and grants-in-aid—"an unbelievably large sum when we consider that a very small percentage is from endowed sources."[57]

The only action taken on this report was to slightly reduce scholarships and grants-in-aid in the next budget. Rudolph Sippola, the only full-time business manager the college had ever had, resigned in May 1951 to accept a position elsewhere. The trustees appointed Lee Carl Underwood, associate professor of accounting, to be "Acting Treasurer, effective June 1, to handle the essential routine of the Business Office until a successor to Mr. Sippola is appointed."[58] Then, incredible as it may seem in the light of the Winters's report comment written before Sippola left that "business administration leaves much to be desired, primarily because of insufficient assistance," the board did not

---

56. C. L. Winters, Jr., "Survey Report: Davis and Elkins College," May 20, 1951, pp. 9-10.
57. *Ibid.*, p. 28.
58. Trustee Minutes, May 14, 1951, p. 275.

appoint a new business manager until April 1, 1953, nearly two years after Sippola resigned.[59]

The result, as could have been expected, was that the proper administration of business affairs was sorely neglected. Bills owed to business firms in Elkins and elsewhere went unpaid, tuition and fees were often uncollected or partially collected, and at times faculty and staff salaries could not be paid on time. Nevertheless, in September 1951, the trustees voted "to borrow money from the General Fund for use of the Gymnasium Fund."[60] Even after a Faculty Committee revealed in 1952 that intercollegiate football was costing a great amount of money, the most that the trustees would do was to recommend "that only a limited schedule of approximately six (6) games of football be undertaken in the fall of 1952," thus delaying for a year the discontinuation of that drain on college funds. Wesleyan had dropped football a year earlier as had many other colleges throughout the nation.[61]

In March 1952, the Executive Council on Higher Education of the Southern Presbyterian Synod of West Virginia met to review the situation at D&E. After noting with satisfaction the great progress made since 1945, the council voted to call "most urgently to the attention of the Trustees and Administration of the College" the need to "discontinue inter-collegiate football unless it ceases to be a drain on the finances of the College" and the need for "an able and qualified business manager and public relations man."

Finally, early in 1953, the financial situation reached a critical stage. The Trustees' Executive Committee met on February 26 at the call of Dr. David K. Allen who had succeeded H. P. Mullennex as president of the board on May 8, 1950. The committee voted to direct the new business manager, Jacob E. Nicholson, to "provide the Executive Committee with a monthly statement of receipts and disbursements on each item in the budget." The title of treasurer and business manager was then changed to that of "Comptroller." College officials were authorized to borrow up to $36,000 to meet the March payroll and pay some creditors, and were "instructed to delay any commitments in football contracts for the ensuing year." The next day and evening, the committee,

59. *The Senator*, March 11, 1953, p. 1.
60. Trustee Executive Committee Minutes, September 28, 1951, p. 50.
61. *Ibid.*, April 30, 1952, p. 51; *The Senator*, May 20, 1953, p. 1.

augmented by four other trustees, interviewed various people, and held a long discussion in regard to conditions at the college. The result was a decision to prepare a report and "to call a special meeting of the entire Board of Trustees as soon as convenient to consider and take appropriate action upon the report."[62]

It was readily apparent that some people desired to lay the whole blame for the financial mess on the college president. Certainly he was to some degree responsible in that he did not keep himself and the board adequately informed about the affairs of the treasurer's office and that he did not insist on a competent, full-time replacement of the business manager immediately after Sippola's resignation. However, in view of the known facts and circumstances, it seemed to most of the faculty and to some trustees that a "demand for the President's head" was grossly unjust. Consequently, at the request of several of their colleagues, Professors DuBose, Long, and Ross prepared a letter to the trustees which was signed by all but three or four of the faculty members and then sent to the board. The purpose was to show support and confidence in Dr. Purdum, despite his admitted shortcomings in the existing situation, and to suggest that some solution be sought short of immediate dismissal of the president.[63]

Apparently the faculty's views made some impression. One trustee wrote "your thoughts were very helpful to the supporters of Dr. Purdum" and another expressed the hope that the faculty would feel that the board's actions "were in keeping with the spirit of your letter and for the best interests of the school."[64]

The "Board's actions," not fully revealed to the faculty at the time, included a decision at its regular meeting on May 12, 1953, to accept "with reluctance" Dr. Purdum's resignation "for the sake of my health." The trustees provided that "in consideration of the great and meritorious service rendered by Dr. Purdum to the College during the past twenty-eight years . . . and of his loyal efforts on behalf of the Board" he was to have a year of sabbatical

62. Minutes of the Executive Council on Higher Education, March 6, 1952; Trustee Executive Committee Minutes, February 26, 27, 1953, p. 53.

63. Twenty-eight faculty members to the board of trustees, Elkins, W.Va., March 19, 1953.

64. Harry M. Gray, Fulton, N.Y., to Thomas R. Ross, May 13, 1953; George H. Vick, Charleston, W.Va., to Thomas R. Ross, May 13, 1953.

leave with full pay beginning July 1, 1954. For the period from May 1953 until his leave, he was to "give his full time to public relations," while retaining the title of president. The authority and responsibility of his office was transferred to a "full-time Executive Vice-President" who was to be appointed later "to administer the affairs of the College."[65]

Thus, Raymond B. Purdum, president in name only in 1953-54, completed his twenty-ninth year of service to the college to which he had given his entire adult life. He also served as president of the West Virginia Foundation of Independent Colleges, an institution he had helped establish. His resignation was not publicly announced until January 1954. Later that year, he accepted a professorship in chemistry at Presbyterian College in South Carolina.

A longtime member of the board of trustees, one of Dr. Purdum's most severe critics, stated what many knew to be true, when he asserted that "Purdum saved the College in 1943 and had been a major force in doing so in the thirties." Looking at the record a quarter of a century after his resignation as president, it is difficult to deny that R. B. Purdum and his associates, especially Benton Talbot, deserve great credit not only for D&E's survival in the 1940s, but for providing the foundations for progress made in the years since the frustrations of 1953—progress which would not have been possible without the accreditation gained in 1946 and the subsequent achievements of the Purdum-Talbot era.

65. Trustee Minutes, May 12, 1953, p. 283.

Dr. David K. Allen and Dr. Andrew R. Bird, Jr., at the inauguration of Dr. Allen as president.

VIII

Retrenchment, Reform, and Renewal: 1953-64

By the early summer of 1953, Dwight D. Eisenhower, who had succeeded Harry Truman as president of the United States in January, was able to announce that the peace negotiations which President Truman had initiated in Korea in 1952 had been concluded with a truce. Demobilization, prevention of a recession, and retrenchment rather than reform preoccupied the new administration in Washington.

Retrenchment *and* reform were the major concerns of the trustees and faculty at Davis and Elkins College as the board concluded its annual meeting in May 1953. After acting on the resignation of President R. B. Purdum, the trustees appointed a special committee composed of Dr. David K. Allen, Dr. Andrew R. Bird, Jr., and Dr. James R. Henry (all Presbyterian clergymen) to seek an executive vice-president for the college. The same committee was instructed to begin "preliminary work with a view of securing a new President of the College." Before adjourning, the board also authorized an increase in room and board charges, and ordered that no student could register for another semester, receive a transcript, or be graduated until his account owed the college had been paid in full. The awarding of grants-in-aid was restricted and a motion was adopted that "as an economy measure football be discontinued as an intercollegiate sport for the ensuing season." The trustees also decided to ask the appropriate committees of the Presbyterian Synods to request additional financial aid amounting to seventy-five cents per church member per year for five years to meet D&E's need for emergency funds for debt liquidation.[1]

1. Trustee Minutes, May 11, 12, 1953, pp. 284-85.

Four days later, at a special meeting, President Purdum informed the faculty that the trustees "had considered it advisable, in view of the existing situation and the approaching 50th Anniversary of the College, to create a new office," that of executive vice-president. No mention was made of his resignation. After reviewing other actions of the board, Dr. Purdum introduced Dr. David Allen, the trustees' president, who stated that he was present to "confirm the report of the President." In addition he announced decisions to discontinue football and to change the title of the business manager to that of "Comptroller." Inasmuch as the college owed $146,000 in unpaid bills, he stated that no one was permitted to make any purchases without the comptroller's permission.[2]

The failure to explain frankly to the faculty what had been decided in regard to terminating the Purdum presidency as of July 1, 1954, or to involve the faculty in the plans and process of selecting a new chief executive were mistakes not unlike the board's errors of the 1935-40 era in connection with the appointments of successors to James E. Allen and Charles E. Albert. A second blunder was in overemphasizing the authority of the new comptroller, a man with no prior experience in college administration. Before taking time to reflect on the implications of his actions, J. E. Nicholson published a notice in *The Senator* that students with unpaid accounts could not take final examinations. He then discovered that approximately 250 students would be affected and thus within a week, he had to rescind his decree. Faculty members quickly reminded him that it was not a prerogative of his office to determine who could or could not take examinations. Final examinations would be administered as the faculty might determine—though, of course, transcripts and final grade reports might later be withheld. A motion was passed that if, at the end of the semester, there was a desire that grades not be given to students with unpaid accounts, then "instructions to that effect must come from the President's office."[3] Although in itself a minor matter, this episode was symptomatic of the strange failure of so many to realize the vital importance of morale. Financial problems of institutions can be solved rather easily as compared with the difficulty of dealing with problems of

2. Faculty Minutes II, May 16, 1953, pp. 167-68.
3. *Ibid.*, May 23, 1953, p. 169.

shattered morale whether of a nation, an army, or a college faculty.

The administrative situation at D&E during the late spring and the summer of 1953 was awkward to say the least. In July, the Executive Committee of the Board of Trustees elected Dr. David K. Allen to serve as executive vice-president of the college "until Dr. Purdum's resignation takes effect on June 30, 1954." The vice-president was instructed to "perform all duties entrusted to the President by the Constitution and By-Laws of the College," except that Dr. Purdum was to continue to hold the title of president and to represent the college on all social and academic occasions.[4]

Apparently the special committee, in the limited time it had had for its search, had not been successful in finding anyone willing to accept the office of executive vice-president. Thus, the Executive Committee drafted Dr. Allen. He had sought and gotten the promise of support from both of the Presbyterian Synods and had then agreed to accept the position effective September 1, 1953, with the understanding that he would spend as much time as he could at the college in July and August.[5]

A native of Ohio and a combat veteran of World War I, David Kell Allen had received his Bachelor of Arts degree at the College of Wooster in 1922 and had then studied for the ministry at Western Theological Seminary in Pittsburgh where he was awarded the degree Bachelor of Sacred Theology. While at Western, he had won a scholarship for study abroad which enabled him to earn a Ph.D. degree at the University of Edinburgh in Scotland. He had served as minister of Presbyterian churches in Erie and Johnstown, Pennsylvania, for more than thirteen years prior to accepting a call to the First Presbyterian Church in Fairmont, West Virginia. There, where he was the minister for twelve years, he had become one of the leaders of his Presbytery and Synod and a member and president of the D&E Board of Trustees. He and Mrs. Allen had a married daughter and a son in Princeton Theological Seminary at the time he accepted the appointment as executive vice-president of Davis and Elkins College. A man of vision, with the courage of his convictions, a good

---

4. Trustee Executive Committee Minutes, July 6, 1953, p. 58.
5. *Ibid.*, July 6, September 15, 1953, pp. 58-60.

sense of humor, and a great capacity for hard work, Dr. Allen approached each task with confidence.

To undertake the assignment given him at D&E was an act of courage, involving considerable risk and requiring much faith on the part of David Allen. Not only did he give up a successful career in the profession for which he was trained and which he dearly loved, but he knew something of the magnitude of the task confronting him at D&E.

First of all, of course, the financial crisis and the morale problems at D&E were very serious and appeared to be almost insurmountable under the best of conditions. However, the new vice-president was in the rather awkward position of having been both president of the board when the crisis developed and a member of the special committee appointed to select an executive vice-president and begin the search for a new president. Of course, no one who gave thought to the matter could assume that he had given up his pastorate merely to accept the temporary post of vice-president. The faculty realized that, again, the board had selected a president of the college without involving the faculty in any way in the process. Moreover, Dr. Allen was thrust suddenly, without previous experience in academic affairs, into a position of leadership in a faculty where professional loyalties, longtime relationships, and family ties were strong.

Probably neither Dr. Allen nor the majority of the trustees understood at the time—if they ever did—the impression which the board's actions in 1953 created in the minds of many faculty members and friends of the college in Elkins. Basically this was that since the college treasurer and business manager was responsible to the board which retained the authority to appoint and remove that officer, their negligence in finding a competent replacement for Rudolph Sippola (even after receiving the Winters's Report pointing out the deficiences and problems in that office) was the root cause of the existing financial disaster. That, plus the perennial failure of the trustees to attempt to get endowment funds essential for the financial health of the institution, many believed to be of far greater significance than whatever fault might properly have been attributed to President Purdum in the 1951-53 period. Under the circumstances, to have brought in any trustee as executive vice-president to supplant R. B. Purdum and pay him a beginning salary (even though it was no more than his salary as a minister) in excess of what any president had ever received was bound to create some unfavorable reactions.

Furthermore, it was decided to replace S. Benton Talbot as dean of the college. For some time there had been some criticism directed at him for his tolerance of certain activities by a few faculty members and of rather loose admission standards for students. That, in addition to his long and close relationship to Dr. Purdum, led the board to think that he ought not to be continued as the chief academic officer. A popular lifelong resident of Elkins and then the senior professor at D&E with a formidable following among faculty, alumni, and students, as well as in the town, Dr. Talbot was not one whose status could be lightly disregarded. That he was tenured as professor of biology meant that he would remain a faculty member. The fact that he retained the chairmanship of his department and was given the same salary he had had as dean was not much solace, for he had always been underpaid. Moreover, the displeasure of his supporters was in no way appeased by the decision to terminate the faculty appointments of Richard Talbott, the dean's brother, then a member of the West Virginia Legislature, as instructor in mathematics, and of Mrs. Richard Talbott as a member of the Education Department.[6]

As is so often the case, it is not what is true but what people believe to be true that motivates them. Thus, though it later was clear that in those troubled times at D&E, there were no villains—only victims; there were those who looked for the former. No one embezzled any money; there was no "conspiracy of Presbyterian preachers" (as some people claimed) to take control of the administration; there was no post-Purdum faculty cabal plotting to embarrass the new administration (as some professed to believe). There were many "victims." In fewer than five years, Benton Talbot was dead and a few months later R. B. Purdum died. Some of their relatives and friends could not help but believe that their experiences in 1953-54 contributed to shortening their lives, since neither was beyond middle-age at death. The bitterness of some in the community marred the early years of the Allens's residence in Elkins to the distress of Dr. and Mrs.

---

6. *Ibid.*, September 15, 1953, p. 61. Richard Talbott, already under contract when dismissed, insisted on remaining for the 1953-54 academic year and the trustees agreed that he could.

Allen who felt that, in some social circles at least, they were not treated with the respect and kindness normally expected. All of those in the faculty who had been hostile to Dr. Purdum soon left, finding the new administration as strongly committed to the educational and religious concepts they criticized as the old, if not more so. Some of those who had been as a matter of principle most outspoken in support of Dr. Purdum and critical of the board's procedure were "suspect" in the eyes of the "powers-that-be" for a year or two and felt keenly the injustice of such an attitude—some lamenting, some resenting it.

A major loss to the college in the summer of 1953 resulted from the decision of Dr. Daniel Rhodes, who had loyally supported Dr. Purdum, to resign from the faculty to accept a professorship at Southwestern College in Memphis. He had served well as dean of students and was regarded as an outstanding teacher of Bible and philosophy. Thus, when it was decided that Dr. S. Wilds DuBose should replace Dr. Talbot as Dean of the College, he was also assigned Rhodes's duties as dean of students. Inasmuch as he was also chairman of the Religion and Philosophy Department, Dr. DuBose was to bear a very heavy workload during his first years in the deanship.[7]

In addition to Dean Rhodes and Mrs. Talbott, ten other members of the faculty left D&E in the summer of 1953. These included David E. Warner in physical education; Dr. Friend E. Clark in chemistry and David L. Haught in education, both of whom retired; Floyd DeNicola in history; Milan D. Stoller in engineering; and Lee Carl Underwood in accounting, as well as others who had been at the college for a brief period. Eight replacements had to be rather hastily recruited during July and August, with four places being left vacant as an economy measure. Among those appointed in 1953 were two alumni: Ralph Ray Booth in chemistry, and Harry L. ("Bud") Shelton, a former faculty member, who returned after a thirteen-year absence to teach physical education, and to replace "Ace" Federovitch as basketball coach. Also Dr. Howard A. Redmond and Dr. Claude King Davis were appointed to the Religion and Philosophy Department and Dr. Davis was named the first college chaplain. Mrs. Claude King Davis became director of the college choir.

---

7. *Ibid.*, September 15, 1953, p. 61; Letter from S. Wilds DuBose, Staunton, Va., to Thomas R. Ross, Elkins, W.Va., July 28, 1979.

Dean S. Wilds DuBose and President David K. Allen.

Raymond Ford of the English Department succeeded Floyd DeNicola as Book Store manager.

When the fall semester began, the enrollment was 511 (427 men, 84 women) including 16 Korean War veterans. The resident women lived in Halliehurst Hall except for nine who were housed in the Sylvia Inn on Randolph Avenue. Greenbrier Hall and Graceland Hall, as well as the "T-House" sheltered the males who did not live in off-campus fraternity houses or private homes in Elkins. The three fraternities, a year or two earlier, had arranged to acquire houses on Buffalo, Boundary, and Second streets where upperclass members lived.

At the first faculty meeting in September, the committee structure was reorganized to some extent. An Assembly Committee was created under the chairmanship of Dr. Redmond to plan for and manage chapel and convocation programs which were henceforth to be held twice a week in the Memorial Gymnasium. The function of the two former committees on curriculum and on educational policies were combined under a new Educational Policies and Curriculum Committee, chaired by Professor Ross, and charged to make a study of the future of the college and to devise a "Ten Year Plan" outlining the aims and needs for the decade ahead as well as to consider immediate changes in academic policies. A new committee on Social Life and Student Activities was created to attempt to maintain a "social calendar" and coordinate campus activities. Professor Carrie Brittain was the head of this committee. The net result of the reorganization was to reduce the number of committees to thirteen.[8]

In October, the Executive Committee of the trustees met to hear a report of George Renneisen, treasurer of the board of Christian Education of the Presbyterian Church, U.S.A., who had come to the college to review the conditions in the business office and offer suggestions regarding a new accounting system. He urged that "good budgetary procedures" be adopted and pointed out that to meet the standards of the General Assembly, the college "must have an annual audit made by an independent certified accountant," asserting that "the Trustees are responsible for seeing that such an audit is made." Renneisen also suggested that the business manager ought to be "responsible to the President" and stated that "the President should not become involved in administrative matters except in the matter of broad policy. His major job is raising money."[9]

It was at that meeting that Dr. Allen suggested that each Synod ought to nominate "one key woman for membership on the Board." There had never been a women trustee. (Although Hallie Elkins had been made an "Honorary Trustee" shortly before her death, she had never attended a meeting.) The committee voted to recommend that in the future women be considered "for vacancies which might occur on the Board of Trustees."[10] As a result of this, two years later Mrs. C. E. Stetson of Weirton and Mrs. James M. Laird of Lewisburg became the first women trustees at D&E.

The board held a called meeting in December 1953. After electing Dr. Andrew R. Bird, Jr., to succeed Dr. Allen as board president, the trustees considered an offer from the West Virginia

8. Faculty Minutes II, September 29, 1953, pp. 170-72.
9. Trustee Executive Committee Minutes, October 23, 1953, pp. 65-66.
10. *Ibid.*, p. 67.

Coal and Coke Corporation to deed the unincorporated town of Norton, some eight miles northwest of Elkins, to the college. This grant included approximately seventy acres of land and 113 houses. The company representative explained that West Virginia Coal and Coke was closing its mining operations in the area, but wanted to keep the town intact, provide housing for the workers employed by the man who had bought the mines and prevent "the town from being infected with undesirable establishments such as beer joints." The company hoped to achieve all of its goals, plus gaining certain tax advantages, by donating the town to the college which would benefit either from renting or selling the houses to their occupants. After having H. K. Higginbotham, the college attorney (since the death of E. A. Bowers in 1950), review the legal implications, the board voted to accept the offer.[11] Dr. Allen, who had learned of the company's interest in disposing of the town and had initiated the negotiations, recalled that "some friends of the College reacted negatively, predicting that the gift would be worthless. On the contrary, through the generous efforts of Clay Whetsell and W. R. Cromwell, the properties were subsequently sold for over one hundred thousand dollars."[12] This was the first major gift the college had received from a corporation and the first fruits of Dr. Allen's efforts to begin to acquire new resources for D&E aside from his initial success in getting the Synods to promise to increase their financial support.

While in session in December, the trustees voted to elect Dr. David Allen to be president of the college effective July 1, 1954. This was to be announced publicly soon after the January release of the news of Dr. Purdum's resignation. The board also authorized the creation of the office of assistant dean and dean of women which was to be filled by the end of the academic year.[13]

During the fall and early winter construction of two tennis courts, on the lower campus on the site of some of the recently removed barracks, was completed. This was a joint project sup-

---

11. Trustee Minutes, December 8, 1953, p. 286. (Henry Higginbotham became "Associate Counsel" for the College in 1950 with D. H. Hill Arnold. Since Mr. Arnold's death in 1955, he has been the college attorney.)

12. Letter from Dr. David K. Allen, Boca Raton, Florida, to Thomas R. Ross, Elkins, West Virginia, February 22, 1979.

13. Trustee Minutes, December 8, 1953, pp. 288-89.

ported in part by the city of Elkins, the state highway department, the Elkins Limestone Company and a Clarksburg construction company all of which contributed labor and material. The local Lions Club contributed the lighting and fencing for the courts.[14]

At the first faculty meeting in January 1954, Dr. Allen presiding for the first time as "President-elect," spoke at some length on the fact that "Davis and Elkins College is a child of the Church" and stressed that D&E is "a liberal arts college which, if it is to be successful, must secure a larger general endowment fund and must continue its building program." He indicated that an application was being made for a government financed dormitory.[15] Earlier in the month, Dr. Allen had given an address during National Education Week which won him much respect from faculty members and others. He had discussed the cultural and economic value of the college to Elkins and the need for the citizens who benefited from "Elkins greatest industry," D&E, to support it. Admitting that the college "has been struggling for fifty years," he suggested that those who ask "What is the use? Why keep trying?" should remember that "the progress made in these fifty years is tremendous, and especially have great strides forward been made in the past ten years." He also pointed out that in 1954, D&E ranked third in size among the twenty-three colleges supported by the Southern Presbyterian churches, but had the smallest endowment of all of the four-year colleges in the denomination. In conclusion, he asserted his belief that D&E "is potentially strong" and that with the support of "all friends of the College" it could be developed into "one of the greatest liberal arts Christian Colleges."[16]

Campus morale was also improved somewhat by the early success of the basketball team coached by "Bud" Shelton in the winter of 1953-54. Paul Wilcox, a talented six-foot five-inch freshman, playing center, was the sensation of the season. He scored 46 points to lead D&E to a victory over Wesleyan on January 12 and by the end of January, D&E was tied for second place in the conference. Unfortunately, both Wilcox and Miles Runner, another star freshman player, became scholastically ineligible at

---

14. *The Senator*, December 2, 1953, p. 1.
15. Faculty Minutes, January 23, 1954, p. 183.
16. *The Senator*, January 20, 1954, p. 1.

the end of the first semester and D&E's record at the season's end was 14 wins to 13 losses. Other outstanding players included Page Brake, Bob Juback, Bob Seem, Mario Regent, Bruce Phares, Stan Wilmoth, and Dorsey Sherman.[17]

The Heiress, directed by Claire Fiorentino, was the senior class play for 1954 with "Tish" Davis, Bob Bender, and Ronnie Bova in leading roles. Later in the year, "Tish" Davis placed second in the National Speech Contest in Baltimore despite the fact that D&E was the smallest of the colleges and universities participating in the annual event.[18]

In order to stress a renewed emphasis on the religious commitment of the college, the Faculty Committee on Religious Life proposed, and the faculty adopted, a recommendation that arrangements be made for "Faculty people to get together for social fellowship and intellectual and spiritual stimulus." Later in the year, after a visit to the faculty by Rene Williamson, editor of *The Presbyterian Faculty Newsletter*, who discussed the Faculty Christian Fellowship movement, a chapter of that group was organized. Also, the Religious Emphasis Week speaker in the spring of 1954 was one of the outstanding writers and lecturers of the period, Dr. Kenneth J. Foreman, who made a very favorable impression on both faculty and students.[19]

As a means of strengthening the college's ties to the Southern Synod as well as to provide a needed service to high school and college students, the Projects Committee of the Men of the Church of the Greenbrier Presbytery suggested that a Presbyterian Vocational Guidance Center similar to those at Centre College in Kentucky and Flora McDonald College in North Carolina be established at D&E. Dr. Allen arranged for Professor Thomas R. Ross, a member of the Projects Committee, to present the proposal to the Trustees Executive Committee in February 1954. Dr. Hunter B. Blakely, then secretary of the Division of Higher Education in the Southern Presbyterian Church, was present at the meeting and supported the proposal commenting that "here is one area in which Davis and Elkins can render vital and dramatic service to its students and constituency." In May,

17. *Ibid.*, p. 3; The 1954 *Senatus*, pp. 100-103.
18. *The Senator*, May 3, 1954, p. 1.
19. *Ibid.*, February 10, 1954, p. 1; Faculty Minutes II, November 24, 1953, and May 17, 1954, pp. 175, 191-92.

the full board gave approval and voted to include funds in the budget to support the center.[20] Subsequently, the Guidance Center, jointly sponsored by the college and the Synod, was established in Halliehurst. Under the early direction of such able counseling psychologists as Dr. William G. Meyer, Dr. C. R. Thayer, Dr. William Gross, and Miss Margaret Ann Murphy, and more recently of Dr. Joseph Martin, the center has proved to be an exceedingly valuable addition to the college as well as to the youth of the Synod.

On the same day that the Trustees' Executive Committee gave initial approval to the Vocational Guidance Center proposal, the chairman of the Educational Policies and Curriculum Committee of the faculty presented the committee's preliminary recommendations relative to "A 10-Year Plan" to the Trustee Special Committee on the future of the college. In summary, these included: (1) That Davis and Elkins College shall place primary emphasis on developing and maintaining a strong liberal arts program; (2) That the vocational and pre-professional training offered "be based on a sound core of liberal arts in order that all graduates be properly educated and not merely trained to earn a living"; (3) That the college seek to attain a stable enrollment of not fewer than nine hundred nor more than one thousand students; (4) That it remain co-educational, and that "every effort be exerted to obtain a better numerical balance between male and female students; (5) That a program of general campus improvement be undertaken in the following order of priority: blacktopping of the campus roads, construction of adequate residence halls, renovation of the Liberal Arts and Science halls, erection of a student union, a library, a chapel-auditorium, and a fine arts building. The special committee approved the recommendations "relative to the size of the College and its liberal arts emphasis" as presented by Professor Ross and voted to continue study and discussion of the matters related to roads, and buildings as well as such other items as faculty salary scales, scholarship assistance, and a public relations program.[21]

---

20. Trustee Executive Committee Minutes, February 16, 1954, p. 72, and Trustee Minutes, May 10, 1954, p. 293.
21. Trustee Executive Committee Minutes, February 16, 1954, pp. 69-71. On October 26, 1954, President Allen and Professor Ross presented the plan to the full board. Trustee Minutes, October 26, 1954, p. 81, of Executive Committee Minutes.

On March 4, 1954, the faculty held a long evening meeting to consider the recommendations of the Educational Policies and Curriculum Committee relative to several reforms. The committee had discovered that the college was losing much money by permitting students to carry an unlimited number of credit hours per semester without extra charge and that many students had low grade averages because they attempted to do four years' work in three, that is, they got eight semesters of credit for the price of six. Thus, the faculty approved a new rule which fixed the maximum number of hours for which a student could register at seventeen per semester, unless he could get special permission from the Administrative Committee to carry excess hours in which case he must be charged twelve dollars per hour for each hour in excess of seventeen carried.

Then the faculty debated and adopted thirteen specific recommendations designed to establish a core curriculum in the liberal arts for all candidates for degrees. Briefly stated, these recommendations were intended to implement a renewed emphasis on the primacy of the college's purpose as a liberal arts college. Henceforth, for many years, with minor modifications, all students were expected to complete eight hours in Bible, twelve hours in English, two hours in public speaking, three hours in philosophy, three hours in psychology, six hours in history, six hours in economics, three hours in American government, six hours in mathematics, eight hours in one natural science, and two hours in physical education. B.A. and B.S. degree candidates must complete six to twelve hours in foreign language (depending on proficiency), and all males must complete at least eight hours of air science (unless veterans or otherwise exempt).[22] The exempting of the students in the specialized degree programs from the foreign language requirement was not pleasing to many of the faculty, including the committee chairman, who presented the report and supported it; but that compromise was necessary both for existing financial reasons and in order to muster the votes needed to get the other measures adopted. The other major defect was the failure to include work in the fine arts in the core, but at that time neither adequate faculty nor facilities was available.

At the 1954 commencement an LL.D. degree was awarded to Michael Benedum, the famous oil millionaire and philanthropist.

---

22. Faculty Minutes II, March 4, 1954, pp. 187-88.

The first AFROTC cadets to complete the program received their commissions as second lieutenants in the United States Air Force that year. Among those receiving bachelor's degrees were Charles J. Farmer, Richard Griffith, Frank R. Rightmire, and Lewis W. Wilson, all of whom later returned to their alma mater as faculty or staff members. James A. Towler, Jr., of Elkins, a popular senior who died not long before graduation day, was awarded his degree posthumously.

During the summer, a special committee headed by Professor Ralph Booth, was requested to study the eligibility rules governing participating in extracurricular activities. The report of the committee was presented and adopted by the faculty at its first meeting early in September. Aimed at correcting abuses of the past which had sometimes proved embarrassing to coaches or had involved exploiting students by allowing them to spend so much time in activities that they failed their courses, the new rules were specific and inclusive and were followed with much benefit for more than fifteen years thereafter.

As had been the case the preceding year, faculty "turn-over" was great and there were twelve new faculty members in the fall of 1954. Silas M. Vaughn, a young Texan who later became president of Montreat College, succeeded J. E. Nicholson, with his title being changed back to business manager and treasurer. Jane Little began her duties in the new office of assistant dean and dean of women and John Smart became the first development officer. Dr. William G. Meyer succeeded Dr. Georgiana Stary as professor of psychology and became the first director of the Presbyterian Vocational Guidance Center. John Venable Moore replaced Leila Johnston in the Religion Department and Richard DeHart was appointed head of the Physical Education Department and assumed coaching duties which had been "Ace" Federovitch's. Emily Wilmoth Opel, a retired public school official, joined the faculty to teach education and Latin. In 1954, also both Harold R. Henry and Louise Linhart began longtime service as faculty members, the former in business administration, the latter in physical education. Both would subsequently devote full time to administrative duties.

Dr. David K. Allen was formally inaugurated as the eighth president of the college on October 26, 1954. Dr. Arthur S. Flemming, then director of the Office of Defense Mobilization and later a cabinet member, gave the principal address. More than eighty colleges and universities and various learned societies and ecclesiastical bodies sent representatives to participate in the colorful ceremony. The theme of President Allen's inaugural address was "Christian Commitment." He asserted that such commitment "requires a high standard of academic work, that the College should help its students to become the finest men and women they are capable of becoming, which requirement in turn means that the undergraduate must be given at least an introduction to the best which has been written, spoken, or done in all the major fields of human achievement . . . that this commitment requires that the college community should strive to realize and defend Christian ideals."[23]

If, in the beginning fifty years before, Hampden-Sydney, Washington and Lee, and Davidson colleges had served as models for D&E in the minds of the founders, early presidents, and faculty leaders, surely in the decade after 1954 the College of Wooster was used for a somewhat similar role during the administration of David K. Allen who especially revered his alma mater, Wooster. The emphasis in his inaugural statement on high academic standards, a strong liberal arts curriculum, and Christian commitment represented the ideals which D&E sought to realize in the decade of his presidency and beyond.

In January 1955, the first issue of *The Davis and Elkins Forward* appeared. A publication prepared by the Development Office, the *Forward* has for a quarter of a century presented news of interest about alumni, campus affairs, and college program as well as timely messages from the president. In that month, too, President Allen announced that the college debt had been reduced by more than seventy thousand dollars during the preceding fifteen months and that he had hopes that the financial condition was sufficiently improved to enable the college to qualify for a government loan to finance the building of a men's dormitory.[24]

The year 1954-55 was a good year for Coach Shelton's basketball team. Having regained their eligibility, Paul Wilcox and Miles Runner joined Captain Bob Seem, Dorsey Sherman, John Sanzari, and Pete Bezzini in a combination which won 17 of 24 games for a second place conference record. Wilcox scored 863

23. *The Senator,* October 20, 27, 1954, p. 1.
24. Faculty Minutes II, January 13, 1955, p. 217.

points and was named to the All-Conference Team and also won honorable mention for All-American. The women's varsity basketball team, coached by Louise Linhart, also had a good season, the star players being Aurilla Scherbaum and Jo Ann Little Twig.[25]

Other campus activities also flourished, there being an unusually large number of able and interested student leaders. Especially active were the Student Christian Association led by James Parsons and Glen Shackelford, the Westminster Fellowship under the presidency of Richard Hepburn; the radio station managed by Maxwell Morgan and Harry Houser, and the Women's Athletic Association sparked by Rosalie Blacka and Aurilla Scherbaum. The head cheerleader was a male, Jack Blacka, who was also first vice-president of the student body. *The Senator* was sufficiently impressed with the caliber of campus leadership that year to devote an entire issue of photographs of and comments of about thirty of the leaders, including, in addition to those mentioned above, Edward Gardella, Ronald MacDonald, Richard Edwards, William Leist, Frank Cooper, Patricia Davis, John Halloran, John Stein, Robert Shea, Frank Cooper, Kenneth Taylor, and Jackson Winter.[26] Winter, who was president of the class of 1955, was largely responsible for arranging for reconstruction of the stone pillar at the entrance to the campus, a project paid for by the senior class as its gift to the college.

Certainly one of the more memorable and lasting accomplishments of the year was the paving of the campus roads with blacktop for the first time in the history of the college. As one trustee remarked: "Now that we are out of the mud we can make better headway."

It was during this period that the faculty women and the wives of faculty members, at the suggestion of Mrs. David Allen, organized a group called the "D and E Dames." For many years this group was active in sponsoring social affairs, helping new faculty get settled in Elkins, etc. At its annual meeting in May, the board of trustees approved a faculty recommendation presented by Dean DuBose that D&E participate in the "Tuition Exchange Plan for Faculty Children." This program, designed at Williams College, provided that sons and daughters of faculty

---

25. The 1955 *Senatus*, pp. 35, 69; Kessler, *op. cit.*, p. 270.
26. *The Senator*, May 25, 1955, p. 1.

members in colleges participating could attend other colleges in the "Plan" without payment of tuition, providing there was a reasonable degree of reciprocity. At the same meeting the trustees voted to resume participation in intercollegiate football and to authorize the appointment of an assistant dean and dean of men. The board was informed that financial support from the churches had increased from $45,000 in 1952-53 to $70,000 in 1954-55.[27]

At the 1955 commencement, honorary D.D. degrees were awarded to Warner DuBose, Jr., minister of the Davis Memorial Presbyterian Church, and to Arnold B. Poole, a trustee. An LL.D. was conferred upon Edward L. R. Elson, the minister of the National Presbyterian Church in Washington, D.C., who was notable for having recently baptized President Eisenhower. The valedictorian was Glenn Allen Shackelford of Elkins who later became a prominent Lutheran pastor in Virginia.

During the summer of 1955, plans were made to convert the old Swimming Pool Building into a Student Union and for the construction of a new residence hall for men on the site of the Old Bowling Alley. Also that summer, as in the two preceding summers, it was necessary to recruit several new faculty members—twelve in all. Among them was Marshall Emm, appointed to the new position of dean of men and also as assistant professor of history to teach courses usually offered by Professor Ross, who had been granted a special leave to accept a Danforth Teacher Study Grant for a year. Jonathan Keith Hiser began his long and useful career as a D&E faculty member in the fall of 1955 as instructor in physics. He later became chairman of the department and in 1979 was the senior member of the science faculty. An excellent teacher, Keith Hiser became noted for his work in developing the Science Fair and in directing the Planetarium and the Observatory. James Welshonce, now chairman of the Economics Department, also joined the faculty in 1955 as a part-time instructor. Active in committee work and in community affairs, Professor Welshonce in 1979-80 served as district governor of Rotary International. R. H. Carder in business administration, Donald Vosburgh in sociology, and Robert Phillips as assistant coach of football, were other new faculty members who served well, but for only a few years.

27. Trustee Minutes, May 9 and 10, 1955, pp. 298-302.

Another famous member of the faculty "Class of '55" was Lois Latham, associate professor of English until her retirement. A talented writer as well as classroom teacher, she inspired several generations of students to develop an interest in and love for literature, especially the work of Shakespeare and of the great English poets.

Student enrollment increased to 569 in the fall of 1955—a gain of 70 over the preceding year. There was much interest in the construction of the new $300,000 men's dormitory, named James E. Allen Hall in honor of the fourth president of the college. In an editorial, *The Senator* observed that "the step taken by the College in the construction of a new dormitory has been the greatest improvement since the College moved from its former location to its present site. This is the first big undertaking by the Trustees since the completion of the Memorial Gymnasium."[28]

Professor J. Keith Hiser in the planetarium.

On December 13, the first "Boar's Head Dinner" was held at D&E, establishing a tradition that has become an elaborate and unique ceremony at the beginning of the Christmas season each year.[29] The preceding day, the Ford Foundation informed President Allen that it was granting D&E $111,000 for use in increasing salaries for faculty—an announcement which brought much "Christmas Cheer" to the campus.

During the fall semester, the Educational Policies Committee (chaired by Professor Ralph Booth in 1955-56), working with Professor Jesse Reed, developed a proposal to provide a major in art. This significant step was approved by the faculty on December 10, 1955. Subsequently that year the music curriculum was

28. *The Senator*, November 9, 1955, p. 2.
29. *Ibid.*, December 14, 1955, p. 1.

revised and majors in that department were redefined. The aim was to strengthen the fine arts.

Early in 1956 the lawsuit filed against President Allen and the college by Professor Stephen P. Toadvine was settled by compromise on the initiative of Toadvine's attorney without going to trial. Toadvine, who alleged that he had been improperly dismissed from his tenured position in 1955 had sued the president for $100,000 and the college for $50,000 in "damages." He settled for $5,000, essentially the year's salary which he had been offered when his appointment was terminated for cause, in accordance with AAUP procedures, in the first place. The main significance of the case was that it led the trustees to approve faculty recommendations defining in writing for the first time the personnel and tenure policies which, with minor modifications, have been in effect since. These included the definition of membership and authority of the faculty, procedures for appointment and promotion, a definition of tenure, and the sabbatical leave policy.[30]

The resumption of participation in intercollegiate football in 1955-56 was voted by the board without faculty approval. The reasons which had brought about dropping football in 1953 had not materially changed. The 1955 season was a disaster—D&E lost seven games out of seven. The next year was little better with only one victory and in the 1957 and 1958 seasons not a single game was won. "Bud" Shelton had transferred from the physical education to the mathematics department and was appointed assistant director of development in 1955 after coaching his last basketball team in a 17 to 7 season. In 1956 the D&E cagers, coached by Dick Dehart dropped to ninth place in the conference and in 1957 and 1958, they finished last place both seasons under coaches Ron Knapp and Mel Greer, respectively.[31] There was an increased interest in intramural sports in those years, however, and in campus activities.

In the spring and summer of 1956, a Presbyterian "Survey of Higher Education in West Virginia" was undertaken. Directed by Dr. Donald Agnew, the aim was to determine the needs of

30. Faculty Minutes III, March 24, 1956, p. 2; Trustee Minutes II, September 6, 1955, p. 1; May 8, 1956, p. 7; October 30, 1956, pp. 23-25. (The policy statement was drafted by Silas Vaughn and T. R. Ross for a special committee which included Dean DuBose, Professors Booth, Meyer, Ross, Vaughn, and Wilson. It was adopted by the faculty and approved by the board.)

31. Kessler, op. cit., p. 271.

D&E and of certain church-sponsored agencies at West Virginia University and Marshall College. The report was not altogether complimentary to D&E, pointing out numerous weaknesses, but it helped to pave the way for a major financial campaign later by concluding that "there was nothing wrong with Davis and Elkins College which a few million dollars will not cure."

Before the "Survey" had gotten under way, however, what appeared to be a major disaster occurred on May 22 when a bolt of lightning set fire to the Science Hall. Because of a lack of water pressure, the Elkins Fire Department was unable to bring the blaze under control before all but the first floor and the outer walls were destroyed. No one was injured except President Allen who suffered a broken toe in helping remove furniture from the building. Science classes had to be held in various places (including the high school during the fall semester), but immediately after commencement in May, plans to restore the building were made and construction soon was under way. The emergency aroused the interest of the townspeople and alumni and a successful campaign was launched in Elkins to raise $145,000 to help with the rebuilding of the Science Hall. The student body set a goal of $7,500 to be given by students for the purpose of furnishing a biology laboratory. Walter Cerrato, the 1956-57 student body president, Peggy Chandler, and Fay McGee led the student effort. The faculty pledged $11,000. In all, more than $155,000 was pledged—the first time in history that a D&E financial campaign ever reached—much less exceeded—its goal.[32]

Gene Penn was the valedictorian in 1956 as well as having served as president of the student body. The commencement speaker was Dr. James E. Allen, Jr., commissioner of education of the state of New York, who with his brothers, visited the campus for the dedication of the new men's residence hall to the memory of their father. Among the outstanding seniors were Constance Altfather, Franklin L. Kittle, Gerald Maynard, John J. McKenzie, Mary Lou Secrist, Richard Plant, John J. Rector, J. K. Hiser (who had already begun teaching at D&E), B. Jeff Coberly (who soon became the college's chief accountant), Frank W. Rogers and John Campbell (both of whom were appointed instructors in engineering at their alma mater) and Margaret A.

32. *The Senator*, October 24, 1956; January 23, 1957, p. 1; Faculty Minutes III, October 13, 1956, p. 38.

Isner (later to be secretary to the dean of the faculty). Later in the summer, George R. Triplett, Circuit Judge of Randolph County in the 1970s, received his B.S. degree.

The first sabbatical leave ever granted at D&E was awarded to Professor Richard G. Long for the summer and fall of 1956. This initiated a program which for more than twenty years has been of great benefit to dozens of faculty members.[33] The board's approval of the Educational Policies Committee's long-range plans and of the faculty's recommendation's relating to personnel and tenure policies (which had included provisions for sabbatical leaves) symbolized a much improved relationship between the faculty and the trustees. This was due in large measure to the efforts of President Allen who rather quickly came to understand the vital importance of the faculty in college governance and who, as a former trustee for more than a decade, also had rapport with board members and some insight into both the proper and the improper functions of that body. Another factor doubtless was the addition to the board in the decade of the fifties and early sixties, as others retired, of several very able new trustees. Board President Andrew R. Bird and such senior members as Jennings Randolph (a former faculty member), Dr. George H. Vick, Dr. J. Howard Anderson, Dr. James Henry, Dr. William Ferry, George Ward, and Dr. James W. Witherspoon had usually shown concern for faculty problems. They were supplemented by such more recently elected trustees as Dr. D. Alton Gilmore, Dr. Paul E. Francis, Dr. David Bell, L. E. McWhorter, H. Arthur Stroud, Paul S. Hudgens, Judge Frank Taylor, Henry B. Wehrle, Jr., George Stevenson, Cary Blain, Cary Adams, Merritt Davis, Herschel Mosier, Joseph E. Hodgson, Mrs. C. E. Stetson, Mrs. James M. Laird, Dr. Walter W. White, William R. Cromwell, Jr., Charles B. Gates, Jr., Judge Ben R. Honecker, Dr. Hubert T. Marshall, Dr. Arnold B. Poole, Dr. Robert A. Pfrangle, Elwood Davis, John D. MacLeod, Dr. G. Ousley Brown, and Judge David E. Cuppett. Several of these were alumni. From 1954-55 on, it is evident in their minutes that the board repeatedly consulted with faculty members, acted favorably on faculty recommendations, and voted to involve faculty members in various studies, surveys, and campaigns. During 1956 the trustees acted to provide retirement funds for the future benefit of Dr. Charles E. Albert and

---

33. Trustee Minutes II, May 8-9, 1956, p. 3 of insert following p. 8.

Miss Anna Parmesano, both of whom had devoted much of their lives to the college, but who had not been eligible, because of age, for inclusion in the College Retirement Plan established earlier.[34]

Among the new faculty appointed in 1956 were Evan and Ann Kek of whom President Allen often said, "One of the best things that ever happened at D&E in the 1950's was the coming of the Keks—he as Business Manager and she as Professor and Registrar." Both were graduates of Indiana Central College where they had subsequently served as faculty members for more than two decades. Both had M.A. degrees from Indiana University and she had a Ph.D. from Cornell. They served D&E until their retirement in the 1970s. Dr. B. C. Harrington also joined the faculty in 1956 as head of the Department of Education. A graduate of Princeton and Columbia universities, he had already had a distinguished career as an educator and as a missionary and college president in India. Dr. William E. Phipps, a Davidson graduate with a doctorate from Saint Andrews, became chairman of the Religion and Philosophy Department that year and his wife, Martha Ann, joined the faculty in chemistry. Dr. Phipps, an able teacher and committee chairman, has published more books than any other D&E faculty member, the most famous being *Was Jesus Married?* Among others of the thirteen named to the faculty in 1956 were Dr. Louis E. Mattison (chemistry), Margaret Kump Roberts (mathematics), Norman L. Sheets (physical education), and William Wood (sociology and anthropology), each of whom served for several years.

A notable event of the fall semester was the October visit of Adlai E. Stevenson, Democratic nominee for president, to the campus for the Forest Festival. Because of inclement weather, he had to deliver his address in the overcrowded gymnasium and was then unable to leave town on schedule because his plane could not land. He recalled having been a guest in Graceland Hall earlier in the century when he visited the Davis and Lee families.

The headline-making event in November was a "raid" on Halliehurst Hall by a group of Wesleyan College students and the attempted retaliation by some thirty D&E men on a women's dormitory at Wesleyan later the same night. Although the D&E boys never reached the Wesleyan campus, being apprehended by the Wesleyan dean of students and advised to return to Elkins,

34. *Ibid.*, October 30, 1956, p. 28.

they did have an interesting adventure. After turning back, following the Wesleyan dean's advice, they were stopped by the Buckhannon police, arrested for disturbing the peace, thrown into jail for the night, and then rescued the next day by President Allen and Dean DuBose. The Elkins *Inter-Mountain* ran a front-page editorial two days later, entitled "We Do Things Differently Here," blasting the Buckhannon authorities for their conduct and hoping "that the several hundred dollars collected from Davis and Elkins boys in fines and costs will be put to some purposeful use."[35] The students—at least those not jailed—enjoyed the whole episode. August Vilseck told a *Senator* reporter that "D&E has finally become a full-fledged college. The raids are great for school spirit." Mike Dakes, a spectator at the Halliehurst brawl, said it was "the best thing to happen here in years. We should have attendance like that at the football game!" One girl said of the raid on Halliehurst: "Wow!" Another said: "Tremendous!" And one wondered "how Dean Little made out during the raid?"[36]

In February 1957, the board of trustees met in Parkersburg to receive a report from a Joint Committee of Trustees, Faculty and Synod Representatives which had been directed to develop a campus building plan. The committee recommended that three buildings be constructed as soon as possible—a women's residence hall, a library, and a chapel-auditorium. The board approved and agreed to employ Ward, Dreshman, and Reinhardt to direct a financial campaign as soon as the Synods of West Virginia voted to sponsor such a fund drive for higher education. The Synods subsequently authorized a $1,080,000 campaign—$1 million for D&E, sixty thousand dollars for an Interdenominational building at Marshall and twenty thousand dollars for the Westminster Foundation at West Virginia University.[37] Designated as "The Christian Higher Education Fund Campaign," the drive began with a Joint Synods' Rally in Charleston on April 12. George C. Leslie, a Charleston attorney, and H. Ar-

35. The Elkins *Inter-Mountain,* November 10, 1956, p. 1.
36. *The Senator,* November 14, 1956, p. 3.
37. Trustee Minutes, February 8, 1957, pp. 41-48. The Joint Committee included Evan Kek, chairman; Thomas R. Ross, secretary; David K. Allen, S. Wilds DuBose, Robb Keyser, Clay B. Whetsell, Arnold Poole, Dr. J. Howard Anderson, and H. P. Mullenex.

thur Stroud, promotion manager of the Monongahela Power Company, served as co-chairmen. Keynote speakers at the "Kick-Off Dinner" were Dr. James McCain, Dr. E. Fay Campbell, and Dr. Warner Hall.[38] Although the stated goal was pledged, many pledges were never paid and the amount actually received by the college was not adequate to finance the three buildings projected. The women's residence hall, later named Gribble Hall, was the first of the three to be constructed.

Meanwhile a library consultant, William H. Jesse of the University of Tennessee, made a study of the D&E library and

The library when located in Liberal Arts Hall—Miss Virgie Harris (standing right).

prepared a report which was helpful both in terms of proper reorganization of the staff and procedures and in the planning of a new building. The "Jesse Report" urged that the faculty should elect a library committee to "provide the College with a continuing, responsible, interested group which will constantly be trying to improve the library situation and constantly evaluating it." The consultant was emphatic in underscoring the necessity for greatly increasing expenditures for books and periodicals and for

---

38. *The Senator*, April 3, 10, 1957, p. 1.

both improving and enlarging the professional staff. Subsequently, a faculty committee spent several months in preparing plans for the architect's guidance in developing blueprints for a library building not to exceed $288,000 in cost.[39] Construction of that much needed facility began late in 1958 and was completed in 1959. Some years later the building was named Jennings Randolph Hall.

The Science Hall fire in 1956 and the response of friends of the college to the resulting emergency can be seen in retrospect to have given impetus to efforts to raise funds for the construction of campus facilities in addition to the rebuilding of the Science Hall. Gribble Hall (the first women's residence hall) and the library, as well as necessary improvements in roads, pipelines, etc., were financed largely from the money derived from the "Christian Higher Education Fund Campaign." Subsequently, between 1959 and 1963, Darby Hall (the first "co-educational dorm," so constructed that one end was for women, the other for men), and Benedum Hall were completed. The latter, a multipurpose building originally included the Dining Hall and Student Union as well as the College Book Store, the Campus Post Office and the Faculty Lounge. The Benedum Foundation donated $250,000, the largest gift ever given up to that time, and the Federal Community Facilities Administration provided a loan of $285,000 to finance what at that time was the most expensive building on the campus. David L. Johnson, then vice-president and secretary of the Benedum Foundation, was the principal speaker at ground-breaking ceremonies, on October 31, 1961, which were also attended by Senator Jennings Randolph, a member of the board of the Benedum Foundation.

Meanwhile, many matters other than the construction of buildings required attention. The examination by the North Central Association representatives, Byron K. Trippet and Donald M. Mackenzie, in January 1957 resulted in the college's accreditation being threatened. Recognizing that D&E was emerging from a "crisis of recent years," the examiners prefaced their report with the observation that "the remarkable thing,

---

39. William H. Jesse, "A Report on the Library of Davis and Elkins College," May 1957; Trustee Minutes, February 28, 1958, pp. 66-67. The committee which planned the library building consisted of Professor T. R. Ross, chairman; Evan R. Kek, S. Benton Talbot, Knox Wilson, Carrie Brittain, and Virgie Harris.

however, is not so much that the problems are pressing but rather the fact that in view of the recent history of the College they are not much more acute." The basic weaknesses cited by the report may be summarized as follows:

1. That D&E claimed to be a liberal arts institution, but was in fact providing "extensive offerings in vocational and professional or pre-professional areas" and had "heavy enrollments for majors in those areas and "limited enrollments" in the more traditional disciplines of the "liberal arts." The report was critical of the fact that four specialized degrees were offered in addition to the B.A. and B.S. degrees.
2. That many of the students were "inadequately prepared and poorly motivated for a liberal arts education."
3. That there was a "large and rapid turnover in faculty personnel" and that "a high percentage of faculty members" lacked advanced degrees.
4. That faculty salaries and the library budget were too low.
5. That current funds were used "to meet indebtedness for capital improvements" and that the basic financial problem (lack of endowment) seemed to result in emphasis on "administrative leadership in financial rather than academic matters" and that "the financial uncertainties and the lack of vigorous academic leadership . . . have left their marks on the faculty.
6. That department heads did not participate to a significant degree in the appointment of new faculty and that "there is some evidence that members of the board of trustees have taken a direct hand in the matter of reappointments from time to time."

That examiners were impressed with the fact that the personnel policies, including provisions for tenure, retirement, and sabbatical leaves, initiated by the faculty, had been approved by the board and observed that "there is a small group of devoted Faculty members who have been at the College for an extended period of years and are very competent. The examiners are convinced that this small group of half-a-dozen or so has served the College well in holding it together and in maintaining standards in the difficult times through which the College has passed."[40]

Having its accreditation questioned by the regional accrediting agency was a serious matter, but like the Science Hall

---

40. B. K. Trippet and D. M. Mackenzie, "Report to the Board of Review of the North Central Association: Davis and Elkins College," January 11 and 12, 1957, *passim.*

fire the year before, in the long run it stimulated action and strengthened the hand of the president and the "small group of devoted Faculty" who were working for reform. Furthermore, the "Pilot Study" made during the winter of 1957-58, by an evaluation team of educators representing the Presbyterian Church, U.S.A., headed by President Theron B. Maxon of Hastings College, offered additional adverse criticism. The Maxon report began with the observation that "the College apparently strayed far afield from its educational objectives and aims. It permitted a cheap degree to be given where much of the work was in vocational and special interest fields." It also suggested the need for higher admission standards and that "the Dean of Students should be responsible to the Dean of the College for most effective coordination of the administrative responsibility." As had the North Central report, the Pilot Study praised the work of the president, the business manager, the director of the Presbyterian Guidance Center, and cited the strengths and weaknesses of the faculty as follows:

Faculty

It appears that the Head of the Department of History and Political Science and Chairman of the Educational Policies Committee, is an exceedingly able and effective chairman of this committee. The effectiveness of the committee work can be significantly attributed to his leadership. There seem to be a number of able faculty. Good leadership seems evident in Biology, Chemistry, History and Political Science, Mathematics and Teacher Education, although the latter professor has already been retired from another institution.

There are too many faculty who hold only the bachelors degree. There should be far more with the masters degree and preferably some additional faculty with the doctors degree. There is considerable reason to believe that the assignment of academic rank needs very careful restudy.[41]

As a result of the impact of these reports, and in order to eliminate or mitigate the factors which threatened the continuation of accreditation, the faculty and trustees in 1957 and 1958 approved a series of recommendations dealing with specific weaknesses cited.

First of all, as soon as the North Central Report was received,

---

41. T. B. Maxon, Leo Nussbaum, F. N. Rudolfson, H. Jensen, "Presbyterian U.S.A. Pilot Study Report: Davis and Elkins College." February 20-22, 1958, *passim.*

it was read to the faculty at a special meeting. On passage of a motion that he do so, President Allen appointed a special committee consisting of Professors Ross (chairman), Miller, Sheets, Wilson, Dean DuBose, Evan Kek, and himself to study the implications and "make suggestions that might meet with North Central approval" when the president and dean appeared before the Board of Review in Chicago in April.[42] This committee recommended that in the future, no person be appointed to the faculty without a master's degree at least, that those faculty members who did not have such a degree "be required to pursue a program of graduate study which will assure the attainment of the master's degree at the earliest possible date" (except for any members of long service whose age might make such a program unfeasible); that the trustees be urged to adopt a salary schedule for the faculty "which will provide incentive for continued service and professional growth"; that "only the degrees Bachelor of Arts and Bachelor of Science be granted" effective with the class admitted in 1958; that the college begin participating in the National Sophomore Testing Program in 1958; that comprehensive examinations of seniors be required beginning with the graduating class of 1960.[43] These recommendations were approved by the faculty and proved to be helpful to the president and dean when they pled the college's case for continued accreditation before the North Central Board of Review. The Board of Review decided to place the college on "probationary" status, requiring an annual report for 1958 and 1959 with the understanding that "accredited status will be reconsidered in 1960."[44] In May, the trustees approved the recommendations of the special committee, and in addition directed that the faculty remove "from the curriculum any and all curriculum offerings which are not essential or valuable in producing a quality liberal arts and science program." The board also invited the faculty "to recommend to the Board any additions to the curriculum which may be needed to strengthen our liberal arts and sciences and outline our fine arts program." The salary scale established ranged from $3,300 for beginning instructors to $5,100 for senior professors, with the understanding, strongly emphasized by President Allen, that such salaries were inadequate, that annual

42. Faculty Minutes III, March 22, 1957, p. 70.
43. *Ibid.*, March 28, 1957, pp. 75-76.
44. *Ibid.*, April 4, 1957, p. 77.

increments were necessary, and that the college could never attract and keep enough good faculty to attain the academic quality desired unless much larger salaries could be paid.[45]

Subsequently, the board established a Development Commission, under the chairmanship of H. Arthur Stroud, to "enlist and develop the interest and support of all the publics of the College" and especially to help in the securing of "Living Endowment" funds to help meet current expenses each year. This commission worked hard and well for several years and secured many annual gifts from alumni, parents of students, business and industry, and others.[46]

During the year following the special committee's report, the Educational Policies Committee was assigned the task of preparing revisions of curriculum, degree requirements, and policies to implement the changes authorized. Professor Ross was chairman of that committee, but great credit for the work accomplished belongs to Professors Ann Kek, Fred Miller, William E. Phipps, Jesse Reed, and Louis Mattison, and to Dean DuBose who gave much support to the committee. Specific resolutions relative to the discontinuation of special degrees in business, engineering, education, and physical education, and provisions for new requirements for majors and a liberal arts core for all students were prepared and in due order adopted by the faculty. This core, required of all students, provided greater flexibility but included courses in foreign languages and the fine arts which had not been required of all students previously.[47]

In view of the criticism that admissions standards were low and that D&E was getting the reputation of being a "second chance" college for transfer students, the faculty voted to require applicants for admission to present CEEB and similar test scores, tightened the probation and eligibility rules, and defined the basis for admitting transfer students and the acceptance of credit by transfer. Elizabeth Millard was appointed director of admissions, effective July 1, 1957, filling a post left vacant during the preceding year since Raymond Kiser had resigned to accept a similar position at West Virginia Wesleyan College. Miss Millard (who later became Mrs. Jesse F. Reed) was deeply com-

45. Trustee Minutes, May 7, 8, 1957, pp. 49-52.
46. *Ibid.*, February 28, 1958, pp. 67-68, Appendix "A".
47. Faculty Minutes III, April 21, May 3, May 19, 1958, pp. 115-36.

Professor Richard Grant Long (in white) visiting with Dr. Talbot and students at commencement reception a few months before his death. The Reverend and Mrs. Frederick Valentine and Professor Emily Opel (foreground).

mitted to the policy of improving the academic quality of the college and thus sought in every way possible to recruit an increased number of students qualified for and interested in college-level academic studies. For more than a decade she served the college with devotion as director of admissions, later becoming assistant professor of mathematics.

Anna Dale Kek, who had joined the faculty in 1956 as professor of English, succeeded Fred A. Miller as registrar in the summer of 1957 and also became secretary of the Educational Policies Committee. She worked tirelessly in both positions, as well as professor of Latin and chairman of the Language Department, to assist in upgrading the academic program of the college and to help correct some of the deficiencies criticized by the accrediting agency and the Maxon "Pilot Study."

In mid-March of 1957, the college community was saddened by the death of Professor Richard G. Long. A popular faculty member and the founder and first director of the College Placement Center, his death at age fifty-five was a severe loss to D&E. His friends and former students established a memorial fund to purchase books for the library. Hundreds attended the memorial service which was held in the gymnasium on March 19 and *The Senator* printed in the editorial column the entire memorial address which concluded with the observation that Professor Long had "lived a life of commitment. Whatever he did, as churchman, as patriot, as professor, or friend to mankind, he sought to follow the admonition of St. Thomas Aquinas that it is our duty to strive honestly to help man to know what he ought to believe, to know what he ought to desire, to know what he ought to do."[48] Professor Miller took charge of the Placement Office for several years after the death of Professor Long.

Inasmuch as Daniel B. Gerhardt and Suzanne Underwood had exactly the same grade point average, they were named co-valedictorians for the class of 1957. Three Elkins girls, all excellent students and campus leaders were graduated in that class. They were Elizabeth Butt, Fay McGee, and Julia P. Wilson, daughter of Dr. and Mrs. Knox Wilson of the faculty. Honorary D.D. degrees were awarded to trustees, Paul E. Francis and Robert A. Pfrangle, and an LL.D. was conferred on Nelson S. Knaggs, a noted explorer, writer, and business leader who later became a valued member of the board of trustees.

Including Elizabeth Millard, mentioned above, there were twelve new faculty members at the beginning of the academic year 1957-58. Two of them, Dr. William Tolstead in biology and Dr. C. R. Thayer, director of the Presbyterian Guidance Center and chairman of the Psychology Department would remain until they retired. The others, except for Miss Millard, stayed only two or three years. It was in September 1957 also that, in an effort to improve the preparation and serving of meals, the Slater Food Service was brought in to operate the College Dining Hall. This proved to be a very satisfactory arrangement which was continued for twenty-two years.

In October the four-story barn built by Senator Elkins in 1900 burned to the ground. Located on the back campus (near the site of Hermanson Campus Center), this landmark was a magnificent wooden structure which at the time was being considered for possible use, after remodeling, as a theater.[49]

The major play presented in 1957-58 was *Death of a Salesman.* Several talented students were in the cast, including Ed Praul,

48. *The Senator,* March 27, 1957, p. 2.
49. *Ibid.,* October 23, 1957, p. 1.

Ruth Herbert, Dick Huggins, and Jack Armitage in major roles as well as Earl Jarvis, Bob Genther, Gene Slota, Bill Hancock, Betty Fletcher, and Judy Beckham in supporting parts.

A "first" in the history of D&E athletics was the award of a varsity letter in 1957 to a co-ed, Carol Douglas, an outstanding tennis player.[50] The first Pre-Law Seminar was organized in 1957-58. Of the original six members, four completed law school and became successful attorneys, two (Ken Deegan and Herb Wallace) in New York, one (Michael DiMario who became a D&E student body president) in Maryland, and Fred Fox II, a judge in West Virginia.

Miss Virgie Harris died in April 1958. An alumna of the college, she had been a faculty member for most of the time since 1922, first as registrar and later as associate librarian. A painting of her by Professor Reed was hung in the reading room of the new library during a memorial ceremony for her shortly after the building was completed.

In April 1958, Dr. S. Wilds DuBose announced his resignation of dean of the college, effective June 1. President Allen stated what should never be forgotten when he said: "Davis and Elkins College will always owe a debt of gratitude to Dean DuBose because of his service beyond the call of duty through the rough years since he took office."[51] After a well-deserved sabbatical leave, Dr. DuBose returned as professor of religion and philosophy in the spring of 1959 and later also served as chaplain until his retirement.

At its meeting in May, the board of trustees elected Dr. Thomas R. Ross to succeed Dr. DuBose as dean of the college. A graduate of Park College in Missouri, with M.A. and Ph.D. degrees from Harvard, Professor Ross had been a member of the D&E faculty since 1949. He accepted the appointment with great reluctance, much preferring to teach and write and being at the time in the process of reading galley proofs for his first book which was due to be published in October 1958. However, President Allen insisted, and persisted in arguing that, with accreditation threatened, someone who had served so long as chairman of the Educational Policies Committee and was familiar with the problems faced, as well as being well acquainted with the

50. *Ibid.*, April 2, 1958, p. 1.
51. *Ibid.*, April 17, 1958, p. 1.

faculty and the trustees, was needed as dean. Evan Kek and senior faculty members aided the president in his persuasive efforts and so on June 1, 1958, T. R. Ross began what proved to be more than twelve years of service as academic dean.

At the same meeting at which they elected the dean, the trustees also approved establishing the TIAA Retirement Plan effective September 1, 1958. They voted to amend the constitution to provide for enlarging the membership of the board to thirty, including three alumni and three members-at-large and established a "rotary rule" which made a trustee ineligible for reelection after serving two consecutive three-year terms until he had been out of office for at least one year. Mr. Kek reported that, in accordance with a request made by the board earlier, the T-House and other temporary buildings had been removed from the front campus and that the Graceland "Ice House" had been torn down. All recommendations from the faculty relative to terminating the awarding of the specialized degrees were approved and the board reaffirmed "its unqualified support" of the program "to raise the academic level of the Student Body to high standards."[52]

The 1958 commencement was of considerable sentimental interest. Dr. DuBose participated for the last time as dean. Dr. Charles E. Albert having decided earlier to retire, was given an honorary Sc.D. degree and proclaimed "Mr. D & E" in recognition of his many years of service since he first joined the faculty in 1911. The recently reconstructed Science Hall was named "The Charles E. Albert Hall of Science" in his honor. Mrs. Albert also retired at that time, as did Professor Emily Opel. The Reverend John Charles Wynn, a close friend of President David Allen, was awarded a D.D. degree and Dr. Hunter B. Blakely, long a powerful ally of the college, received an honorary Doctorate of Literature. Outstanding student leaders graduated included Harvey Lozman, the valedictorian; Nancy Malone, one of the most distinguished of the long line of *Senator* editors; Tom Krogel, president of the student body; Peggy Chandler, Neil Irons, Harold Arner, and George Buschman. Natalie Barb, then secretary to the business manager and more recently the very able director of financial aid, received her bachelor's degree.

The progress reported to the North Central Association for

52. Trustee Minutes, May 7, 8, 1958, pp. 78-90.

1957-58 was commended by officials of that agency, but much remained to be done to insure that the reexamination in 1960 would result in reaccreditation without qualifications. Thus, among the matters to which President Allen asked the new dean of the college to give attention in the immediate future were (1) stabilizing and upgrading the faculty and reducing faculty "turn-over"; (2) improving the efficiency of some phases of administration in the academic and student personnel areas; (3) smooth implementation of policies recently adopted in regard to degree programs and curriculum; and (4) raising scholastic standards for students. The president began to devote most of his time to helping with the fund-raising efforts of the Living Endowment campaign then under way—an undertaking which in the beginning, as Gerald Larson of Ward, Dreshman and Reinhardt said, "was not what the Company considered a successful drive."[53]

The first task in the summer of 1958 was to find qualified faculty to fill the positions vacant because of deaths, retirement, and resignation. Inasmuch as Dean Little and Dean Emm had resigned effective July 1 and as the Maxon Report had suggested that a dean of students should be made responsible to the dean of the college, it was decided to restore the position of dean of students and appoint Dr. Norman L. Sheets to that office. An able, dedicated, and energetic young assistant professor of physical education, Dr. Sheets also served as director of athletics and department chairman and proved to be an effective and popular administrator. Miss Carrie Belle Vaughan was appointed counselor for women to assist Dr. Sheets and to be in charge of Gribble Hall. New faculty included Dr. Walter S. Hartley as head of the Music Department, Dr. James E. Dow to replace Professors Long and Emm in history and political science, Patty R. Petty to succeed Mrs. Albert in English, and Susie E. Odor to succeed Mrs. Opel in education. The last two remained on the faculty until retirement, the first two for a decade. Dr. Winifred Shannon in languages stayed several years until she had to resign because of poor health. Ira Blankenship in physical education served six years before accepting a position at Concord College. Several of the new faculty held doctorates and all, including Lt. Col. Roger Sanders, new commandant of the AFROTC Unit, had master's degrees.

53. Trustee Minutes III, October 28, 1958, p. 94.

Lt. Col. Roger Sanders introducing the queen of the Military Ball and her attendants.

It was in this period, too, that Professor Harry L. Shelton became executive secretary of the Alumni Association, a division of the Development Office. Harold Henry was appointed to be assistant to the president in Development. Professor Shelton brought Mrs. Vernie G. Roy into the Alumni Office as secretary, a position she filled with effectiveness and devotion for many years thereafter. At about the same time, Mrs. Mary Elizabeth Simmons began her more than two decades of faithful service as secretary to the registrar.

The college and the town were shocked and saddened at the unexpected death of Dr. S. Benton Talbot on July 17, 1958. An alumnus of the college, he, like Miss Harris and Dr. Albert, had devoted most of his life to D&E. Always especially interested in the college preparation of students who intended to go to medical school, Dr. Talbot had a great influence on the lives of many who became physicians and dentists, as well as on many others. At memorial services held for Dr. Talbot in the fall semester, Dr. E. E. Hutton of Elkins, his former student, said that Dr. Talbot was "an educator who believed that happiness resulted from what a man had in his head, not in his pockets." Dr. Albert stated that Dr. Talbot was a professor "who constantly encouraged his students but never let them relax since he always pointed the way to higher achievement."[54]

With the resignation of Dr. Purdum, the retirement of Dr. Albert, and the deaths of Miss Harris and Dr. Talbot, the gallant few who had served from the era of James E. Allen in the 1920s were all gone. Indeed, none from the 1930s and only a few from the 1940s were still on the faculty.

Inasmuch as the old swimming pool building had to be removed in connection with the construction of the library, arrangements were made during the summer to move the Student Union into the servants' wing of Halliehurst Hall. This was used until Benedum Hall was built and then the dispensary was established in that section of Halliehurst. Virginia L. Henry was the very efficient manager of the Student Union and Book Store in those days.

As to the matter of implementing the revisions of the academic program, it is interesting to note two decades afterward that the Maxon Report of early 1958 had stated that:

> One of the greatest difficulties faced by the President and the Faculty is restructuring curricular offerings and degree programs so fundamentally different from the present, in the face of opposition from a number of Faculty who were attracted to the institution by its special degree offerings. Some of them are literally incapable of comprehending the academic significance or the desirability of such a change. In order to accomplish this, it may be necessary to release certain Faculty who cannot be reconciled to the liberal arts nature of the institution.[55]

In fact, however, the changes recommended by the Educational Policies Committee were perfected and adopted in every case by the votes of a large majority of the entire faculty after free and full debate. It was not "necessary to release" a single faculty member, nor so far as is known did anyone leave because he could not "be reconciled to the liberal arts nature of the institution."

During 1958-59, a plan providing for written and oral comprehensive examinations for seniors was adopted, effective with the class graduating in 1960. The dean appointed a special com-

54. *The Senator*, October 9, 1958, p. 1.
55. Maxon, *et al., op. cit.*, p. 8.

Professor Jesse F. Reed, *left,* and Miss Carrie L. Brittain, *seated,* at a reception for a visiting lecturer.

mittee to encourage able students to prepare for graduate study and to advise and assist them. Dr. Louis Mattison, chairman of the Department of Chemistry, with the aid of Dr. Nelson S. Knaggs, developed a program of research for outstanding majors, which provided significant financial stipends for those qualified. A Special Programs Committee, under the chairmanship of Professor Jesse F. Reed, arranged to bring several outstanding speakers to the campus and was subsequently created as a standing committee of the faculty to arrange for lectures, concerts, and other events for the cultural enrichment of the college community.[56]

The college had barely recovered from the shock of the January 10 death in an airplane crash of Lt. Paul E. Ash, Jr., one of the most popular members of the ROTC faculty, when news came of the death in South Carolina of Dr. R. B. Purdum on Feb-

56. *Ibid.,* October 16, October 30, 1958; May 21, 1959, p. 1.

ruary 4, 1959. He was fifty-nine and had seemed to be in excellent health.[57] He had enjoyed his work at Presbyterian College since leaving D&E. However, while in Elkins during the 1958 Christmas holidays, he had come to the campus to visit Dean Ross and before leaving had expressed the hope that if a vacancy should occur in the Chemistry Department, he could be considered for it, as he said he would like to spend the remaining years of his professional career at the college he loved best where he had begun teaching thirty-three years earlier. Arrangements were made for Mrs. Purdum to complete her degree requirements at D&E in subsequent years without cost, and she became a teacher in a private school in Virginia. Later Margaret Purdum Goddin, younger daughter of the Purdums, was invited to join the faculty as an instructor and in due time was promoted through the ranks until she became a full professor. Undoubtedly, Dr. Purdum would have been proud that she ultimately was appointed dean of the faculty and long used the office desk he had used as president of the college.

Several factors contributed to a significant rise in "school spirit" in 1958-59. For one thing, the *Senator* maintained a very positive attitude, constructively critical, but supportive of both student government and the faculty and administration. Wendell Cramer and Judy McCullough, the editors, together with Art Heldman, for two years probably the best editorial writer the paper has had, and their staff published a first rate collegiate newspaper. Of course, the fact that students were actively involved in the Living Endowment campaign, that the new women's residence hall was soon ready for occupancy, and that the library was visibly under construction were morale boosters. Jack Armitage, student body president, and Priscilla ("Pat") Weaver, a leader in many campus organizations, worked hard for the Living Endowment drive as well as to support improvements in the academic and extracurricular activities. Another factor was doubtless the forming of a campus society known as the "Rotanes" for the purpose of "promoting school spirit on the campus." Led by such exuberant characters as Dick Huggins, Bruce Donaldson, Bob Genther, Wendell Cramer, Barry Bova, Jim Ruyak, Dick Matz, Ed Hunt, Dick Stoeltzing, Ed Blacka and

---

57. *Ibid.*, January 15, February 12, 1959, p. 1.

Dave Meserve, the "Rotanes" kept things lively, especially at athletic contests.

The return of Paul Wilcox, after a two-year absence while on military duty, helped to make the 1958-59 basketball season the best for many years. Miles Runner, who had re-entered D&E the preceding February after overseas service, was co-captain with Bob Back of a squad which included Jack McDonald, John Warren, Tom Schreiber, Jim Lloyd, Herb Wallace, Gene Filippi, Bob Ferrell, and Don Fowler. As managers, Tharon Jack and Charles Fletcher were of significant assistance to Coach Mel Greer and the season ended with 16 wins and 12 defeats—a big change from the total of 5 wins and 45 losses in the preceding two years. The big thrill, however, was that Paul Wilcox, who scored 70 points in one game to break all single game scoring records in the state, finished the regular season with a total of 773 points (an average of 33.4 per game) to become the leading scorer in the entire nation. He not only won the national scoring title, but he also led the nation in rebounding and was the first player in history to win both titles. He was named to the All-Conference Team, the All-Tournament Team, and also to the Little All-American First Team.[58]

Paul Wilcox

Other developments which pleased many students and faculty included the election of Trustee Jennings Randolph to the United States Senate in 1958, the gift of the use of several dozen billboards throughout the state (arranged by L. E. McWhorter, president of the Standard Advertising Corporation) showing Liberal Arts Hall and the stone arcade in color and publicizing D&E as a liberal arts college; the decision of the trustees to adopt a faculty recommendation giving Dr. Albert the title, professor-emeritus (the first D&E faculty member so honored); the extend-

58. *Ibid.*, February 19, March 26, 1959, pp. 1-3; Kessler, *op. cit.*, pp. 271-72.

Local members of the Development Commission
at the president's house in 1961.

ing to the dean of the college the opportunity to attend and participate in all board meetings (except for voting); and the adoption of procedures providing for a faculty committee to participate with a trustee committee in the selection of persons to be nominated for honorary degrees.[59]

In May 1959, the board approved a "Fifteen-Year Plan" for the development of the college. Prepared by a joint Faculty-Trustee Committee on Long-Range Planning under the chairmanship of Dr. William M. Ferry, this plan incorporated the recommendations of the 1954 "Ten-Year Plan," brought up-to-date. In addition, it included such aims as giving "the Faculty a larger share in the academic government of the College"; increasing the number of faculty with doctorates; provision of a salary schedule of a nature to be "an incentive for continued service and professional advancement"; attainment of a student-faculty ratio of 12 to 1; better provisions for sabbatical leave and tenure; a student body "stabilized at between 750 and 800; suitable minimum

---

59. *The Senator*, November 20, 1958, p. 1; Trustee Minutes III, October 28, 1958, p. 95; and May 6, 7, 1959, p. 100.

standards (high school record, S.A.T. or A.C.T. scores, I.Q. scores, and letters of references) for admission of students; scholastic standards in regard to eligibility and probation, sophomore and senior examination programs; provisions for increasing the number of volumes in the library; reorganization of the board of trustees, and a building program to provide for four residence halls, a chapel-auditorium, faculty housing, a student union-dining hall, and improvements of Liberal Arts Hall and roads and parking lots. The plan envisioned raising at least $105,000 annually from Living Endowment and launching a major fund drive for $2,735,000 "sometime within the period 1963-1965."[60]

At the suggestion of Professor Shelton, the custom of granting an honorary degree to an alumnus each year was begun at the 1959 commencement with the award of an Sc.D. degree to Nathan I. Hall, Jr., of the class of 1930. Bachelor's degrees were conferred on Captain Charles A. Gover of the AFROTC faculty; James F. Cain (now prosecuting attorney of Randolph County), James A. Davis, Thomas Eidell, and George D. Vandenbergh, (now all active in business affairs in Elkins) and on such outstanding student leaders as Ronald Hinkle (class valedictorian), Ken Deegan, Bob Genther, Art Heldman, Ruth Herbert, Herb Wallace, Priscilla Weaver, John Armitage, Rolf T. Hammer, Michael Dakes, Mariwyn McClain, and Charles D. Dickey.

During the summer of 1959, the library collection was moved from Liberal Arts Hall into the new library building. James M. Turner had been appointed head librarian in January and he supervised the move, with the assistance of Miss Brittain and Mrs. Fred A. Miller, who joined the library staff in 1958. Shortly thereafter, Mrs. Robert Wall was added as periodical librarian.

There were only four new faculty members in the fall of 1959. One of these was Dr. Laura Jean McAdams (who had served in the 1930s) as associate professor of languages. Another was Sidney Hamilton Tedford who succeeded Mrs. Claude King Davis as director of the college choir. An able and talented young man, Professor Tedford was a valuable associate of Dr. Walter S. Hartley, a noted composer and pianist, who had become chairman of the Music Department the preceding year. Professor Tedford's wife, Barbara, joined the faculty in January 1960 to teach English.

60. Trustee Minutes, May 7, 8, 1959, pp. 104-9.

Dedication of the long-awaited new
Library Building, 1959.

The year 1959-60 also saw the arrival of Arthur Southwick as assistant director of admissions, after his retirement as director of admissions at the College of Wooster. A man of wide experience, he was of great help in the effort to develop a more selective admissions program and it was at his suggestion that Dean Ross made arrangements to develop the Washington Semester Program with American University in 1961.

The 1959 faculty conference.

Stephen Martin retired as superintendent of campus maintenance at the beginning of the fall semester in 1959, after having served for twenty-six years. He was succeeded by Ellery J. Hinkle who continued in the post until he had to retire because of illness.

On October 10, 1959, the college held the first "Parents' Day," an affair which has become an annual event of interest to increasing numbers for two decades.[61]

A result of the efforts of Ann and Evan Kek in the early winter of 1959 was the establishment of a major new facility known as the Modern Language Laboratory located on the second floor of the Liberal Arts Hall in space formerly occupied by the library. At the time of its installation, it provided D&E students "the most advanced type of equipment obtainable for the purpose, equipment which is not currently in use in any other college in the state."[62] For several years this laboratory was supervised by Mrs. Ruth Hinkle.

The Campus Drama Society presented *Sons of Adam* in December. Said to be a type of drama never presented before at D&E, it involved "modern dance movements and poetry, rather than the usual prose." Students with leading roles included Rita Campbell, Joyce Blacka, Gary North, Douglas Gilbert, Ed Hunt, Ed Simpson, Gail Lewis, and Bruce Chadwick.

There was much activity in intramural athletics, but D&E had little success in either football or basketball in this era. Bob Ferrell, the basketball team's leading scorer, broke his hand in mid-season of 1959-60, a factor accounting for a conference record of 8 wins to 16 losses.[63] That season a group of alumni, aided by "Bud" Shelton, decided to select a "D&E Team of the Decade" from among basketball players who had participated from the 1949-50 through the 1959-60 season. They chose Carl Payne, Paul Wilcox, James Harold ("Hap") Huey, Lycurgus ("Skip") Hill, and Joseph Pukach, Jr. Later in the spring, Carol Ann Douglas was awarded the "All Sports Trophy" for the "most all around athlete of the year."[64]

A debate team was organized in 1960 for the first time in many

61. *The Senator* October 15, 1959, p. 1.
62. *Ibid.,* November 19, 1959, p. 1.
63. *Ibid.,* February 4, 1960, p. 3.
64. *Ibid.,* February 25, 1960, p. 3; March 31, 1960, p. 1.

years. Coached by Professors Fiorentino and Dow, the team included Trish Bethany, Thomas Wroldson, Grier Haslam, Lucius Quintus Cincinnatus Lamar, Sam Topal, and Paul Billups. The following year the affirmative team (Dennis Weidner and Grier Haslam) placed first in the state finals. In March 1963, the D&E team (Grier Haslam, Dennis Weidner, Ann Boisclair and Michael Harris) took first place in the Middle Atlantic States Debate Tournament at Hampton Institute in Virginia. Dennis Weidner also won the trophy for being the best affirmative speaker.[65]

A new activity was developed on the campus in the winter of 1960-61. This was skiing on the hillside below Inspiration Point near the Ross house. A Ski Club was organized under the leadership of Major Robert Rippey and much interest was developed in the sport.

During the spring semester, the faculty adopted comprehensive rules governing class attendance which gave juniors and seniors in good academic standing a significant amount of freedom. The faculty also revised and liberalized the provisions for sabbatical leaves and recommended them to the trustees, who approved the program at the May board meeting.[66] The North Central Self-Study Committee, under the chairmanship of Dr. William E. Phipps, devised a program for course evaluation which could be used on a voluntary basis in all classes. This was adopted by the faculty and was used by many for several years. Acting on recommendations from Dr. Phipps's committee, provision was also made for "Independent Study" by qualified students in courses numbered "391," and for the establishment of a "President's Seminar" for selected freshmen students to meet with faculty members for discussion of important books.[67] Later, in 1960, a "Great Issues Seminar," open to a limited number of seniors, was formed. Like the president's seminar for freshman, the students met with a few faculty members in a faculty home once or twice a month to discuss topics of major significance. The First Scholarship Dinner to honor Dean's List students and the highest ranking student in each of the four classes was held in the spring of 1960. Sponsored by the college and the AAUP Chapter, this became an annual event.

65. *Ibid.*, April 12, 1961; April 5, 1963, p. 1.
66. *Ibid.*, May 5, 1960, p. 1; Trustee Minutes III, May 4, 1960, p. 126.
67. Faculty Minutes III, February 8, March 21, 1960, pp. 27-38.

The best news of the year was that the North Central Association examining team had prepared a favorable report and that D&E had been released of the necessity of making an annual report and was no longer on "probation."[68]

At its May meeting, the board of trustees, noting that President Allen would soon reach retirement age, voted to ask him to continue to serve on a year-to-year appointment and appointed him president for the 1961-62 year. He was permitted to take an extra month of vacation each year in lieu of a sabbatical leave year and any unused portion of the leave would be paid as terminal pay when he retired. The board also authorized the renovating and enlarging of the Ross house on the back campus during the summer of 1960. It was reported that only $609,990 of the Christian Higher Education campaign pledges had been paid and that more than $426,000 remained to be collected before the pledge period terminated on June 30, 1960.[69] Not enough of those pledges were paid to enable the college to build the chapel-auditorium as planned.

The death of Captain Robert F. Blaess in a plane crash in the summer of 1960 saddened his many D&E friends. He had been an assistant professor of air science since 1957. Inasmuch as both Dr. Shannon and Dr. McAdams had to resign because of problems of health during the preceding year, two replacements in the Language Department were appointed during the summer of 1960. One, Professor Tatiana Jardetzky who had served previously and had left in the mid-fifties to be in New York City with her husband, returned to teach French and Russian, this time to remain until retirement. The other was Ernest Thomas Schwarz, Jr., who was named instructor in German. Dr. Michael J. Alexander replaced Professor Carder, who retired, as chairman of the Economics and Business Department. Two additions to the faculty were Charles P. Cullop in history and E. H. Hunter Davis in English. Both soon completed their doctorates and remained for several years. Dr. Franklin Thompson was also appointed associate professor of Spanish. In August, Patty R. Petty became dean of women, a position she was to hold until her retirement in the late 1970s.

The coordinator of Liberal Arts Studies, Professor Robert E.

68. *Ibid.*, January 4, March 21, 1960, pp. 6, 38.
69. Trustee Minutes, May 4, 1960, pp. 127, 129.

Bader, visited the college in October. His report was heartening, to say the least, especially his comment: "Seldom have I visited such a vital College. I believe that the many changes which have been made in the last few years have been in the right direction ... I envy the students at Davis and Elkins. They have the usual student complaints, but they are aware of the excellent educational opportunities which they have."[70]

Although there was much interest in the 1960 presidential election on the campus, one could not have detected it from reading *The Senator*. Not a word about the campaign or the outcome of the election appeared in the campus paper all fall. Quite a contrast to the *Senators* of previous years! The debate club discussed the issues over the campus radio station, and many students, impressed by the "youth" of Senator John F. Kennedy, were delighted at news of his election.

In December the National Science Foundation awarded D&E $57,000 to support a 1961 Summer Institute in Science and Mathematics to be directed by Professors Louis Mattison and Fred A. Miller.[71] This was the first of several similar grants for such institutes secured through the efforts of Dean Ross and the Science Faculty early in the new decade. Subsequent institutes were directed by Professor Keith Hiser.

President Allen's report to the board in May 1961 summed up the highlights of the year as follows:

> The Faculty is probably as fine as we have ever had in our history. Forty per cent have the earned doctor's degree, and Professors Cullop and Davis hope to achieve their doctorates this summer. These figures are especially significant when we remember that the average per cent of doctors degrees in West Virginia is twenty-seven, and if that West Virginia University and Marshall University are omitted, the percentage falls to seventeen.
>
> Among the things which have indicated academic progress in the past year are the following: The acceptance of Davis and Elkins into institutional membership of the American Association of University Women (which meant that women graduates of D & E could become members of the AAUW for the first time in her history); the approval of the College for participation in the Washington Semester of American University; the recognition

---

70. *The Senator*, November 21, 1960, p. 1.
71. *Ibid.*, December 14, 1960, p. 1.

given to D & E in a survey of Modern Language Facilities and teaching in West Virginia; . . . the recognition given Dean Ross through his invitations to share with selected other Deans of America in the Pugwash Conference in Nova Scotia and in the Institute for College and University Administrators at Harvard.[72]

Dr. Claude King Davis and Dr. B. C. Harrington retired at the end of the 1960-61 academic year. Dr. Davis was named chaplain

Dr. B. C. Harrington and Dr. C. K. Davis, *standing center* between Dr. C. E. Albert and Dr. W. E. Phipps, at reunion for Church Vocation Alumni. Mrs. Davis and Mrs. Harry Shelton, *seated.*

emeritus. Dr. DuBose succeeded Dr. Davis as chaplain and Dr. Harrington became a part-time assistant to the president for a few months. He was replaced as chairman of the Department of Education by Dr. William B. Axtell, former president of the West Virginia Institute of Technology. Dr. Norman L. Sheets resigned as dean of students to accept a position at Temple University and was succeeded by Dr. Charles P. Cullop of the History Department. At the same time, Dr. James E. Dow was appointed director of the library and Mabel Phares began her service as secretary to the dean of the college, a position she filled for more than a decade thereafter. During the summer of 1961, Cornelia Brock

72. Trustee Minutes, May 3, 1961, Appendix B following p. 145.

was employed as residence hall counselor for women, thus beginning a long association with D&E.

As the future was unexpectedly to prove, the efforts made in the summer of 1961 by Dean Ross and Professor Fred Miller, director of athletics, to assist Professor E. H. Hunter Davis in making arrangements to organize and coach a soccer team were of great significance in D&E's history. Soccer was a new sport at D&E and in most West Virginia institutions in the early 1960s, but interest was increasing at West Virginia University, Fairmont College, and Wesleyan, which had organized teams. D&E had a number of foreign students as well as a few from Northeastern states who knew the game and wanted to make it a major activity at D&E. Dr. Davis, associate professor of English, who had starred in soccer as a student, offered to coach a team if arrangements could be made for a place to practice and for some contests to be scheduled on a home-to-home basis with two or three nearby colleges.

Thus, in the fall of 1961 some non-varsity level games were scheduled. The D&E "booters" won the first intercollegiate soccer game in the college's history, defeating Wesleyan 2 to 0 on October 18, 1961, on the old athletic field where the chapel now stands. Later, in the final game of the year, D&E beat a West Virginia University team 5-0. As a *Senator* sports writer commented at the end of the first season: "The soccer team has set two school records: We have never been defeated at home and we have never been scored upon at home." Outstanding players included Gary Horvath, Dave Vivian, Dave Clapp, Jim Douglas, Rich Sennhenn, Bill McQuary, Jim Fishel, Jim Bushyeager, George Scott, Dennis Bye, Bob Maitan, Joe Seid, Duncan McGill, Jim Nunn, and Alvi N. Saeed. Only two were seniors and next year, when the team gained varsity status, it posted a 3-5 record with the addition of Karl T. Herrmann as co-coach and of such players as David Heron, Andy Maros, Roger Hailes, Bob Lennox, Stewart MacSherry, Richard DeLisser, Roger Shipley, Ronald Mars, Robert Allen, and Sandy Wright. The year 1963 was the first winning season ending with a 6-3 record. New players who helped the veterans win were Francois Muyumba, Khosrov Ardalan, Keith Trewick, Bill George, Allen Freimauer, and Henry Nefflen.[73] Thus began a new chapter in the long history of athletics at D&E.

---

73. *The Senator*, October 1961-December 1963, *passim.*

Financial exigencies and changing times finally ended an earlier chapter which might better have been concluded a decade sooner. In November, Professor Miller, chairman of the Athletic Committee, brought to the faculty the committee's recommendation that D&E discontinue participation in intercollegiate football. The faculty approved and at its next meeting the board of trustees agreed, with reluctance on the part of some members, "to drop football."[74] The 1961 football team won only two games, but did boast some outstanding individual players. Tony DeMotto was an All-Conference end as he had been in the year before, and received honorable mention for Small College All-American and Joe Harris was named an All-Conference guard. Tex Lee Boggs was listed both as second team Scholastic All-American and on the All-Conference second team. Other outstanding players included Woody Davis, Don Fowler, "Fuzz" Jones, and Don Bainbridge.[75]

The basketball team did not rate any winning seasons in the early sixties, but it too had some star players with distinguished individual records. In addition to Bob Ferrell, already mentioned, there were such men as David Kirk, Richard Shreve, Frank Holsclaw, Don Fowler, Craig Felber, Mike Maiden, Jim Cook, Stan Kokie, Art Wheatley, Norman Pingley, and David Norcutt.

The swimming team, coached by Karl Herrmann in 1962-63, placed second in the West Virginia Conference. Andras Maros and Gil Fitzsimmons broke five conference records and Maros was selected to compete in the National Inter-Collegiate Athletic Association Championship meet at Bartlesville, Oklahoma, in the spring of 1963.[76]

As a result of the increase in the number of co-eds, a new sorority was formed under the leadership of Professors Gloria Payne and Claire Fiorentino. Beginning as a local named Kappa Lambda, this group became a chapter of national Zeta Tau Alpha in December of 1962 with Mary Spivey as the first president.[77]

Other new organizations formed in this period were the Madrigal Singers, directed by Professor Sidney Tedford; the Ski

---

74. *Ibid.*, November 23, 1961, p. 1; Faculty Minutes, November 13, 1961, p. 8; Trustee Minutes, May 2, 1962, p. 2.
75. *The Senatus*, 1962, p. 112.
76. *Ibid.*, March 14, 1963, p. 1.
77. *Ibid.*, January 17, April 5, 1963, p. 1.

Some notable members of the Green Room Society in 1963.
Professor Claire Fiorentino, *inset*.

Club sponsored by Major Robert Rippey, and the Netherworld Explorers, a spelunking club first led by Charles Grabe. Professor Tedford and Lewis Wilson of the library staff, were also the leaders in establishing the tradition of forming a community-college chorus to perform the Messiah each Christmas season in the Davis Memorial Church. The *Adum*, a literary magazine, began publication in 1962.

The Green Room Society, successor to the venerable Playcrafters since 1962, sponsored several successful dramatic productions in the early sixties. Directed by Mrs. "F," the more memorable of these were *Tartuffe, Hedda Gabler, Christ in the Concrete City, The Rainmaker, Taming of the Shrew,* and *Antigone*. Outstanding participants in this era included John Benjamin (later to be director of Theatre West Virginia), Calvin Morgan (later famous for stage designs), Lorna Dale and Cynthia Wands (both of whom became professional actresses), Al Andrews, Gary North, Bob Gracey, Judy Mewha, Jean Humason, P. A. Adams, Joyce Houser, and Richard Mower.

During the 1962-63 year, various irregularities in the fraternity pledging system and in the conduct of those living in off-campus fraternity houses led to the appointment of a special committee to investigate fraternity matters. The result was a recommendation that the Inter-Fraternity Council be reorganized and that the fraternity men be required to move on the campus as soon as arrangements could be made to house them.

Two events of national significance made an impact on the campus in 1962 and 1963. The first was the Cuban Missile Crisis, which led the Civil Defense officials to designate the basements of Graceland Hall and Halliehurst Hall as "fallout shelters." *The Senator* took an "opinion poll" as to the government's policy and reported on November 1, 1962, that "the main thoughts were that Kennedy was right and that we cannot now back down . . . that Davis and Elkins students . . . in the event of war are behind their President, their nation, and their ideals to help build a free and peaceful world."[78]

The second event coming just slightly more than a year later was the assassination of President John F. Kennedy. *The Senator* carried the headline "Fatal Shot Heard 'Round the World" and devoted much of the front page and the editorial page to the tragedy. Professor Dow took a carload of students to Washington, D.C., for the funeral; college classes and other activities were canceled and almost the entire student body attended a non-required memorial service on Monday, November 25, in the gymnasium.[79]

Dr. Cullop decided to return to full-time teaching in 1963 and Dr. Axtell was appointed vice-president for Development and Public Relations. Succeeding Dr. Cullop as dean of students and Dr. Axtell as chairman of the Department of Education was Dr. Edward V. Perkins who joined the faculty in the fall of 1963. He was a conscientious and hard-working dean of students, serving in that difficult position until the end of the decade, and an able and effective professor of education and director of the Teacher Education Program until his death in 1979.

To encourage well-qualified faculty to come to D&E and remain, the following policy was implemented in the fall of 1963. "Sons and daughters of regular full-time Faculty members above

---

78. *Ibid.*, November 1, 1962, p. 1.
79. *Ibid.*, November 27, December 4, 1963, *passim.*

Faculty and seniors at the first Boar's Head Dinner to be held in the new dining room in Benedum Hall.

the rank of Instructor who attend accredited liberal arts colleges other than Davis and Elkins College will receive from Davis and Elkins College financial assistance toward the payment of tuition at the colleges of their choice in an amount not to exceed the tuition being charged at D&E." Of course, faculty dependents could still also attend D&E without payment of tuition.

In this period, too, the college was successful in getting several matching grants from the Board of Christian Education of the Presbyterian Church, U.S.A., which enabled faculty members to spend a year in study toward their doctorates. These grants, in addition to funds from the Danforth Foundation and the National Science Foundation and the Regional Council for International Education for faculty summer institutes, seminars, and study abroad, made possible the broadest and most useful program for professional development the college had ever had.

Faculty members still on active duty in 1979 who joined D&E in the early 1960s included Dr. John P. Martin (chemistry), Dr. Georgiana Vazquez (Spanish), Dr. Anna Jean Tallman (physical education), Mrs. Mary Margaret Woodward (library science), and Dr. Margaret P. Goddin (English and education). Dr. Alfonso Vazquez, professor-emeritus of biology and Miss Evelyn V. Crouch, recently retired catalog librarian, also came in that period. Dr. Vazquez had had a distinguished teaching career in Cuba prior to the rise of Castro and had also been a leader in the Presbyterian Church in Cuba. He and his wife both became valuable additions to the D&E faculty. Others who stayed less than a decade included Dr. Jerald L. Wagener, who served ably in the Physics Department and helped establish the first computer program; Jean Wagener who taught mathematics; Dr. John Pavlos (chemistry), the late Dr. Paul C. Bibbe (chairman of the Biology Department), Avis L. Partain (chairman of the Physical Education Department and director of athletics), and L. Gregory Myers (physical education and outstanding soccer coach). Staff members who came at that time were Frank Rightmire, Jean Talbott, Cleva Harrold, and Carolyn Black in Admissions; June Steele, Eleanor Harrison, and Marion Godwin in the Business Office; Lucille Booth, Mrs. Karl Herrmann, Judith Moore (later Mrs. Grady Guye), and Margaret Heron as college nurses; and Mrs. Cornelia Brock, Mrs. George Hull, Mrs. Bessie Fisher, Mrs. Nina Phillips, Mrs. Fuda Hamrick, and Mrs. Eli Koppel as residence hall counselors. (Mrs. Koppel also assisted in the

Some "Housemothers" in the new Dining Hall in 1963.

library.) In January 1963, Louise Linhart became director of activities in Benedum Hall and advisor to the Campus Social Committee. She was ably assisted for several years by Tillie Montoney.

With the special emphasis placed on improving admission standards and upgrading scholastic standards in the years after 1958, it is not surprising to find a number of students with outstanding ability and distinguished academic records being graduated in the sixties. Although in mentioning some, others will inevitably be unintentionally overlooked, it is surely as important to cite examples of distinguished achievement in scholarship as in extracurricular activities. Often, of course, the student with excellent grades was also a leader in other campus activities as well. The following are representative of "Dean's List types" who brought honor to their respective classes in their day: Patricia ("Trish") Bethany, Jean P. A. Toureille-Lichtenstein, Elizabeth Reed, Yih Tang Ling, Sally Taylor, Dorothy Jean ("Gaby") Garner, Gary W. North, Kenneth O. White, Carolyn V. Black, Charles W. Reid, John G. Thompson, Tex Lee Boggs, William Cline, Carol Rice, James Crowl, Sarah Grabe, Pamela Verner, Suzanne Rose, Mary Spivey, John Dunsmore, Barbara Frank, David Kurtz, Carolyn Roberts, Victoria Zepp, Gail Hagerman, Nancy Rogers, and Harley Sandford.

It was in the fall of 1963 that an off campus problem of concern to the college arose when it was discovered that African students and American black students were unable to get their hair cut in Elkins in the barber shops. The Administrative Committee and Student Council began what proved to be a prolonged effort to persuade the barber shops and other businesses which discriminated against blacks to change their policies.[80]

The effort of the Special Programs Committee to bring cultural enrichment to the campus, despite limited funds to finance its work, bore fruit. Notable visitors to the campus included Dr. James Bulloch of Edinburgh University, the Trio Italiano D' Archi, Lionel Wiggam, Sir Hugh Foot, the New York String Sextet, Donald Andrews, and T. H. White. Of course, the visit of former President Harry S Truman to the campus during the 1962 Forest Festival was an event of major interest, but it was not sponsored by the Special Program Committee.

80. *Ibid.*, October 23, 1963, p. 1.

President Allen in this period, obtained three grants totaling $45,000 for the purchase of library books—one from the Kellogg Foundation—each to be spent over a three-year period. He also obtained a $25,000 grant from the Richard K. Mellon Foundation for the purpose of initiating the financing of four faculty houses on the Harpertown Road. The first two of these were completed in 1963-64 and were rented to Professors Fred A. Miller and Charles P. Cullop.[81]

In October 1963, the board of trustees appointed a committee known as the "Sixtieth Anniversary Five-Year Advanced Program Committee for Capital Funds." The aim was to raise "several million dollars for endowment." George Stevenson was appointed chairman of this committee and it immediately began to make plans for a financial campaign. In its first report to the board, the committee recommended that during the first phase (1964-68) of the campaign, efforts be made to obtain at least $3 million to $4 million and that during a second phase (1968-69) a goal of $1 million to $2 million be set.[82]

At the same meeting at which the "Sixtieth Anniversary" Committee was established, the board also appointed a "Committee to Seek a New President." President Allen, having already served two years beyond normal retirement age, had informed the board that he wished to retire as of June 30, 1964. His view was that the Five-Year Financial Drive would continue until 1969 "long after I will have reached the age of compulsory retirement" and that "it would be foolish for the College to enter upon this program knowing that it would need to change leadership in the middle of it." Dr. Allen, aware of past problems of transition, advised the trustees to include faculty members on the Search Committee and gave notice of his intention to retire many months in advance in the hope that a new president could be elected before July 1, 1964. The board selected Dr. William M. Ferry, its new chairman, to be chairman of the committee to seek a president. Other members were Charles B. Gates, Jr., James W. Witherspoon, David E. Cuppett, Jr., James E. Allen, Jr., Evan R. Kek, and Thomas R. Ross.

The committee began its work immediately. After widely distributing a description of the qualifications needed for the posi-

---

81. Trustee Minutes, October 29, 1963, May 6, 1964, *passim*.
82. Trustee Minutes, October 29, 1963, p. 20; May 6, 1964, p. 38.

tion and requesting applications and nominations from many sources, the committee received numerous suggestions and applications. By March 12, 1964, the committee was able to report to the trustees a unanimous recommendation that Gordon E. Hermanson of Storm Lake, Iowa, Vice-President for Development of Buena Vista College be appointed president of Davis and Elkins College. The board then voted to accept President Allen's resignation "with sincere regret" and to elect Mr. Hermanson in accordance with the terms recommended by the committee. The board president, Dr. Allen, and others conferred by telephone with Mr. Hermanson and received his verbal acceptance. It was then agreed that before the news was released to the public, Dr. Allen should inform the faculty of his retirement and Dr. Ferry should formally notify the faculty by letter of the election of Mr. Hermanson.[83]

President-elect Hermanson attended the spring meeting of the board of trustees on May 6, 1964, and was warmly received by all present. At that meeting, the trustees accepted the resignation of Dr. Andrew R. Bird, Jr., a longtime member and former chairman of the board, who had moved to Virginia. He was made an honorary trustee, a distinction previously bestowed on Senator Jennings Randolph, Dr. James R. Henry, and Dr. Lloyd M. Courtney, for outstanding service.

The dean was requested to present a report for the Committee on Long-Range Plans reviewing the progress made since 1954 toward the achievement of the goals of the "Fifteen-Year Plan." In summary, this review revealed that the committee had found:

(1) That the goal of aiming for a stable enrollment of 750 to 800 students by 1969-1970 was sound and that in 1964 the numerical balance between male and female students was much better than it had been in 1954.

(2) That the Faculty had been substantially improved since 1954. Then 21% had had earned doctorates whereas in 1964, 50% had doctors degrees. The sabbatical leave program, a tenure system, financial assistance for travel to learned society meetings, and for dues, and other fringe benefits envisioned in 1954 had been achieved before 1964.

83. *Ibid.*, March 12, 1964, pp. 25-28; letter from David K. Allen to all members of the faculty, March 13, 1964; letter from William Ferry to the faculty and staff of Davis and Elkins College, March 16, 1964.

President-elect Gordon E. Hermanson and retiring President David K. Allen with the board of trustees in 1964.

(3) That whereas the *average* Faculty salaries in each rank had been $4,000, $3,360, $3,175, and $2,810 in 1954, the *minimums* for each rank in 1964 were $8,000, $7,000, $5,400, and $4,800.

(4) That despite the progress made, Faculty salaries were far below the national average and below those paid at Bethany and West Virginia Wesleyan and thus that it was essential to acquire a productive endowment of at least five million dollars by 1970 with plans to increase that to seven and one-half million by 1980 if D & E was to become a "quality college with a student body of 750 to 800 students."

(5) That financial aid for students (scholarships and grants-in-aid) was inadequate and that by 1970 "approximately two million dollars of the endowment funds should be used for scholarships and grants to students."

(6) That of the physical plant improvements cited in 1954 as essential, three of the five fire-proof residence halls, the College Union Building, the Library Building (and grants totaling more than $45,000 for books), the renovation of Liberal Arts Hall and Science Hall, the paving of the roads and walks, had all been achieved by 1964, but that still needed were a Chapel-Auditorium, a Fine Arts Building and a Greenhouse.

(7) That the curriculum revisions and the renewal of emphasis on the liberal arts proposed in 1954 had been accomplished by 1964.[84]

Following the completion of routine business, the trustees voted to elect Dr. David K. Allen, president emeritus and to appropriate a substantial sum to help purchase a retirement home for him and Mrs. Allen. Dr. Allen was the first of the eight men who had been presidents of the college to serve until retirement age and the only one to be honored with the title president emeritus. Despite great obstacles and difficulties faced in the early years of his presidency, Dr. David K. Allen and his associates had succeeded in accomplishing most of the major goals established at the beginning—except for the chapel-auditorium and the acquisition of an adequate endowment. More permanent buildings were built, more money was given, a better trained faculty was recruited with far better salaries and fringe benefits, higher standards of admission and eligibility for students, and a curriculum of greater breadth and depth was

---

84. Trustee Minutes, May 6, 1964, pp. 29-33.

developed between 1954 and 1964 than in the preceding half century. There was still much to do in the years ahead, but the way was clear for expansion and innovation in the future as the Allen administration ended.

IX

Years of Expansion and Innovation: 1964-79

Looking back on it fifteen years afterward, one finds the year 1964 to have been of portentous significance in American history. A Civil Rights Act was passed outlawing discrimination in public accommodations and in federally funded projects and establishing an Equal Opportunity Commission. The Twenty-fourth Amendment outlawing poll taxes as a means of preventing citizens from voting in federal elections was ratified. Martin Luther King, Jr., became the youngest man ever to win a Nobel Peace Prize. Riots in Panama resulted in the deaths of twenty-five persons and set in motion negotiations which culminated in the Panama Canal Treaties of 1978. The "War on Poverty" began and the Tonkin Gulf Resolution, which became the basis for unlimited American participation in the Vietnam War, was adopted by the Senate. Lyndon Baines Johnson and Hubert H. Humphrey were elected president and vice-president by a landslide in the 1964 election, a fact which was to mean much in terms of future federal financing for higher education, including both scholarship and loan funds for students and grants and loans for construction of facilities for colleges and universities.

In 1964, D&E was sixty years old. Little notice was taken of that fact, however, and there was no "diamond jubilee" observance. Of greater interest was the first serious effort to establish an honor system. During the 1963-64 academic year, the North Central Self-Study Committee, chaired by Dr. William E. Phipps, and the Student Council, under the leadership of David Kirk and Samuel Dunlap, presidents of the student body in 1963-64 and 1964-65, respectively, drafted an honor code. This was discussed at length in the late spring and early fall of 1964 and seemed to have broad-based support. However, when finally presented to the student body, the plan was rejected by a vote of 80.6 percent against to 19.4 percent in favor.[1] This matter had been of interest to various groups over the years since the early 1920s, but had not before been presented as a realistic proposal. Its defeat in 1964, in large measure by freshman and sophomore votes, was a great disappointment to students, alumni, and faculty who believed that an honor system was desirable on the campus of a Presbyterian college. Not much more success resulted from the continued efforts of the college to get local barbers and beauticians to cease discrimination against blacks by refusing to serve them. However, in time these efforts did bear fruit, whereas in 1979 D&E still did not have an honor system.

Less controversial was the establishment of a "Reading Period" each semester prior to examination week. This allowed time for students to review and reflect on course work before plunging into final tests. In terms of provision for professional development, the initiation of D&E's participation in the activities of the Regional Council for International Education enabled several faculty members in future years to attend summer institutes in Europe and the Far East. The RCIE also funded special area studies programs on the campus, and promoted faculty conferences at the University of Pittsburgh and elsewhere. In addition, as a result of the college's membership, several students were able to spend a Study Year abroad in Switzerland, Austria, and Italy. Also in 1964, under the sponsorship of a group of faculty wives led by Mrs. Charles E. Albert, Mrs. William E. Phipps, Mrs. John Pavlos, and Mrs. Thomas R. Ross, a Student's Wives Club was organized. Arrangements were made for them to meet in faculty homes and for each student wife who wished to do so to enroll as an auditor without charge in one college course per semester.[2]

Most notable of all campus events in 1964 were the retirement of David K. Allen and the election and subsequent inauguration of Gordon E. Hermanson as the ninth president of D&E. Commenting on Dr. Allen's retirement, *The Senator* observed that

1. *The Senator,* February-November 1964, *passim;* November 12, 1964, p. 1; Faculty Minutes, October 5, 1964, p. 14.
2. *The Senator,* September 24, November 25, 1964, p. 1.

Student body president Samuel Dunlap introducing new students to President and Mrs. Hermanson at the faculty reception in 1964. Robert Hermanson, *at left.*

"during President Allen's years of service so many changes have taken place that the College has been transformed both in the physical aspects of the campus and in the quality of its intellectual life."[3] To expand the physical plant, to enlarge the student body, and through innovations to make more attractive the social atmosphere and intellectual life of the campus were among the aims of Gordon E. Hermanson in the summer of 1964 as he began what was to be a presidency exceeded in length only by that of James E. Allen earlier in the century.

A native of Chicago, Gordon Hermanson was educated at Wheaton College and received his divinity school training at New York Biblical Seminary. Subsequently he earned a master's degree from Temple University and studied extensively at Columbia University. Ordained a minister of the Presbyterian Church, U.S.A., he served in churches in New York and Pennsylvania and for three years was director of Youth Work and Christian Education in the French Cameroons, West Africa, for the Commission on Ecumenical Mission and Relations of the Presbyterian Church. He later served as associate field director of the Synod of Pennsylvania and field director of the Board of

3. *Ibid.,* March 19, 1964, p. 1.

Dr. James Witherspoon, chairman of the board of trustees with Dr. Hermanson at the latter's inauguration as president.

Christian Education of the United Presbyterian Church, U.S.A., for four metropolitan New York presbyteries. From 1962 until he came to D&E, he had been Vice-President for Development of Buena Vista College in Storm Lake, Iowa. He and Mrs. Hermanson had a son and daughter in college and a son and daughter in public school at the time they came to Elkins. The younger son, Robert, entered D&E as a freshman in 1964.

In his first address to the faculty on September 4, 1964, President Hermanson paid a gracious tribute to his predecessor and then described the style of leadership he hoped to provide for D&E. Emphasizing a desire for collegiality and cooperation, he asserted that "if the College is to achieve new heights, *we* shall bring it to pass." He stressed his desire for "Christian" and "democratic" principles and procedures and for "openness" and concern for "evaluation" as characteristics of his "style of leadership." In conclusion, he discussed the needs of the college for new sources of income, for finding "more efficient ways to use our resources," and for working cooperatively "towards more closely approximating our goal as a Christian College."[4]

It was an interesting coincidence that in the September during which the sixtieth anniversary of D&E's opening occurred, exactly 600 students registered. This compared with 526 in 1963 and included 377 men and 223 women. Nineteen states and six foreign nations were represented in the student body. The teaching staff (in addition to the dean, registrar, dean of students, dean of women, two librarians, and three AFROTC officers—all of whom taught courses) totaled forty full-time faculty and two part-time instructors. New faculty, in addition to President Hermanson, included Margaret P. Goddin, L. Gregory Myers, Evelyn Crouch, Dr. and Mrs. Jerald Wagener, and the inimitable Han-sheng Lin, a Chinese scholar soon famous for teaching Western "Gee" (as he called his course in freshman history).

Impressive inaugural ceremonies were held on October 15 in connection with the installation of Gordon Hermanson as president of the college. Speakers included Dr. Harold K. Schilling, Dr. Frank H. Caldwell, and Dr. Hubert C. Noble. Honorary degrees were awarded to Dr. Schilling and Dr. Noble as well as to the Reverend Albert A. Leininger, a longtime friend of President Hermanson. Dr. James W. Witherspoon, chairman of the board

---

4. Faculty Minutes, September 4, 1964, p. 4 ff.

of trustees, presided at the ceremonies and the inaugural prayer was offered by Dr. Harold H. Viehman, secretary of the Division of Higher Education of the United Presbyterian Church, U.S.A. An eloquent and inspiring speaker, President Hermanson made a favorable impression in his inaugural address as he had in his September remarks to the faculty.

His topic was "Commitment To Learning" and he began by quoting John Gardner that "Learning is risky business!" and Robert Hutchins that "Education can be dangerous." He then continued by stating:

> I am deeply committed to the conviction that a College is primarily a place for this kind of learning.... Learning is life long! Learning is life encompassing! Learning is exciting! Learning is demanding.
>
> I believe that this kind of dynamic learning demands equally dynamic teaching which shares the same characteristics. I believe that teaching inevitably involves the inculcating of subject matter; the conveying of information; the passing on of man's cultural heritage. I believe that teaching is much more than this: it is inciting to action; it is arousing curiosity; it is inviting to debate; it is motivating to study; it is compelling to think; it develops understanding. This kind of teaching leads to true learning....
>
> I believe in a program of higher education which has its roots deeply set in the liberal arts tradition. I interpret this tradition to be a program of undergraduate study in the basic academic disciplines of literature, history, philosophy, religion, the arts, mathematics, and the sciences. This education must provide opportunities for teaching and for learning at such depth and breadth as will make possible an intellectual maturity which will inseparably join together a love of truth, freedom, and a dedication to social responsibility.

In addition, President Hermanson affirmed his belief in "the private institution of higher education," and in "a program of higher education which is distinctively and uniquely Christian in its purposes." He described a Christian college as "an institution where Christ is existing in the community of Faculty and students—and where there are "Christian concern for the individual" and "opportunities for the enrichment of spiritual life." He concluded his brief but excellent statement with the assertion of his convictions that "institutions of higher education must be responsively related to the needs and the aspirations of the people within the community in which it exists—town, state, and country," and that a program of higher education is enriched by the discovery of channels for "meaningful service."

Suzanne Rose, editor of *The Senator*, wrote an editorial praising the president's speeches and describing him as "a warm, friendly person" who was interested "in the students and their welfare."[5] President and Mrs. Hermanson began entertaining students and faculty in their home in order to get acquainted as quickly as possible and Mrs. Hermanson's fame as a culinary artist par excellence as well as a fine helpmate to her husband soon spread. In 1965, President Hermanson was awarded the honorary Doctor of Divinity degree by Buena Vista College. Later, in 1970, he received an honorary Doctor of Laws from Concord College.

The Spiritual Emphasis Week speaker in the fall of 1964 was Dr. William A. Benfield who had recently returned to his native West Virginia to become pastor of the First Presbyterian Church in Charleston. He subsequently became a member and chairman of the D&E Board of Trustees and later served as moderator of the General Assembly of the Presbyterian Church, U.S. Others who began service on the board of trustees in the mid-sixties or late sixties were Arch Cantrall, John W. Doane, Donald G. Lester, Kenneth Stettler, David L. Francis, David C. Crawford, Mrs. E. I. Dansereau, Robert B. Woodworth II, Nelson Knaggs, James E. Allen, Jr., Lindsay J. Phares, Walter G. Koupal, Alvey B. Rushton, Royce K. McDonald, Jefferson Monroe, Carl W. Channell, L. Newton Thomas, Ralph S. Shepler, Donald G. Miller, Sam R. Hoover, John H. Strock, Frederick P. Stamp, Jr., Henry Gassaway Davis III, Lawrence A. Zwicker, Samuel J. Marshall, D. Reginald Thomas, James R. Jackson and William C. Killgallon. One of President Hermanson's aims was to broaden the membership of the board and to increase the interest of trustees in, and their support of, the college. To a significant degree, he met with marked success in so doing and the financial contributions of individual board members, as well as the assistance of many in enabling the president and Development

---

5. *The Senator*, October 15, 22, 29, 1964, *passim*. The quotations from the inaugural address are from the pamphlet entitled *The Inauguration of Gordon E. Hermanson as Ninth President of Davis and Elkins College: Texts of the Addresses*, Elkins, October 21, 1964, pp. 22-24.

Office to obtain other funds, have greatly increased in the past decade.

In 1964-65, however, the board failed to follow up on the proposals of the "Sixtieth Anniversary Five-Year Advanced Program Committee" for a financial campaign to raise $5 million to $6 million mainly for endowment (see chapter 8). Plausible reasons such as the nation's involvement in war in Vietnam; the loss of board leaders such as Dr. Andrew R. Bird, Jr., chairman of the Long-Range Planning Committee, and Dr. William M. Ferry, president of the board, both of whom moved to other synods in 1964; current financial deficits at the college; and possible conflict with other church-related fund drives, were advanced to justify postponement. Postponement, however, in reality, resulted in abandonment of the plan and so D&E continued to seek to survive in the 1960s and the 1970s as she had in every previous decade, from current income based largely on tuition and with a totally inadequate endowment.

Whether or not the decision not to try to raise funds for endowment was the only realistic option, in view of the circumstances, seemed debatable. Of a certainty it was a grave disappointment to those who had expected that the board would implement the Stevenson Committee report which had been approved on May 6, 1964. It was a major factor, among others, which produced a crisis in confidence on the part of many faculty members by 1966 and interrupted the increasingly good relations between the faculty and the trustees which had been established in the preceding decade. Instead of proceeding with a serious effort to promote a campaign for endowment funds, the board soon set aside the previously adopted goal of attaining a productive endowment of at least $5 million by 1970 to undergird a quality program for an enrollment of 750 to 800 students. Without the participation or approval of the faculty, the board voted to establish our enrollment goals as follows:

1967-68	825 students
1968-69	925 students
1969-70	1025 students
1970-71	1125 students
1971-72	1200 students

It was understood, of course, that the implementation of these goals would be dependent on the concurrent expansion of faculty and facilities needed.[6]

Those who had given long and careful study to the matter in previous years expressed the conviction that there was a grave inconsistency in the board's voting on the one hand "that we continue to emphasize the overall objectives of Davis and Elkins College as . . . a quality liberal arts" institution and that "we accept the objectives of an improved quality of students accepted for admission" and then on the other hand voting to establish the above enrollment goals—goals which many doubted could be achieved short of an "open admissions" policy, if then. No one ought to have objected to seeing the enrollment increase. That was surely essential to survival. It was not the "goals" but the method of fixing them and the implications of willingness to continue the precarious policy of depending too much on student tuition instead of increasing endowment income that caused serious disharmony. Unfortunately, those who sincerely questioned the board's methods and doubted the feasibility of the new enrollment objectives were regarded by some as being mere obstructionists opposed to any change. Soon misunderstandings, feelings of insecurity, personality conflicts between the president and some faculty members, disputes over faculty participation in decision-making vis-a-vis board powers, the general unrest in *academe* characteristic of the mid-sixties, and miscellaneous other matters, often trivial, combined to bring turbulence to the atmosphere at D&E for several years.

It is bootless to dwell on what might have been. If everyone directly involved were apportioned his full share of blame, there would still be some left for distribution among casual sideline observers who reveled in rumormongering. What is of lasting importance is not the transient harm and heartache but that D&E continued to survive and to serve. Inevitably, some very valuable people were lost to the college in the last years of the decade and some became embittered. Others, equally able and loyal to their convictions, remained and served as a stabilizing influence, providing perspective and moderating the tension always generated

---

6. Trustee Executive Committee Minutes, September 21, 1966, p. 2, and Appendix "B," Trustee Minutes, October 1966.

by the necessity for maintaining continuity of purpose in a time of change.

During 1964-65 the faculty voted to require each student accepted for admission to read three paperback books during the summer prior to their matriculation and be prepared to discuss them during orientation meetings in the fall semester. Recognizing the needs of some high school graduates who showed potential for college work but who might be handicapped because of deficiencies in English or mathematics, D&E also established a summer "College Preparatory Program" for prospective college students. A forerunner of the later College Orientation Program ("C.O.P.") and of the William James House Program, this was an effort to provide "special remedial training in the mechanics of English expression, writing, reading, and mathematics." For each group of twenty-five students there were two English instructors and one mathematics instructor as well as two "mature student residence counselors to live in the residence halls with the students, help with study problems and with the recreational activities."[7]

Coach Greg Myers with the 1964 swimming team.

7. Faculty Minutes, November 2, 1964, p. 19 ff.

Although the 1964-65 season's records in varsity soccer and basketball were mediocre, the women's hockey team coached by Jean Tallman was undefeated and the swimming team won all but one of their meets. Ed Jones, a freshman swimmer, broke the conference record in the five-hundred-yard free style race. D&E's debate team, coached by Ed Moore (since both Dr. Dow and Mrs. "F" were on sabbatical leave), won trophies for the "Best Team" and "Best Negative Team" in the tournament. The negative team (Michael Harris and Dennis Weidner) won eleven of the twelve contests entered during the year. Stowell V. Kessler and Barbara Mercer, the affirmative team, were less successful, but overall, the record was excellent.[8]

Three D&E students, Stowell V. Kessler, William Abraham, and Glenn Long, went to Selma, Alabama, in March to participate in a rally supporting voting rights for Negroes and were among those chased out of town by police using cattle prods.[9] There was increasing student interest both in the civil rights movement and in the Vietnam War policies. Also, during the year, the Circle K Club received its national charter and became an active campus service organization.

In July 1965, Captain Edward Anaka, a popular instructor in air science, was killed in an airplane crash. He was the third D&E AFROTC faculty member to die in an air accident in six years.

During the summer, new faculty members were appointed to replace those who retired or who were to be on leave in 1965-66 and three were added to the regular faculty. The most notable of these were Dr. Dorothy F. Roberts, associate professor of history and political science, and Dr. Donald M. Walter, assistant professor of religion and assistant to the dean of students. Dr. Roberts, a graduate of Park College with a Ph.D. from the University of Chicago and a LL.B. from Columbia University, later became the first chairman of the Department of Political Science. An outstanding teacher, much in demand as a guest lecturer both on and off the campus, she also served as advisor to pre-law students and founded the Political Science Club. Dr. Walter earned his undergraduate degree at Lafayette College and his advanced degrees at Princeton Theological Seminary. A distinguished scholar, writer, and traveler, he taught Greek and

8. The 1965 *Senator, passim; The Senator*, March 25, 1965, p. 1.
9. *The Senator*, March 25, 1965, p. 4.

Dr. Donald Walter with some students.

Dr. Gloria M. Payne in class.

geography as well as religion and various interdisciplinary courses. Both have served the college well for the past fifteen years and have been leaders in the local and state work of the American Association of University Professors.

It was at this time, too, that Miss Mabel Woodward, an alumna of D&E and a retired high school teacher, began to assist in the library and that Gerald L. Morrison ("Gerry") took charge of the Campus Post Office. Gloria M. Payne, who had begun her teaching career at D&E in 1945, was appointed chairman of the Department of Economics and Business, a position she had held on an acting basis for three years. Under her leadership, that department grew to have the largest number of student majors in the college and to offer several important programs both for degree candidates and for those wanting one or two years of special training. She also made the Beta Alpha Beta annual awards dinner an outstanding community event and her initiative in developing the tradition of selecting an outstanding businessman and secretary in Elkins each year to honor at the banquet has done much to promote good "town-gown" relationships. By 1979, she had served on the faculty longer than anyone, having held each rank from instructor to professor.

In the years from 1963 to 1969 the D&E faculty, in terms of education, ability, and experience, was the best overall in the history of the college. In 1965-66, for example, 50 percent of the faculty engaged in teaching held earned doctorates. Except for one Sc.D. and one Ed.D., all of the doctorates were Ph.D.'s and most had been earned at some of the most prestigious graduate schools such as Harvard, Princeton, Cornell, Chicago, Virginia, Carnegie, Duke, Minnesota, Saint Andrews, Nebraska, Southern California, New York, Rochester, and Pennsylvania. The other faculty, with the exception of one, held master's degrees and most had extensive graduate work beyond that.

The student enrollment at the beginning of the fall semester in 1965 totaled 689 (394 men and 295 women), with 194 from Pennsylvania, 144 from New Jersey, and 87 from West Virginia. Construction of New Women's Hall, on the hill between Gribble Hall and Halliehurst, was begun that fall, but living quarters on campus were inadequate in 1965. Thus, 30 freshmen men were housed in a former funeral home on Randolph Avenue—promptly named "Mortuary Hall" or "The Morgue" by the students—under the supervision of Dr. Donald Walter as "housefather." A score more were quartered in the Tygart Hotel and more than 90 roomed in private homes in Elkins.

In early October *The Senator,* edited by Elizabeth Leahy, took an informal poll of campus opinion on the war in Vietnam. The report stated: "We did not find any student or Faculty member who was happy about our role, but most agreed that it was a necessary evil which must be engaged in." It is interesting to note, however, that two outstanding faculty members, who were quoted, were well ahead of the nation in seeing the error of America's involvement in that conflict. Professor William E. Phipps stated "I lament that we did not learn from the French the futility of fighting to protect the Vietnamese from domination by Communist leadership inasmuch as there is little evidence that South Vietnam has any interest in democratic reforms." Professor James E. Dow asserted that "unless we are prepared to fight a major war of extermination, we shall eventually have to come to terms with what those guerillas call communism ... I do not think we should fight a war of any kind without a clearly defined and attainable goal. I do not see such a goal in Vietnam."[10]

Other major topics of student interest during the year appear to have been fraternity and sorority discrimination against Negroes, the college rules against use of alcoholic beverages, and required attendance at convocation. The faculty was concerned with the student attrition rate between the sophomore and junior years, with the necessity of revising the air science curriculum as a result of an Air Force decision to provide ROTC training only for juniors and seniors who desired to earn a commission, and with the implications of changing relationships between the trustees and faculty and in the administrative structure.[11]

In May and October of 1966, the trustees revised their by-laws to provide that the treasurer of the board should be a board member instead of the business manager of the college, redefining the method of selection of business manager and dean, changing the title of the academic dean from dean of the college to dean of the faculty, making the dean of student affairs responsible to the president instead of to the dean, making the director of admissions responsible to the dean of student affairs, and creating a

10. *The Senator,* October 5, 1965, pp. 1, 4.
11. Faculty Minutes, January 24-November 7, 1966, *passim.*

"President's Cabinet" to be composed of the president, the dean of the faculty, the business manager, the dean of student affairs, and the vice-president for development.[12]

The position of vice-president for development which had been vacant for two years was filled by the appointment of William F. Engert in the spring of 1966. His staff included Harold R. Henry, associate director of development, and John Frost, the newly appointed director of public relations, who has for nearly fifteen years provided continuity in the Development Office and rendered outstanding service in whatever position he has been assigned.

New faculty appointed in 1966 included Dr. Ellis Gale Shields as chairman of the English department to succeed Dr. Knox Wilson, who had reached retirement age, and Joseph Daniels who was added to the English faculty as an instructor. Both of these men remained for several years. An interesting addition to the Student Affairs staff was David Fyock who (with his delightful Chinese wife) served as residence counselor in Allen Hall and later as dean of men.

A major interest in the 1966-67 year was the first Founders Day observance. Designed to commemorate the founding of the college and to honor the Davis and Elkins families, this ceremony, conceived by President Hermanson, became an annual event. Thomas Davis Lee, grandson of Senator Davis and nephew of Senator Elkins, and his gracious wife, Sue, were present to represent the founders. The first Founders Day award was given to Dr. Charles E. Albert, professor emeritus of physics and engineering. An honorary degree was conferred on Dr. James W. Witherspoon who had recently retired as chairman of the board of trustees after serving nineteen years as a faithful board member. Following an address by Dr. Benfield at convocation, the first Founders Day was concluded in the afternoon by the dedication of the new $550,000 Women's Residence Hall. *The Senator* noted Dean Ross's comment praising the idea of the Founders Day ceremony and quoting Edmund Burke that "people will not look forward to posterity who never look backward to their ancestors."[13]

Perhaps of greater interest than that generated by Founders

---

12. Trustee Minutes, May 1966-October 1966, *passim.*
13. *The Senator,* September 27, 1966, p. 1.

Dr. Hermanson greeting Vice-President Hubert H. Humphrey in front of Halliehurst.

Day, was the visit of Vice-President Hubert Humphrey to the campus in October to participate in the crowning of the queen of the Forest Festival. President and Mrs. Hermanson entertained Vice-President and Mrs. Humphrey and Governor Hulett Smith, as well as Senator Randolph and other distinguished guests and senior faculty members at a luncheon in the faculty lounge in Benedum Hall prior to the coronation ceremonies.[14]

The following week, the convocation speaker was Senator Joseph D. Tydings of Maryland who "enthralled" the campus, according to Charles Potter, *The Senator* editor, a student from Maryland, who specialized in interviewing statesmen.[15] Potter, later a student body president, was one of the ablest of the editors of *The Senator*. He frequently devoted a whole page of the campus newspaper to recording a personal interview with some newsworthy political personality such as Congressman Gerald R.

14. *Ibid.,* October 4, 1966, p. 1.
15. *Ibid.,* October 18, 1966, p. 1.

Ford, Governor Spiro Agnew, or Senators Jennings Randolph, Robert Byrd, Mark Hatfield, Daniel Brewster, and Edward Brooke.

President Hermanson was able to announce a fifty-thousand-dollar gift to D&E from the United Presbyterian Church of Wheeling in October of 1966. This was the first of many gifts he would secure in the years to come. The income from this was designated to be used for scholarships for West Virginia students.[16]

In November, Lance Pledger won the state cross-country meet for D&E. Pledger, a deeply religious young athlete, hoped to qualify to represent the United States at the next Olympic games, and he trained constantly throughout his years at D&E. Although he never achieved his greatest ambition, he did bring fame to his alma mater as a result of his achievements each year as a runner. He was named conference "Runner of the Year in 1966."[17]

Although the 1966 soccer team, coached by Jack McDonald, did not win the conference title, three members were named to the first WVIAC All-Conference Soccer team. They were Francois Muyumba, a popular African student; Ed Jones, and Joe Carroll. This inspired Dr. Hunter Davis to select a "D&E All Star Team" from among those who had played since the college had first participated in varsity soccer competition. His selections included Dave Clapp, James Douglas, Dennis Bye, Joe Carroll, "Sandy" Wright, James Bushyeager, Jim Hill, Dave Herron, Dave Vivian, Al Freimauer, Jim Fishel, Bob Lennox, Mike Sedlak, Andy Maros, and Francois Muyumba[18]

The major dramatic production of the year was *Candida*, directed by Claire Fiorentino, and starring Patty Roy, Craig Rupp, Jane Elliot, Jim Enterline, John Davidson, and Nick Morgan. It was even more successful than *Fantasticks*, produced the preceding year.[19]

What was hoped would be the first of a series of annual "International Weeks" was observed in early December. The emphasis in 1966 was on Russia and speakers included the Reverend John

16. *Ibid.*, October 25, 1966, p. 1.
17. *Ibid.*, November 15, 22, 1966; May 14, 1968, p. 4.
18. *Ibid.*, November 22, 1966, p. 4.
19. *Ibid.*, December 13, 1966, p. 1.

Nehrebecki, rector of the Orthodox Christian Church of Christ in New Jersey, an alumnus of D&E; Professor Tatiana Jardetzky, a native of Russia; and Dr. James Bailey, a professor of Russian from Michigan who had recently toured the Soviet Union. *The Senator*, usually critical of convocation programs, had an editorial commending these presentations.[20] Later in the year, the secretary of the French Embassy visited the campus for two days, Charles Potter published an interview with the Venezuelan Ambassador to the U.S.; Dr. Tetsuro Saski of Tohoku University in Japan spoke at convocation; and Sukich Nimmanheminda, Thailand's Ambassador to the U.S., was awarded an honorary degree at special ceremonies in Benedum Hall at which he delivered a major address.[21] Part of the credit for the unusual number of outstanding concerts, lectures, and other programs was due to the work of the Special Programs Committee chaired by Dr. Dorothy Roberts, and part was due to the efforts of the Campus Social Committee which as *The Senator* editor stated "has soared to new successes . . . under its new chairman, Don Baldwin."[22]

In April 1967, President Hermanson was honored at the Temple University Founders Day dinner in Philadelphia by being given the Conwell School of Theology Alumni Award. This award was presented annually to the alumnus "who has made an outstanding contribution to the university, the Alumni Association, the community or his profession."[23]

During the same month, a chapter of Phi Beta Lambda was established at D&E. Sponsored by Professor Gloria Payne, this organization is the college division of the Future Business Leaders of America.

In May, eight D&E students were invited to the White House to discuss the Vietnam War with presidential adviser John P. Roche. Those participating included Charles Potter and Stowell V. Kessler, who made the arrangements, and student body president Robert Baird, Norman Christiansen, Anne Hickling, Susan Hillick, Carl Wartenburg, and Daniel Daniels.[24]

20. *Ibid.*, December 13, 1966, pp. 2, 3.
21. *Ibid.*, February 7, May 9, 1967, *passim*.
22. *Ibid.*, February 14, 1967, p. 2.
23. *Ibid.*, April 11, 1967, p. 1.
24. *Ibid.*, May 9, 1967, p. 1.

The renovated "Ice House."

It was during this same spring that President Hermanson conceived the idea that the old Halliehurst ice house might be renovated and made into a "unique student gathering place for conversation, relaxation and perhaps entertainment." Dr. Nelson Knaggs, then a trustee of D&E and the senior vice-president of the Hilton-Davis Chemical Company, a noted explorer, photographer, and writer, immediately envisioned the possibilities and took the lead in developing the project. His imaginative suggestions, dynamic leadership, and generous financial support brought the dream into a reality. President Hermanson, Bill Engert, and others provided local leadership and the Benedum Foundation awarded a grant to help with funding. A student committee led by Judy Eadson, Russell Allen (later to be a trustee), Jim Rimmer, Sandra Love, and Ed Alexander organized a "Project Ice House" Committee to raise money from the student body.[25] In due time, the reconstruction was completed, a

---

25. *Ibid.*, May 2, 1967; November 12, 1969, p. 1; Trustee Minutes, October 23, 1968, p. 103 ff.

Dr. Nelson Knaggs presenting a gift to President
and Mrs. David K. Allen.

plaque honoring Dr. Knaggs was installed, and the Ice House has become a popular, attractive, and much used campus facility. In 1968, Dr. Knaggs was the donor of a fine 16 mm Bolex camera which enabled the Development Office to prepare film clips of college events for use by television stations. The following year, he obtained a ten-thousand-dollar gift from Sterling Drug Company to help finance the Science Center construction. Dr. Knaggs was also influential in getting the trustees to provide more financial support for the college's intercollegiate athletic program in the early 1970s and has been a generous contributor of both ideas and money.

A new Long-Range Planning Committee held its first meeting in the spring of 1967. David L. Francis was named chairman and members included trustees, churchmen, businessmen, and faculty members. The committee was created "to recommend and help chart precise goals for a long range plan of development." Richard Dober, a campus planner from Cambridge, Massachusetts, Richard Troxell of the College Building Advisory Service from Chicago, and Richard Bennett, a Morgantown architect, participated in the meeting. Subsequently, Dober prepared a campus plan suggesting the location of future residence halls on the ridge to the left of the Observatory, a chapel in the center of the former Soccer Field, and the Science Hall and Campus Center in the areas where they all were later erected.[26]

During the summer of 1967, the Benedum Foundation awarded the college a matching grant to be used for renovating the Dining Hall. New furniture, carpeting, drapes, and light fixtures as well as repainting, were completed by the end of the Christmas holidays. The first D&E computer—a teletype "hook-up" to a large computer at Carnegie-Mellon University—was installed that summer. Dr. Jerald Wagener developed a course in computer programming which was first offered in the fall semester.

Evan R. Kek who served as full-time business manager longer than anyone else.

Having completed more than a decade of distinguished service as registrar, Dr. Anna Dale Kek retired from that position on June 30, 1967, to devote full time to her duties as chairman of the Language Department and of the Educational Policies Committee and to teaching Latin and English. Later in the year, Evan Kek resigned as business manager and after he and Dr. Kek returned from a spring and summer sabbatical leave in 1968, he served as associate professor of history until his retirement in the mid-1970s. Charles Potter, editor of *The Senator*, devoted an editorial entitled "THANKS TO THE KEKS" enumerating the contributions they had made to D&E in the preceding eleven years. His commendation of Mrs. Kek's "accuracy and efficiency" as registrar and of the "smoothness with which the office operated" under her administration was well

---

26. *Ibid.*, April 25, 1967, p. 4.

Dr. Anna Dale Kek, registrar, and Dr. Edward V. Perkins, dean of students, join President Hermanson and Professor Jesse Reed in greeting President Omano of Kenya.

deserved as was his observation that "through Mr. Kek's management of the financial aspects, Davis and Elkins College has been able to grow and assume financial stability."[27]

Calvin R. Hobart, who had come to the college to direct an "Upward Bound" program (which did not materialize), succeeded Dr. Kek as registrar. Another new staff officer who came in 1967 was the Reverend Nevin E. Kendell as associate director of development. At first, he was in charge of developing support for D&E in the Presbyterian churches. Subsequently, he became the most successful of all the vice-presidents for development. He has the distinction of serving longer in that important position and of obtaining more funds than all of his predecessors combined. In

---

27. *Ibid.*, September 26, 1967, p. 2.

1979, he was the senior member of President Hermanson's cabinet and one whose value would be difficult to overestimate.

Ralph R. Booth returned to the faculty as associate professor of chemistry after an eleven-year absence during which he had pursued graduate studies, taught at other colleges and served as an editor for *Chemical Abstracts*. Subsequently, he became chairman of the Department of Chemistry and served several years as registrar. Of his work as registrar, President Hermanson once remarked "Ralph Booth is one of those persons who manages to find 25 hours in every day and 8 days in every week. . . . He always gives careful and cautious evaluation of any situation, and we have learned to respect his viewpoints."[28]

Nevin Kendell, vice-president for development.

Another former instructor who returned in 1967 was L. Gregory Myers. He was appointed chairman of the Department of Physical Education and soccer coach. New faculty included Dr. Teresa J. Minguez, a colorful Cuban who began her D&E career as a Spanish teacher, but was soon appointed adviser to foreign students, a position in which she excelled as *"Mama"* to scores of students from South America, Africa, Asia, and Europe. Dr. Lloyd M. Elrod came to D&E after a distinguished career in teaching and research at Westminster College and Northwestern University and has continued to serve as a pro-

Professor Ralph R. Booth

28. Trustee Minutes, October 24, 1975, p. 274 ff.

fessor of biology at D&E for more than a dozen years. Several others who had shorter terms of service joined the faculty in 1967. Among them were Dr. Elaine Ann Dittmar in chemistry, Dr. Robert Wilson, chairman of the psychology department, Emery Krizan, James R. Johnston, Monroe Prellop and David Mikkelson in languages, Carl L. Hartman in physical education and coach of basketball, and Robert Painter as instructor in sociology.

During the summer of 1967, Tom Daniels, who had succeeded Ellery Hinkle as superintendent of maintenance, and his staff converted the entry hall in the front of the Liberal Arts Hall into an attractive carpeted area known as "Founders Hall." A suggestion of President Hermanson, this hall featured portraits of Senators Davis and Elkins with bronze plaques summarizing their careers and glass display cases containing various items belonging to the founding families.

After having been significantly decreased in 1965-66, the cumulative deficit rose to an excess of $101,000 by the beginning of the 1967-68 academic year. Although student enrollment increased by 52 from the preceding year, the September registration of 788 was short of the 825 projected. Despite the discouraging financial situation, 1967-68 was a year of progress and achievement.

The second Founders Day brought Henry Gassaway Davis III, a grandson of Senator Davis, and Mrs. Charles Kelly, a granddaughter of Senator Elkins, as well as Thomas Davis Lee, and other members of Davis and Elkins families to the campus—some for the first time. The award was given to Dr. J. Howard Anderson, longtime trustee of the college, and the principal speaker was James F. Oates, chairman of the Board of the Equitable Life Assurance Company.[29]

Parents Day was well attended and it was in 1967 that the Elkins Chamber of Commerce established the tradition of sponsoring a breakfast in the armory for parents and students.

Later that fall, the Reverend George Ogilvie, who had succeeded Dr. Warner DuBose, Jr., as minister of the Davis Memorial Presbyterian Church, was called to a church in Richmond. A great pastor and loyal friend of D&E as well as a distinguished churchman who served on the General Assembly's

29. *The Senator,* September 26, 1967, p. 1; October 3, 1967, p. 1.

Board of World Missions, George Ogilvie is the only minister known to have refused an honorary degree from D&E. His humility was such that he could not believe that he deserved the honor. To replace Mr. Ogilvie, the Davis Memorial Church called the Reverend Douglas Oldenburg who began his fruitful ministry in Elkins in December 1967. Like all of his predecessors, Douglas Oldenburg took great interest in the college and ministered to many students.

Two important new campus organizations were established in 1967-68. Alpha Phi Omega, the national service fraternity, chartered its Tau Alpha Chapter at D&E in October. The next month, the West Virginia Alpha Chapter of Alpha Chi, a national honorary fraternity, was installed by the president of the national council. The student body voted on the issue of joining the National Student Association and defeated a motion to do so by a vote of 320 to 169 after a long debate.[30]

A faculty decision of the preceding year to establish a Department of Sociology was implemented and a major in that field was developed. In addition, the faculty during 1967-68, adopted recommendations which provided for qualified students to participate in the honors program in science at Argonne National Laboratory, in the semester in the arts program at Drew University, in a cooperative pre-medical technology program with Broaddus Hospital School of Medical Technology, and for broadening the participation in the cooperative pre-forestry program at Duke University. It was during that year also that the Educational Policies Committee, chaired by Dr. William E. Phipps, proposed the new academic calendar providing two twelve-week semesters, and a six-week winter session. This was implemented in 1969. It offered such advantages as ending the fall semester just before the Christmas recess so that there was no "lame duck" session between Christmas and first semester examinations and a winter session long enough to permit students either to complete traditional courses or to engage in experimental courses, off-campus projects, overseas study, or independent study.[31]

In January 1968, Kenneth A. White, Jr., succeeded Evan Kek as business manager. An able and experienced young man, he had

30. *Ibid.*, October 24, November 21, 1967, *passim.*
31. Faculty Minutes, April 22, May 13, 1968, *passim.*

previously served as comptroller at Bethel College in Saint Paul and as director of finance at Florida Presbyterian College.[32] Shortly afterward, Harry Thompson was appointed comptroller in the business office, succeeding Stanley Koon, and beginning a relationship with the college which lasted eleven years.

Acting on a recommendation from President Hermanson, the trustees voted to permit each board committee to meet with three students and three faculty representatives prior to each regular board meeting. This policy was implemented at the May meeting in 1968 and with minor modifications has been continued as a means of facilitating open discussion of matters of general interest.[33]

Although no promotions in rank and only token salary increases could be made in 1967-68 because of the stringent financial situation, only two faculty members resigned at the end of the year and both of them for reasons unrelated to finance. Dr. Cullop accepted an opportunity to teach at the graduate school level and Professor Odor resigned to be with her family in Virginia. Professors Roberts and Evan Kek took responsibility for the courses Dr. Cullop had offered and at the president's request, Dean Ross resumed the departmental chairmanship which Dr. Cullop had held for the preceding three years. Russell Crouse, who had married a D&E graduate, succeeded Miss Odor as assistant professor of education.

In the spring semester of 1968, the college began an experiment which permitted students to choose any twelve of the nineteen convocation programs scheduled for the spring semester. Student opposition to required attendance at convocation had increased greatly during the late 1960s and with the larger numbers to be accommodated, the gymnasium seemed more than ever to be an inadequate setting for worship services, lectures, and other programs.[34]

Regardless of the problems resulting from lack of a comfortable auditorium, the college, through the Special Programs Committee, the Campus Social Committee, and the efforts of individuals, provided a number of very interesting speakers in the late 1960s. Among the most popular were "Jay" Rockefeller;

32. *The Senator,* January 9, 1968, p. 1.
33. Trustee Minutes, October 18, 1967; May 15, 1968, *passim.*
34. *Ibid.,* May 14, 1968, p. 80 ff.

Dr. Dorothy F. Roberts and Judge Robert Maxwell join student body president Charles Potter and President Hermanson in welcoming Senators Randolph and Gale McGee.

Senator Gale McGee; Congressman Arch Moore; William D. Snodgrass, a Pulitzer Prize-winning poet; Dr. Ernest Gordon, author of *Through the Valley of the Kwae*; Dr. George Buttrick and Dr. David Buttrick, and Lionel Wiggam (who had lectured here in earlier years); Dr. James E. Allen, U.S. Commissioner of Education; and various outstanding musical groups.

In May 1968, the faculty revised the faculty committees by abolishing five committees and reorganizing the others. The name of the Administrative Committee was changed to Executive Committee and a new Student Affairs Committee with five student members and six faculty members was created. Other new committees were a Faculty Enrichment Committee, a Committee on Graduate Study and Leadership identification, and an International Education Committee.

At its spring meeting, the board of trustees adopted a recommendation of the Development Committee that a campaign to raise $1.5 million for D&E be conducted in the synods. Of this $1 million was to be for a chapel-auditorium, $350,000 for endowment for maintenance of the building, and $150,000 for a student aid fund. This had already been approved by the Joint Councils of the Synods. Subsequently, the Development Office staff was reorganized and enlarged. Nevin Kendell was promoted to vice-president succeeding Bill Engert on July 1, the latter having resigned to accept a post at Alice Lloyd College. Harold Henry also resigned as of July 1 to return to teaching and Tharon Jack, an alumnus, was appointed director of alumni affairs, and later, associate director of development. Two ministers, C. Cecil Rhoades and Kenneth A. Burris, Jr., were given short-term appointments as associate directors of development to assist with fund raising in the church campaign. This campaign was carried forward with vigor. The members of the board of trustees agreed to establish a goal of $300,000 as the amount they would give to the fund drive and that 100 percent of the members would participate.

As has been noted, ten years earlier, in the Christian Higher Education Fund Campaign, the college had sought from its church constituency funds for the construction of a library, residence hall and chapel-auditorium. The proceeds of the campaign had been sufficient only for the construction of a library and residence hall. When the Chapel-Auditorium Fund Campaign was mounted in 1968 there was some resistance among prospective donors whose participation in the earlier campaign had been based primarily on their interest in the construction of a chapel-auditorium. In retrospect, as Nevin Kendell has pointed out, it may be fortunate that plans for a chapel-auditorium in 1958 were not realized. The plan at that time had been to construct a single large facility that could be used for worship and for all other purposes involving a large gathering. Had this plan been implemented, the college would have been saddled with a facility that would be well-adapted neither for worship, nor for other purposes. Although college officials were still thinking in terms of one large facility when the Chapel-Auditorium Fund Campaign got under way, those plans were soon modified to provide for a separate small chapel that would be appropriate for voluntary worship and for the construction of an auditorium as a separate structure. It probably was fortunate that these facilities were constructed only after it had become clear that compulsory large gatherings were largely a thing of the past, and that worship on the part of the college community, as elsewhere, would be a voluntary matter.

The original goal of $1.5 million included funds for financial aid. However, during the period when the campaign was conducted the college also realized a substantial increase in current operating gift income, sufficient to fund the financial aid program, so that the entire proceeds of the campaign were used for the chapel which was built in 1972 and the auditorium (the latter a part of the Hermanson Campus Center completed in 1976). The financial goal of the campaign was achieved with the raising of approximately $1 million from the church constituency and more than $500,000 from other sources.[35]

In late September of 1968, the third annual Founders Day award was given to Henry Gassaway Davis III, a grandson of the Senator and himself a generous benefactor and trustee of D&E. Shortly before this event, ground was broken for the construction of a $650,000 men's residence hall near the Observatory. The design of this building was a departure from the conventional dormitory as it consisted of three three-story brick buildings joined by a balcony and connected by covered patios. Plans were also being made to construct a somewhat larger residence hall on the same ridge to the north and a grant of $1,055,000 had been obtained from the Department of Housing and Urban Development to finance it.[36] When completed, these building complexes were named "International" and "Presidential."

Mrs. Charles Kelly, granddaughter of Senator Elkins, with Thomas Davis Lee, *right*, and Henry Gassaway Davis III, grandsons of Senator Davis.

During the year, the long awaited completion of the third floor extension of the library building was begun. President Hermanson, with the aid of Senator Randolph, obtained a forty-thousand-dollar grant from the Benedum Foundation which was matched by an additional eighty thousand dollars from other sources, to finance this improvement. Inasmuch as the library collection had

---

35. *Ibid.*, May 15, October 23, 1968, pp. 85-98; memorandum from Nevin Kendell to Thomas R. Ross, August 20, 1979.

36. *The Senator*, September 18, 1968, pp. 3, 4.

increased to more than 51,000 volumes and enrollment in the fall of 1968 totaled 843 students, the additional space was essential. A committee also began work on plans for a new science center but money was not yet available for more buildings that year. A grant from trustee David Francis and his mother enabled the improvement of athletic fields on the back campus near Harpertown.[37]

Although the 1967 soccer team was only modestly successful, Joseph Carroll, D&E's co-captain was named to the All-South Soccer Team—the only player from the WVIAC to be selected for the squad which was composed of players from both NCAA and NAIA institutions. Carroll had been chosen for the All-WVIAC Team for two consecutive years.[38] In 1968, Coach Myers's "booters" were undefeated in the soccer season. Furthermore, they won the District Six championship and then won the NIAI championship at Quincy, Illinois—thus becoming the college's first national championship team. During the season, Rildo Ferreira broke Dave Vivian's 13 goal season to establish a new D&E record of 14 goals. Ferreira and William ("Scotty") Smyth were named to the first team of the All-American soccer squad for 1968. Smyth received the added distinction of being named "Most Valuable Player" in the NAIA tournament. Four players were placed on the All-South squad: Bill Nuttall, Joe Donnelly, Rildo Ferreira, and "Scotty" Smyth. Other members of D&E's first national championship team were John Caracciolo, Hans Wango, Al Grimm, Jim Caulfield, Ekong Etuknwa, William Glenn, Tom Wheeler, John Hutchinson, Jim Semler, Charles Straw, Steve Fletcher, Allan Blaise, Bob Wolfe, Bill Miller, Bob Fitting, Doug Amtsberg, Stu Penman, Tom Martin, and Lew Atkinson.[39]

There was much interest in the presidential election in 1968. Vice-President Humphrey, having visited the campus in 1966, was favorably remembered by juniors and seniors and many faculty members, and the student newspaper supported him (to the displeasure of supporters of Richard Nixon).

Both faculty and students in considerable numbers participated actively in community efforts, led by Douglas Oldenburg

---

37. *Ibid.*, September 25; October 2, 16; November 20, 1968, *passim.*
38. *Ibid.*, January 9, 1969, p. 61.
39. *Ibid.*, January 5, May 21, 1969, *passim.*

The 1968 NAIA National Soccer champions. *Back row:* G. Myers, coach; manager; W. Glenn, A Blaise, W. Miller, R. Fitting, D. Amtsberg, S. Penman, W. Nuttall; manager. *Middle row:* J. Donnally, T. Martin, W. Smyth, T. Wheeler, J. Hutchinson, J. Semler, C. Straw, S. Fletcher, H. Wango, L. Atkinson. *Front row:* A. Grimm, R. Wolfe, J. Caracciolo, J. Carroll (captain), R. Ferreira, J. Caulfield, E. Etuknwa.

and others, to help pass a school levy for Randolph County. The faculty voted to authorize the dean to appoint a special committee to work for the levy and the student body president, William Duncan, headed a student committee for a similar purpose. Dr. Phipps was appointed to head the Faculty Coordinating Committee and faculty members contributed more than four hundred dollars to finance its work. *The Senator* published pro-levy articles, letters, and editorials throughout November and early December. Success crowned these efforts and the college had on this occasion, at least, exemplified that ideal expressed in President Hermanson's inaugural address when he had said "the problems of the community must become the problems of the institution."[40]

In the spring of 1969, the faculty voted to change the comprehensive examination program by moving the oral phase to the junior year and administering the written exams during the winter session of the senior year. The calendar was revised to provide for a fourteen-week fall semester, a six-week winter session,

---

40. *Ibid.*, November 6, December 11, 1968, *passim;* Faculty Minutes, October 9, 1968; January 13, 1969, *passim.*

274

and a fourteen-week spring semester with a minimum of 750 minutes of class sessions as the basis for a semester hour of credit. Modifications in the core curriculum to provide greater flexibility in meeting requirements in religion and philosophy, mathematics, and English were approved as was a reorganization of the chemistry major to provide for three options. During 1968-69, a Faculty Committee (Professors Phipps, chairman; Reed, Roberts, Shields, and Ross, *ex officio*) prepared a faculty constitution which delineated the then existing role and the duties and rights of the faculty. Innovations included the creation of a committee or committees to make recommendations relative to the appointment or nomination of committee membership, the provision for electing some committees, and the addition of students to faculty committees concerned with academic and social policies on which they were not already represented. The constitution was adopted by the faculty without a dissenting vote and subsequently approved by the trustees, as were changes in the trustees' by-laws which reflected the new provisions of the constitution and divided the board's Education Committee into an Academic Affairs Committee and a Student Affairs Committee.[41]

As a result of the serious efforts to control expenditures, the current fund showed a surplus of $35,640 for the fiscal year 1967-68 instead of an anticipated deficit of $30,259. Thus it was possible to promote seven faculty in the spring of 1969 and to provide for increases in salaries, student aid funds, and other areas for 1969-70.[42]

In addition to the loss of Dr. Knox Wilson who died during the Easter recess in 1969, D&E's faculty suffered attrition due to resignations in 1969. The result was the appointment of several very able faculty members to fill the vacancies. Many of the faculty "Class of 1969" were still serving in 1979. Among those who came that year were Dr. Nelson Bard and Professor Douglas D. Oleson, who respectively succeeded Dr. James E. Dow in the History Department and as director of the library; Dr. Phillips V. Brooks and Dr. Trevor Owen who replaced Dr. Hunter Davis and Dr. Wilson in English; and Dr. John Russell Wilson, succeeding

---

41. Faculty Minutes, January 13, May 12, 1969, *passim;* Trustee Minutes, April 30, 1969, pp. 108-9.

42. Trustee Minutes, October 23, 1968; April 30, 1969, *passim.*

Dr. Walter Hartley as chairman of the Music Department. Will Gartmann in German; Harold Blankenship in education; Dennis Lindberg in sociology; W. Russell Studenmund in business, and Claire Wilson in library science, also came in 1969. Others who remained for briefer periods were Stanley Hall as professor of sociology, Dr. John C. Biddle in mathematics, and Dr. James S. McKnight who succeeded Dr. Wagener in physics. Kenneth S. Nelson, who had been serving as dean of men was named as acting dean of Student Affairs replacing Dean Perkins who resigned to devote his full time to his work in the Department of Education. In reporting Dean Perkins's resignation to the trustees, President Hermanson expressed regret at losing him from the administrative staff and observed that under Dr. Perkins's leadership, "all aspects of our Student Personnel Services have been expanded."[43]

Knowing that Dr. Hunter Davis was leaving at the end of the academic year, the soccer team presented him with a plaque and a D&E athletic jacket "for being the number one fan of the D&E soccer team" since 1961. Five D&E athletes were included in the 1969 edition of outstanding College Athletes of America. They were George Burke Kimber, Lance Pledger, Joe Carroll, William Smyth, and Rildo Ferreira.[44]

A note of discord sounded at the time of the trustees meeting in the spring of 1969. A statement signed by 645 students was presented to the board in support of a *Senator* editorial by Donald W. Baldwin expressing concern over certain college policies which, in some cases, students did not understand. Although the 1960s were marked by student riots and demonstrations elsewhere, the D&E students were well behaved and in no case disruptive. They were serious and sincere and when explanations were offered in answer to their criticism, they were generally sympathetic and understanding. Probably they were correct in their belief that "in *loco parentis*" type rules prohibiting the use of alcohol by students, regulating residence hall "hours" for co-eds, etc., were out-moded and that communication problems needed to be solved. Their concern about admission standards, the student-faculty ratio, the functioning of the Student Affairs and Registrar's offices and the need for more classroom

43. *Ibid.,* October 24, 1969, p. 136 ff; *The Senator,* October 1, 1979, p. 1.
44. *The Senator,* May 7, 14, 1969, pp. 1, 4.

Participants in the ceremony naming the library building "Jennings Randolph Hall." *Left to right, front row,* Dr. James E. Allen, Jr.; Dr. Quincy Mumford, Librarian of Congress; Senator Randolph, Dean T. R. Ross. *Back row,* President Hermanson, Dr. Robert Pfrangle, Dr. Douglas Oldenburg.

space were legitimate concerns which were, in fact, of at least equal concern to the president, faculty and trustees.[45] In due time, because of the willingness of President Hermanson and the senior administrative officers to talk patiently and of the mature actions of such student leaders as James Martin, Jerry Smith, Lew Atkinson and others in the months following, many of the issues were resolved. Soon there was a new dean of students, a new registrar, a change in some campus rules, and a new Science Center (which greatly increased classroom facilities).

A highlight of the fall semester in 1969 was the presentation of the Founders Day award to Senator Jennings Randolph followed by ceremonies naming the library building "Jennings Randolph

---

45. *Ibid.,* April 29; May 7, 21, 1969, *passim;* Trustee Minutes, April 30, 1969, pp. 106, 119 ff.

Hall." Dr. James E. Allen, Jr., U.S. Commissioner of Education and assistant secretary of Health, Education and Welfare, spoke at the Founders Day ceremony and Dr. L. Quincy Mumford, Librarian of Congress, was the speaker at the dedication of the building.[46]

The autumn of 1969 was one filled with other matters of interest at D&E. One was the October 15 "Vietnam Moratorium" observance led by Neil Biskar and Mark McMillan and marked by seminars, special anti-war meetings and the issue of *The Senator* without news or other articles—merely peace symbols, verses, Biblical quotations, and brief statements surrounded by much white space.[47]

The Maier Scholarship Foundation established a $100,000 trust fund at D&E in honor of Sara V. Neale, widow of an Elkins druggist who had served for many years as a trustee of the college. The income from the fund was to be used for scholarships for students who otherwise would be unable to attend college.[48]

Perhaps of greatest interest to students was the decision of the board of trustees to "temporarily cancel the convocation and worship program," i.e., required attendance at convocations and chapel, until the new chapel-auditorium could be built. Fraternity members were pleased to learn that the board had decided to postpone, at least until 1971, the implementation of the requirement (mandated in 1959) that all fraternities must be housed on the campus by the fall of 1969.

The board also voted to authorize D&E to participate in a four-college consortium (with Alderson-Broaddus, Salem, and Wesleyan), and approved a budget item for support of the activities of the organization.

The D&E soccer team won the WVIAC championship in 1969, never being defeated throughout the season, and then won the NAIA Area 6 championship by defeating the Alderson-Broaddus "Battlers" 2-1. The 1968 national champion Senators went to Richmond, Indiana, in late November to participate in the NAIA National Tournament. There they won their first games but finally were defeated in the third game 1 to 0 in the second overtime period by Eastern Illinois College. Many of those who had

46. *The Senator*, October 22, 29, 1969, p. 1.
47. *Ibid.*, October 8, 15, 1969, p. 1.
48. *Ibid.*, October 1, 1969, p. 1.

played in 1968 were still on the 1969 team. Newcomers, who starred in 1969 and later, included Hank Steinbrecher, Mike Udofia, Bob Nicoll, Nils Heinke, Gus Bruno, Don Spahr, Nick Pino, Rudy Eppright, Pat Massa, Don Pigan, Lou Laconette, and Steve Smith. Bill ("Scotty") Smyth was voted the tournament's Most Valuable Player for the second time and was named to the All-South squad as was Rildo Ferreira, Mike Udofia, Ekong Etuknwa. Ferreira, Udofia, and Bill Nuttall were all named to the All-Tournament team, and Smyth, Heinke, Udofia, Nuttall, Etuknwa, and Ferreira were all selected for the All-WVIAC team, Ferreira being selected "Player of the Year."[49]

The basketball teams coached by Avis Partain or Carl Hartmann in the late sixties, did not find a winning combination in any season. There were, however, some great games and some fine players. Larry Harding had a brilliant scoring record in his freshman year but was unable to continue in college thereafter. Other notables were Ron ("Bear") Kyle, Andy Fry (also a top scholar), Gary Brown, Jim Pingley, Richard Collins, Don Woodward, Reggie Evans, Glenn Alexander, Gordon Grimm, Jim McClure, Jim Haynie, Bruce Hartley, Steve Savage, Carl Watson, Carl Wartenburg, John Lothes, and Dennis Seger.

During the spring of 1970, several students competed for selection to represent D&E in the General Electric College Bowl television program. The dean appointed Professors Oleson, Gartmann, Johnston, Dittmar, and Dean Nelson to coach the contestants. The team selected for the May 24 appearance consisted of Leola Cheney, Ralph Finley, Martha Leighty, and Paul Osborne, with Mark Anderson as an alternate.[50] Although the team was defeated, the experience was great for the participants and the name of the college was carried into the homes of millions who watched the then popular show.

Various activities and achievements of faculty members also brought favorable national and regional attention to D&E in the latter part of the decade. President Gordon Hermanson was selected to serve a three-year term on the Executive and Planning Committee (The NEXUS Committee) of the Presbyterian College Union in 1968. In the spring of 1970, he was one of ten college presidents chosen to tour Europe for a Study Mission for the RCIE, conferring with leaders of higher education in several nations. Dean Ross served as a member of the General Assembly's

---

49. *Ibid.*, November 14, December 9, 1969; January 14, 1970, *passim*.
50. *Ibid.*, January 21, March 20, April 24, 1970, p. 1.

Board of World Missions of the Presbyterian Church, U.S., and as an associate editor of *The Presbyterian Outlook,* a national publication. Professors Walter Hartley in music and Jesse Reed in art both won several awards and prizes from regional and national societies for compositions and prints or paintings in their respective fields. Dr. James E. Dow's book, *The German Nation: Displacement and Resettlement,* published in 1969, was of major significance as the first study of its kind in post-World War II European history. National magazines and other types of media gave much attention to Dr. William E. Phipps's article entitled "Did Jesus and Paul Marry?" forerunner of his later books *Was Jesus Married?, The Sexuality of Jesus, Recovering Biblical Sensuousness,* and *Influential Theologians on Woman.* He was elected president of the West Virginia Philosophical Society in 1968 and was one of fifty philosophy professors in the United States chosen to participate in a national conference on metaphysics in New York during the summer of 1969. Throughout this period, Professor Sidney Tedford took his outstanding D&E choirs on tours of the eastern states. In 1969, Professor Claire Fiorentino was elected president of the State Intercollegiate Speech and Drama Association.[51]

Dr. William E. Phipps, D&E's most famous author.

Locally, D&E students participated actively in the Presbyterian Education Program (PEP) for handicapped children and Professors J. K. Hiser, Ralph Booth, John Martin, Alfonso Vazquez, and others of the science faculty developed Regional Science Fairs. The Students for Black Interest (SBI) were organized in the late 1960s and were especially active in 1969-70 when they began to observe Negro History Week. I ᵊd by Joseph

---

51. *The Senator,* 1965-70, *passim.*

C. Barnes, editor of *The Senator;* Frances Christian, SBI president; James McClure, an outstanding athlete; Richard Simms, Calvin Mitchell, Michael Hunt, and Patricia Jackson, the SBI's aims were to make the white majority aware of the problems of minority students, to end remnants of discrimination in student organizations, and to urge the appointment of blacks to the faculty and staff of the college.[52]

The six-week winter session in 1970 was unique in several respects. Several students spent much of the term in Harlem, in New York, in a Special Topics course offered by Professor Dennis Lindberg. They lived with Negro families and worked for various social welfare agencies. The Psychology Department provided a practicum which enabled students to work with the mentally ill at Weston State Hospital or with retarded children at an Elkins Day Care Center. On campus, Dr. L. N. Palar, a distinguished Indonesian scholar and statesman who had served his country as its permanent representative to the United Nations and as ambassador to India, East Germany, Russia, and the United States, was a visiting professor. He gave a course on the Problems of International Understanding and was available for talks, interviews, and seminars. *The Senator* conducted a "probe" to discuss student and faculty reaction to the six-week winter term. Every printed response was favorable—especially to the idea of special courses, off-campus work, and such seminars as Dr. Palar's.[53]

Of major concern to the faculty in 1969-70 was the preparation for the decennial evaluation of the college by the North Central Association in connection with the renewal of accreditation. The dean asked the Educational Policies Committee, chaired by Professor Fred Miller, to help prepare for the visitation and appointed Professor Phillips Brooks to serve as chairman of a small committee to help write the final report and coordinate the various forms and questionnaires. The evaluation team (Professors Herman R. Muelder of Knox College, Robert S. Bader of the University of Missouri, and Ralph S. Fjelstad of Carleton College) came in late April for a two-day conference. Their report was generally favorable, noting especially that D&E had "doubled salaries in the last decade," that over the past decade the percentage of faculty holding earned doctorates had "usually been over

---

52. *Ibid.*, 1968-70, *passim.*
53. *Ibid.*, January 14, February 27, 1970, pp. 1-3.

forty," that there was an able corps of faculty "with enthusiasm for assisting in the solution of problems," that fringe benefits for faculty "seem good and thoughtful despite limited financial resources," that seventeen of the faculty taught as many as twelve hours per semester while "all others had a teaching load lower than 12 hours," that since 1956, thirty-nine sabbatical leaves had been granted and that "seven Faculty members are on leave, part or all of this academic year." The team also praised the innovative "14-6-14 calendar," participation in the RCIE and the Washington Semester Programs, the great improvement in the library (building, staff, and collection), and noted with approval the "organization and expansion of the Development Office" and that the great efforts of "the President and people in the Development Office for improving the financial condition of the College are bringing results." The report concluded that "the most obvious weakness is the lack of anything like an adequate endowment." As was anticipated, the evaluation team's report resulted in accreditation being renewed for the next ten years.[54]

Knowing that the North Central evaluation would be completed and the Fifteen-Year Plan adopted in 1954 would be in large measure implemented by 1969-70, Dean Ross had informed President Hermanson on June 30, 1969, that he intended to retire as dean of the faculty at the end of the 1969-70 academic year to return to full-time teaching as Professor of History. He pointed out that he had already served as academic dean longer than anyone else in the history of the college, that he had repeatedly expressed a desire to retire since 1964 but had always yielded to requests that he "stay on" through some "current crisis." He had served not only as dean but as director of the Summer School and editor of the College Catalogue and had seldom had even a summer vacation. Thus, he gave a year's notice in order that there would be adequate time to find a successor.[55]

In informing the trustees and later *The Senator* of the dean's decision, President Hermanson stated "it would be difficult for any of us to be fully aware of the significance of the leadership

---

54. Faculty Minutes, October 6, November 3, 1969; February 3, September 4, 1970, *passim;* Visiting team's "Report of a Visit to Davis and Elkins College for the Commission on Institutions of Higher Education of the North Central Association," April 20-21, 1970, *passim.*

55. Letter from T. R. Ross to Gordon E. Hermanson, June 30, 1969.

which Dr. Ross has provided for Davis and Elkins College in his twelve years as dean and in his twenty-one years as a faculty member.... It would be impossible to overestimate the contribution Dr. Ross has made to the development of the college. He came to the college when its very existence was threatened. He became dean at a time when the North Central accreditation was threatened. We rejoice that so much of the Fifteen-Year Plan established by the board of trustees has been achieved. It has been the faithful, patient, persistent and visionary hard work of Dr. Ross that has made many of these achievements possible."[56] Inasmuch as the dean had never had a sabbatical leave, President Hermanson arranged a twelve-month sabbatical for him with a special grant for travel. The trustees presented him a silver tray and the faculty gave him a picture of "The Ross House in Winter" which they had commissioned Professor Reed to paint as a retirement gift.

President Hermanson appointed Professors Fred Miller, Gloria Payne, Keith Hiser, Margaret Goddin, Donald Walter, Nelson Bard, Phillips Brooks, and Russell Wilson to a "Committee to help the President appoint a new Dean of the Faculty." After working with the committee from January to April, reviewing applications and interviewing, the president decided to offer the position to Dr. Lloyd J. Averill, Jr., who accepted. Dr. Averill, a gifted speaker and prolific writer, had earned his B.A. and M.A. degrees at the University of Wisconsin and B.D. and M.Th. degrees at the Colgate-Rochester Divinity School and had been awarded several honorary doctorates. He had served on the faculty of Kalamazoo College from 1954 to 1967, being for a time academic vice-president, and then as president of the Council of Protestant Colleges and Universities in 1967-68. When he decided to come to D&E, he was director of the Council of General and Cross-cultural Education at Ottawa University and had recently published the widely-acclaimed *Agenda for the Protestant College.* He assumed his duties at D&E in late August of 1970.[57]

Other significant changes in personnel in 1970 included the appointment of James D. Holmes as director of admissions and

---

56. Trustee Minutes, October 24, 1969, pp. 125-28, Appendix "A"; *The Senator,* October 29, 1969, p. 1.
57. *The Senator,* May 8, 1970, p. 1.

Ralph R. Booth as registrar to succeed Calvin Hobart who had reached retirement age. Gary Horvath, an alumnus, was added to the admissions staff as an admissions counselor. William Whyte became director of housing and Cassandra Bolyard (later Mrs. William Whyte) began her D&E career as instructor in art. Dr. J. Melvin Miller joined the Department of Economics and Business, assuming some of the courses taught previously by Harold Henry who resigned. Earlier, Edward M. Carter had succeeded Virginia Henry as Book Store manager, also serving as college purchasing agent. Chanson V. Finney became director of the college choir inasmuch as Sidney Tedford resigned to accept a fellowship which enabled him to pursue graduate study.[58]

The academic year 1970-71 opened the new decade and began an era of accelerated change which was characteristic of the 1970s at D&E, as in the world. Inasmuch as it is unwise for a historian to attempt to record a definitive evaluation of what are still essentially current events, the final pages of this history chronicle only in a general way the major developments of the last few years.

During 1970-71, a committee of faculty, students, alumni, trustees, and townspeople undertook an extensive "Self-Study and Evaluation" of D&E. President Hermanson appointed Professor Phillips V. Brooks as secretary and coordinator of the Self-Study. The chairman of the Study Committee of sixteen members was Professor John Russell Wilson. President Hermanson, in reporting the work of the committee to the trustees, expressed gratitude "to both of these men for the invaluable contribution which they have made to the future of Davis and Elkins College." He gave much credit to Dean Averill for having "been the engine powering this multi-faceted study" and asserted that "without the leadership and the stimulus provided by Dr. Averill we could have done very little."[59] Among the more active participants were Professors Margaret Goddin, Donald Walter, Dennis Lindberg, Russell Studenmund, Douglas Oleson, Hal Blankenship, Nelson Bard, Ralph Booth, Keith Hiser, Ann Kek, Dorothy Roberts, Will Gartmann, Cassandra Bolyard, and William E. Phipps. Several students also participated, including William Humphreys who served as a subcommittee chairman; Blaine

---

58. *Ibid.*, January 14; April 10; September 18, 1970, *passim.*
59. Trustee Minutes, May 14, 1971; President's Report, following p. 172.

Steensland (later to be student body president and then director of admissions and finally assistant to the president); and Judy Littlefield (later an admissions counselor). Dr. H. A. Stroud, a trustee, and Dr. Douglas Oldenburg were especially active and helpful in the development of the study.[60]

As a result of this study, a report was developed, largely influenced by Dean Averill, which came to be known as the "Alternative Futures" program. This provided for a new calendar with two eleven-week terms separated by a four-week term in January and with a four-week term at the end of the second eleven-week term. It abolished the liberal arts core curriculum and provided instead for students to enroll in one "integrated studies" course each year, to meet certain minimum "foundations" course and distribution requirements, and to complete three courses in independent study and a specific amount of "area studies." Various "tracks," including a "contract program," were provided to lead to two-year and four-year degrees. Course and half-course units were adopted in place of semester hours for defining credit and the traditional grading system was altered to eliminate the "F" grade and to allow the use of "Highly Satisfactory," "Satisfactory" or A-B-C-Deferred for reporting grades.

The Alternative Futures program also sought to create several distinctive life-styles in the different residence halls, and, in general, eliminated the last vestiges of *in loco parentis,* including parietal rules. The trustees approved permitting students to have beer in the residence halls "on a trial basis" for the remainder of 1970-71, but stipulated that "under no circumstances shall liquor or beer be otherwise permitted, sold, or consumed on campus." A structure of governance involving the creation of a joint faculty-student-administrative Senate in which students comprised approximately 40 percent of the membership, was substituted for the existing Faculty and Student Government Association units. The faculty committee system was replaced with Senate committees all of which had student members.[61] Experience proved that some aspects of the Alternative Futures program as originally devised were impractical for D&E (e.g., the 11-4-11-4 calendar, area studies, three required courses in Independent Study, the

---

60. *The Senator,* September 18, 1970; February 12, 1971, *passim.*
61. Faculty Minutes, September 4, 1970; February 11, 1972, *passim;* Trustee Minutes, October 23, 1970, p. 155.

non-letter grading option), and they were subsequently modified. A central element of the Alternative Futures program as it evolved was the Integrated Studies series known as the Liberated Life sequence. Beginning with the freshmen course entitled "Human Freedom and the Counterforces," each student in subsequent years examined "World Cultures," "Comparative Ideas," and "The Future," exploring topics and issues of concern to every liberally educated individual. Other significant aspects of the Alternative Futures experiment were the off-campus practicum courses, notably in the Business and Psychology departments, which enabled students to gain practical experience in business, hospitals, and other institutions while studying theory. Overseas study programs for those able to afford the costs were developed in several areas, especially notable being those in the British Isles directed by Professors Brooks and Reed, in Spanish-speaking countries led by Professor Georgianna Vazquez, and in the Carribean area managed by Professor Tallman. One successful and unique feature of Alternative Futures was the optional "Orientation-in-the-Woods" experience each fall. Groups of students and faculty spent two or three days backpacking and camping in the beautiful mountains nearby while getting acquainted with each other and learning about the college. The innovations attracted the attention of other institutions, educational consultants, and various foundations, several of which have provided significant financial support for the college. Favorable publicity was given D&E by both regional and national media, including *Time, The Christian Science Monitor,* the *New York Times,* the *Washington Post* and *Changing Times.*

Dr. Nelson Bard preparing to lead a group for "Orientation-in-the-Woods."

A new tradition suggested by Dean Averill was for the college to grant an honorary Master of Humane Letters degree to each faculty member on the occasion of his being elected to tenure. After this policy was adopted, all those already having tenure

Dean Lloyd J. Averill, *left,* Dr. H. Arthur Stroud (trustee), and President Hermanson, *right,* with Professors Latham, Payne, Shelton, DuBose, Thayer, and Ross—the first faculty members to be awarded M.H.L. degrees.

were awarded the degree in special ceremonies. Thereafter, as one attained tenure, the degree was conferred.

In 1971, at the initiative of Dr. William Tolstead, chairman of the Biology Department, an interdisciplinary major in Ecology and Environmental Studies was developed and subsequently the faculty created a Department of Earth and Environmental Sciences.[62]

The following year, under the inspiration of Professors Phillips Brooks and Douglas Oleson, a new environmental field course was developed for the winter term. This was a three-week long experience in learning something about survival under winter conditions atop Spruce Knob and making studies of environmental characteristics and quality. The first year, this project attracted considerable public attention and a Sunday edition of the *Washington Post* carried a full account with pictures.[63]

Another project, which like the winter field course was con-

62. Trustee Minutes, May 12, 1971, p. 172 ff; Dean's Report, p. 4.
63. *Ibid.,* May 19, 1972, p. 198 ff; Dean's Report, p. 4.

tinued after 1972, was the development by Dean Averill and others of a relationship with the Huttonsville Correctional Center (HCC) whereby college courses could be offered at night by D&E faculty. Initiated in the spring semester of 1972 by Professors Brooks, Lindberg, and Ross, the HCC program has benefited hundreds of inmates, several of whom have continued in college, here or elsewhere, after their release from prison and have earned degrees.

Later in the decade, the college in collaboration with the International Language Institute of Washington, D.C., established a program in English language and culture for foreign students. Designed to prepare both undergraduate and graduate students for entry into American colleges and universities, this program was successfully directed by James Eros for several years and brought numerous interesting students to the campus, some of whom decided to become degree candidates here.

During the decade, there was a growing public interest in the arts and crafts of the Appalachian region. In 1973, acting on suggestions of Mrs. W. R. Cromwell and Professor Jesse F. Reed, Dr. Margaret Goddin took the lead in an effort to develop a summer arts and crafts program at the college. Working with R. Dale Wilson, president of the Randolph County Creative Arts Council, Candace Laird, Scottie Roberts Wiest, Olive Goodwin, Willetta Hinkle, Ruth Ann Musick, Professors R. Nowell Creadick and Claire Fiorentino and others, Dr. Goddin organized the Augusta Heritage Workshop which increasingly attracted persons interested in studying and/or developing skills in Appalachian arts and crafts. Subsequently, the faculty approved the creation of a degree program with a major in Appalachian studies as a part of the regular college curriculum. In 1974, Dr. Myron S. Anderson, a friend of the college, gave funds to establish the Myron S. and Ula Mae Anderson Appalachian Literature Collection in the library room named in his honor.

One of the most recent additions to the curriculum has been the nursing program established in the fall of 1976. This program provides expanded career opportunities, primarily for West Virginia young people, while helping at the same time to meet an acute shortage of nurses in the area. This program, as well as career-oriented programs in the Departments of Business and Education and the extended course offerings at the Huttonsville Correctional Center and increased financial aid for residents of

Participants in the first Augusta Heritage Workshop.

the state, has helped to bring about a significant increase in enrollment of West Virginia students in the latter years of the decade.

Of major interest and benefit to the people of the Elkins area as well as to the college, was the development of the "Impact Program," coordinated by Dr. Phillips V. Brooks. As President Hermanson stated in announcing it in 1976:

> It is appropriate in this year-long birthday of America that Davis and Elkins College also celebrate the opening of its new Campus Center and Auditorium. We inaugurate in this 72nd year of the College not only new facilities but a significant and exciting new cultural and religious enrichment program christened IMPACT . . . a rich and varied program of events throughout the year . . . IMPACT reflects and supports the liberal arts tradition as well as the continuing and broadening belief in the full Christian life. It was Thomas Hobbes who expressed that in a society "without arts, letters, music, and drama, the life of man is solitary, poor, brutish, and short."[64]

Dr. Phillips V. Brooks, coordinator of the Impact programs, with former Senator Frank Moss of Utah.

Supported in part by a Booth Ferris foundation grant, IMPACT brought to the campus each year since 1976 many outstanding artists, speakers, and cultural events. Among the more memorable programs were appearances by the Vienna Boys Choir, the Pittsburgh Symphony, Chamber Orchestra, John Chappell as "Mark Twain on Stage," Jesse Owen, Dr. Nelson Knaggs, the National Opera Company's "La-Boheme," Peking Opera, Calvin Morgan's mounted models, photographs and drawings of stage designs, the Ohio Ballet Company, Morris Udall, and Chuck Magione.

64. *IMPACT: 1976-1977,* Folder announcing the program, Elkins, W.Va., August 1976.

Dr. William L. Tolstead with students in the Greenhouse atop the Eshleman Science Center.

The changes which were most readily apparent, of course, were those resulting from additions to the physical facilities of the campus. Most dramatic of these were the construction of the $2.5 million Eshleman Science Center, the chapel and the Claude King Davis plaza, the $3.5 million Hermanson Campus Center (with its Harper-McNeeley Auditorium, olympic-size swimming pool, book store, bowling alley, game rooms, snack bar, and Student Affairs Center), International Center, the new Maintenance Center, and the President's House. In addition, the old heating plant was converted into the Boiler House Theatre, the ROTC Building was adapted for use as the Communications and Theatre Arts Centre, the Whetsell-DuBose House was remodeled for the Admissions Center and the Ross House was relocated as a faculty house. New entrances to the campus from the Harpertown Road were constructed and extensive additions to the system of campus roads, walks, lighting, and parking facilities were made. With the opening of the Hermanson Campus Center, much of the space in Benedum Hall was attractively renovated for use as lounges, private dining rooms, and conference areas. Because of the availability of modern residence halls, dining facilities, the auditorium, and the improved athletic fields, much use can be made of the campus in the summer months for meetings of Presbyteries, Synods and other church groups, large conventions and conferences, training sessions for athletic groups, bands, cheerleaders, and civic meetings.

By the nature of things a less obvious, but very important, aspect of the decade's progress has been the success of President Hermanson, Vice-President Kendell and their associates in obtaining financial support for the college. Federal grants and loans for building projects, federal money for student aid, and Appalachian Regional Commission funds are examples. Since 1968, foundation grants received have totaled more than $4.5 million. Among the most generous of the foundations have been the Claude Worthington Benedum, the Prichard, the W. K. Kellogg, the Kresge, the Andrew W. Mellon, the Max C. Fleischmann, the Louis Calder, the Carnahan-Jackson, the Booth Ferris, the Charles A. Frueauff, the West Virginia Emulation Endowment, and the Pew Memorial—each of which has contributed at least $100,000 (one more than $2 million, one more than $400,000 and one more than $200,000). Several other foundations have given from $15,000 to $75,000 and numerous grants from $1,000 to $15,000 have been most helpful. The Babcock, Mellon and Kellogg Foundation grants for faculty development and the Carnahan-Jackson grant for the library are among those which have been of notable use for current programs in very recent years. In addition, significant amounts have been received from estates of those who have remembered the college in their wills. In recent years, more than $1.7 million have been bequeathed to D&E. Of course, some of these bequests have been the results of efforts made by Presidents Purdum and David Allen, alumni attorneys, trustees, and others in earlier years as well as of the more recent work of President Hermanson and Nevin Kendell. In 1979, productive endowment funds totaled $2.3 million, an increase of $1,870,000 since 1964. Aside from government and foundation grants and bequests, many hundreds of thousands of dollars in gifts for current operations from churches and individuals have been received.[65]

As stated in the College Catalog, "ours is a 'person-oriented'

65. Reports and summaries furnished by the President's Office and the Development Office, August 22, 1979.

College." This history has sought to emphasize that concept by attempting to mention a cross-section of the persons—founders, faculty and staff, trustees, students, alumni—who have been associated with D&E through the years. It seems fitting to conclude in the same vein with a few words about contemporaries.

Dr. Lloyd Averill resigned after less than two years and was succeeded as dean of the faculty by Dr. John Russell Wilson, chairman of the Music Department and associate dean. Dr. Wilson, an extremely able musician and talented organist, worked hard to implement the Alternative Futures program which he had helped to develop. The onerous duties of his office and the frustrations he faced because of shortages of funds needed led to his decision to resign within less than three years.

Dean John Russell Wilson and his wife, Clair.

In fact, a new financial crisis had developed early in the 1970-71 academic year. The cumulative operating deficit had been reduced to only $5,963 as of June 30, 1970. However, the budget for 1970-71 had been based on a full-time equivalent of 825 students whereas enrollment of new students declined and the FTE was only 747. Also funds received from the supporting churches declined with the result that a deficit of more than $340,000 was anticipated after registration in September. As a result of tremendous efforts both to reduce expenditures and to obtain gifts, the deficit actually amounted to $235,086. This situation meant that in the early years of the decade, salary increases were either impossible to grant or, if made, inadequate; promotions were not made; a moratorium was declared on elections to tenure; some faculty members had to be released; the sabbatical leave program was significantly restricted; and the attractive tuition benefit for faculty children to attend other colleges was limited and ultimately to be phased out.⁶⁶

Dr. Margaret Purdum Goddin, first woman to serve as academic dean of D&E.

Dr. Margaret Purdum Goddin was appointed dean of the faculty to succeed Dean Wilson in 1975. The daughter of a former D&E president, an alumna of the college who had earned M.A. and Ed.D. degrees at West Virginia University and had also studied at the University of Cambridge and Indiana University, Dr. Goddin had begun her teaching career at the college in 1964. She had taught in the Education, Sociology, and English departments and served briefly in the Registrar's Office during the preceding eleven years and had been active in the development of the Alternative Futures program. The first woman academic dean at D&E (or at any West Virginia college), Dr. Goddin had served as chairman of the Educational Policies Committee during Dean Averill's last year. He had written of her as being an "effective, patient, and efficient chairman" and had asserted that "it is in large measure due to her efforts that we have been able to make all of the necessary curricular changes and transitions on time and in good order."⁶⁷ Since becoming Dean, Dr. Goddin has devoted much effort to securing funds and faculty for the nursing program, establishing the academic achievement awards, helping to develop the theater and communication's programs, and to improving professional development programs for the faculty. She has been an active

66. Trustee Minutes, October 23, 1970; May 14, 1971; May 10, 1972; May 17, 1974, *passim*.
67. *Ibid.*, May 10, 1972, Dean's Report following p. 198.

member of the Council for the Advancement of Small Colleges and was elected president of the West Virginia Association of Academic Deans in 1979.

Will Gartmann, assistant professor of German, who was already director of the Summer School and head of the Integrated Studies Program, was appointed associate dean. A fine scholar and experienced teacher, Professor Gartmann had also been invaluable in implementing the new curriculum both as an "idea" man and as a tireless worker giving careful attention to important details. In 1976, he edited a book-length report on D&E's professional development program which was widely distributed among hundreds of colleges.

Professor William Gartmann

When Kenneth White resigned as business manager after years of excellent work, including his participation in the construction of several major buildings, he was succeeded by Harry Thompson, former comptroller, who held the office until the summer of 1979.

So far as implementing the numerous changes resulting from the Alternative Futures goes, an officer who had one of the most difficult tasks was Professor Ralph R. Booth, the registrar. He persevered and faced the staggering problems of records and registration transition with tireless energy and with good humor and thoroughness. In 1976, he resigned to devote his full time to his work as chairman of the Chemistry Department and teaching and to significant duties as a regional officer of the American Chemical Society. John B. Neill, a graduate of King College with an M.Ed. from the University of Virginia, then became the registrar. He has subsequently undertaken the massive task of converting the procedures of his office, including registration, to computer processes.

Those who have served as dean of student affairs since the

resignation of Edward V. Perkins, include Kenneth S. Nelson and David Mikkelson (both as acting dean for one semester), Dr. Carl Swanson (1971-72), Dr. Thomas ("Tam") Polson (1972-77) and Guy Sievert since 1977. Patty R. Petty, a highly respected "veteran" of the Student Affairs Office, retired as dean of women in 1976. Quiet, faithful, and effective, she had served in that position longer than anyone in the history of the college and had had a positive influence on innumerable undergraduates. The titles "Dean of Men" and "Dean of Women" have been discontinued and the functions of those offices given to assistant deans for Student Affairs, Truitt Gilbreath and Roseann Durkin.

Because the college has always been heavily dependent upon student fees for survival, the Office of Admissions has long been extremely important. In the 1970s, D&E was fortunate to have had three unusually able directors of admission—James D. Holmes, Blaine Steensland, and David Wilkey—as well as several excellent associate and assistant directors and such experienced and faithful office staff as Barbara S. Carter and Mary Belle Loy. In the mid-seventies, enrollment began to increase somewhat. In part, this was due to the excellent efforts of Blaine Steensland and his admissions staff. Other factors included the attractive new buildings and campus facilities, the expansion of funds for student aid (especially to West Virginians), a move towards open admissions, and new programs such as nursing, fashion merchandising, computer science, hospital management, Appalachian studies, and environmental studies. The increased income made possible higher salary scales, a resumption of promotions, election to tenure, and a more lenient sabbatical leave policy for faculty.

Blaine Steensland and Dr. Teresa ("Mama") Minguez.

Actually, of course, not only in relationships with students, faculty, and public but also in carrying on the routine work of keeping the institution running smoothly, few persons are more significant than those listed in the catalogues as "staff officials." It would be difficult to overestimate the value of Elizabeth Guye Kittle, since 1964 the executive secretary and administrative assistant to the president. An alumna of D&E and a woman of unusual tact and talent, "Beth" Kittle comes as near to being "indispensable" as anyone on the campus. Another veteran, Mable Phares, also an alumna, served as secretary to Deans Ross, Averill, and Wilson before being appointed secretary to divisions heads. For nearly a decade, Dean Ross depended on her for conscientious and faithful attention to the details of the office and Dean Averill wrote of her at the end of his first year: "Mabel Phares has saved me from many an egregious error of omission or commission during the year and her intimate understanding of all the functions of the Dean's Office has been invaluable to me."[68] Her successor, in the Dean's Office, Margaret Isner Meadows, also an alumna, had previously served in other capacities in earlier years. A post of ever increasing complexity and responsibility, the Financial Aid Office, has been managed with great competence by Natalie Barb who prior to assuming it had earned a degree at the college and had long served as secretary to the business manager. Gladys J. Tierney has provided a peerless example of patient, sensitive, and faithful service during her many years as secretary to six deans of Student Affairs. Though their tenure has been briefer, the efficiency, sense of responsibility and savoir-faire of the following have been notable: Vicki Evans, secretary to the business manager; Donna Weese and Shirley Martin, bookkeepers; Jean Jones, secretary to the counseling center; Eunice McLaughlin and Catherine Baechtel, secretaries to the registrar; Robin Price, secretary to the Vice-President for Development; Barbara Schulz, secretary for Alumni Affairs; Brenda Moore, director of Office Service; Eleanor Harrison, cashier; and Phyllis Stemple, clerk in the Book

Elizabeth G. Kittle

---

68. *Ibid.*, May 12, 1971, p. 172 ff (Dean's Report).

Store. Gary Grose, an alumnus, the able manager of the college Book Store also has served for several years as purchasing agent. Mildred Poling has been the chemistry stockroom supervisor for nearly two decades and Ronald Jones has had the responsibility of custodian supervisor of an ever increasing staff.

Others who have less direct contact with the various "publics" of the college, but whose services are essential include such men as Warren ("Tom") Daniels, superintendent of maintenance for years, and his successor, Ralph Forinash. Some of their staff have served longer than any administrator and longer than all but the most senior faculty members. Notable among them should be mentioned Willard Chenoweth, Richard Byrd, Junior Stevenson, Lawrence and Ricky Plum, Howard and Thomas Shockey, Larry Caywood, and the "night patrol" consisting of Shirley Ervin, Lester Arbogast, and Bill Collins.

Almost everyone has known Gerald Morrison, the friendly "Campus Postmaster." For nearly fifteen years, he has cheerfully carried out the responsibilities of distributing the vast streams of mail and campus messages. Once *The Senator* devoted an editorial to him as one who exemplified Christianity in his daily life and work. Later a *Senatus* was dedicated to him, and most recently the student government president, Andrew McCorkle, presented "Jerry" a red jeep on behalf of the students and the college. There are others, of course, such as Roger Dague and Wayne Harkins and their staffs in the food service at the dining hall, Dr. Samuel Kump Roberts and nurse Frances P. Paden in charge of the health service, W. Earl Bennett, Jr., and Martin Baechtel in the Institutional Research Office, and Thomas Vogel and Anne Stottlemyer in the Development Office. Some like Bonnie Phares, Irene Crawford, Margaret Gutshall, Ruth Chabut, Virginia Harshbarger, Louise Girard, Rita Kyle, Jocelyn Teter Riggleman, Barbara Skinner, Lois Frantz, Dixie Singleton, Shelby Gordon, Sandra Vannoy, Patricia McDonald, and Sharon Skinner, who served in various capacities over the years, left long ago. There are many others who cannot be mentioned because of limitations of space, but who know that their lives too have been a part of the rich history of Davis and Elkins College.

Among the numerous faculty who have come and gone in the 1970s, several have made significant contributions. That Dr. C. Joseph Martin became director of the Presbyterian Guidance

Center in 1970 has been mentioned. Subsequently his title was changed to director of the Career and Personal Counseling Center and he has developed the center as a vitally important agency for the college as well as for the Synod. Cassandra Bolyard Whyte has done outstanding work as director of the William James House program and as Dr. Martin's assistant director. The Placement Office has become a part of the counseling center and has greatly increased its usefulness under the direction of Kenton McCoy, who originally came to D&E as a music instructor and also served as an admissions counselor. Laurie Robinson served as a counselor in the center as well as a residence hall director. Carl Wartenburg, an alumnus, returned in 1971 to serve as student activities director and instructor in Integrated Studies.

In 1971, Edward M. McFarlane succeeded L. G. Myers as chairman of the Department of Health and Physical Education and director of athletics. He coached basketball until 1976 when William G. Camp became head basketball coach. Since then, Professor McFarlane devoted his full time to teaching and administrative duties. His wife, Nancy Johnson McFarlane, joined the faculty in 1975 as women's basketball coach and instructor in health and physical education. Frederick B. Schmalz became soccer coach in 1972, serving with great success, until he resigned in 1979 to accept a similar position at a larger university. Two able young men who served well for briefer periods were Dr. Thomas Plaut in sociology and Dr. Paul F. Kradel in psychology, both appointed in 1972.

Dr. David Seaman also joined the faculty in 1972 as associate professor of French and chairman of the Department of Foreign Languages. He served ably as chairman of the Senate Committee on the College Community and was active in the work of the Integrated Studies program. The following year, David L. Harper was appointed instructor in business administration. Doubtless one of the best teachers in accounting the college ever had, he subsequently earned a CPA and was promoted to assistant professor.

Four able young men began their D&E careers in 1974. Dr. Francis L. Schneider, an alumnus of the college, helped develop the computer program as well as serving as chairman of the Department of Mathematics. Dr. Allan LaVoie, chairman of the Department of Psychology, proved to be both an excellent teacher and an effective committee worker. In the Fine Arts area,

Professor Richard Kadel, *upper left*, and the college choir in the chapel.

Richard W. Kadel, as director of the college choir, continued the tradition established by his predecessors (Irving Miller, Isabelle Mossman, Lola Davis, and Sidney Tedford) of developing excellent singing groups. His accomplishments were especially notable inasmuch as he did not have the advantage former directors had of presenting his choirs frequently to sing at regular chapel services.

Since 1974, Michael A. Pedretti, successor of Claire Fiorentino as Director of Theater, greatly expanded the work in drama. He was able to obtain funds for lighting and other facilities and to produce several excellent plays in the new Boiler House Theater. In subsequent years, he was assisted by his wife, Julie, a technical director, and Terry R. Hayes who became assistant professor of speech and drama in 1977.

Those appointed in the period 1975 to 1977 who have demonstrated their abilities and assumed responsibilities in a relative brief period of service were Dr. Robert C. Weber, chairman of the Department of English, Speech and Drama; Dr. James J. Van Gundy, who enlarged the new Department of Ecology and Environmental Sciences of which he became chairman; Dr. Robert E. Urban, chairman of the Department of Biology; Dr. Douglas D. Bickerstaff, associate professor of mathematics and president of the Faculty Association; Dorothy M. B. Johnson, who headed the new nursing department and aided by Brenda Jackson, Julia F. Hartman, and Frances N. Weese, led in its expansion; Dr. Rita Rice Flaningam, assistant professor of speech and drama, who succeeded Will Gartmann as the head of the Integrated Studies program; Dr. Lois R. Larson in education; Dr. James W. Stone in sociology; Dr. Malcolm Ian Jenness in biology and earth sciences; David F. Simmons in engineering and coaching; Sandra Lindberg, technical services librarian; Douglas A. Kranch, a talented audio-visual librarian; and John Zuboy in psychology.

Because of the increasing numbers of high school youths being graduated without adequate skills in reading and writing, D&E established a Learning Skills Center in 1976 to provide assistance to such students. Willard F. Johnson headed that center, assisted by Dr. Flaningam, Roberta Reith, and others.

During the 1970s more than forty men and women began terms of service on the board of trustees, in addition to several who had served earlier and continued or returned for terms in the seventies. Among the new trustees were men like Dr. Lynn T. Jones who succeeded Dr. H. A. Stroud as chairman of the board in 1972 and Dr. William L. Arthur who became chairman in 1977. Four descendants of the Davis and Elkins families serving as trustees in this period were Henry Gassaway Davis III, Davis Elkins, Mollie Peters, and Elkins Wetherill. Alumni elected to the board during the decade who had not served before were Russell Allen, Ellis MacDougall, William S. Robbins, John H. Harling, and the late Dr. Earl Lyons. From the Elkins community, in addition to Mayor Ralph S. Shepler, W. R. Cromwell, Jr., and the late Carl W. Channell (all of whom had served in the sixties), there were Thomas S. Stafford and Ralph Hess. Miss Emily Gibbes liked to boast that she was a "two-in-one minority representative, being black and female." Other women trustees were Mrs. Agnes Veitch who served as vice-chairman, Mrs. Kathryne Flynn, Mrs. Mollie Peters, and Mrs. Dorothy Yingling. With the restructuring of both the UPUSA and the U.S. Presbyterian Churches, the two Synods of West Virginia became parts of the Synod of the Trinity (UPUSA) and of the Virginias (U.S.). The geographical area from which trustees representing those judicatories came was significantly broadened. Of course, the creation of the category of trustees-at-large also had a similar effect. All of which helped in the achievement of President Hermanson's goal of attracting more persons of wide influence and varied experience to the board than had been possible in previous decades. Other trustees beginning their service in the seventies were David P. Birch, Alex E. Booth, Jr., Willis S. Brown, David B. Buerger, John Campbell, David H. Carnahan, Thomas S. Currier, Robert Y. Frazier, Robert M. Hoag, Robert C. Holland, William B. Jackson, John R. Kennedy, Jr., Donald C. Lum, Herbert Meza, Stephen Reppert, William Robbins, William C. Schram, G. Dixon Shrum, Governor Hulett C. Smith, Holly Spahr, Joseph C. Swaim, Jr., James P. Tannian, and David Wallace. An outstanding trustee in this period was the late Bernard Flynn who served as chairman of the Development Committee of the board. His role in helping to secure funds for the construction of the Science Center was indispensable and in recognition of his services, the Planetarium has been named in his honor.

Most board members faithfully attended at least two meetings each year. Several were extremely helpful in securing major grants for the college or gave generously of their own resources. For example, in 1974, when there were inadequate funds to provide salary increments, trustees contributed some $34,000 to make possible a special salary supplement for all faculty and staff members.[69] Active, interested, committed trustees who generously give much time and effort, without any remuneration, as well as sharing their talents, expertise, and resources on behalf of the college have been of tremendous significance and benefit to D&E.

Student activities, interests, and attitudes in the seventies, at D&E as elsewhere, have differed somewhat from those of the preceding decade. However, an enthusiasm for athletics was one characteristic which remained constant.

Since 1970, when D&E won the NAIA soccer championship for the second time in three years, a series of remarkable soccer teams became contemporary versions of the old Scarlet Hurricanes of the twenties. At the 1970 national tournament at Dunn, North Carolina, Coach Greg Myers's booters defeated arch-rival Quincy College 2-0 in the title game. Mike Udofia, Bill Nuttall, Nils Heinke, and Bill ("Scotty") Smyth were named to the All-Tournament team and Nuttall as the Most Valuable Player in the tournament, an honor that had gone to Smyth in

---

69. Trustee Minutes, 1970-74, *passim.*

The 1970 NAIA National Soccer champions. Record 13-1-1. *Back row:* J. Satterfield, J. Sautter, G. Knittle, E. Dreibelbis, D. Blasczak, D. Stanick, D. Bussi, D. Booth, T. Mumblow, T. Stala, A. Ruttigliano, R. LaMora, W. Eastman, manager. *Row three:* A. Latjerman, E. Walk, D. Spahr, R. Eppright, R. Nicoll, W. Miller, N. Heinke, M. Udofia, L. LaQuette. *Row two:* M. Orofitelli, assistant coach; L. Penman, manager; J. Caracciolo, R. Fitting, A. Blaise, W. Smyth, co-captain; W. Nuttall, co-captain; R. Wolfe, T. Martin, J. Donnally, P. Massa, A. Dickerson, manager; G. Myers, head coach. *Front row:* H. Wango, G. Bruno, H. Steinbrecher, L. Atkinson, J. Caulfield, N. Pino, E. Etuknwa, D. Pigan.

1968 and 1969. In 1971, with Charles Smith as Coach (Myers having resigned to continue work on his doctorate), Quincy College defeated D&E 1-0 in the NAIA Tournament finals. That was "Scotty" Smyth's last year and he ended his amazing college playing career by being chosen for both the All-Tournament and the All-American soccer teams. He, Nils Heinke, and Ekong Etuknwa were named to the All-South team.

Fred Schmalz became D&E soccer coach in 1972. The Senators won the WVIAA and Area 7 Championships and were the runners-up at the NAIA Tournament at Dunn. Unfortunately, after the season ended, it was discovered that Zlatko Tripkovic had signed a professional agreement when he first came to the United States and had had a limited command of English. When D&E officials learned of this, they immediately reported it and, of course, had to forfeit all of the season's victories.

Ten soccer players had graduated in 1973 and Coach Schmalz expected the 1973 season to be one of rebuilding. It proved to be much more than that. Conn Davis set a new record as a Goalie, with 22 "saves" in a game against Howard University which D&E won 1-0. The Senators swept the conference, took the Area 6 Championship, and went to the national tournament where they were defeated in the semi-finals by Quincy. In fact, from 1973 to 1978 Coach Schmalz's teams won the right to participate in the NAIA national tournament every season except 1975. This means that D&E was in the national soccer picture ten out of the eleven years since winning the championship for the first time in 1968. In the summer of 1975, the coach and team were invited to spend two weeks in Poland where they played various Polish teams. After returning in the fall, the team won the conference title, but lost the Area 6 tournament, after 7 overtimes, to Fredonia State University. The 1976 team set records for the most wins (16) in one season and for achieving the highest ranking (ISAA) of any team in the college's history. In 1976, 1977, and 1978, D&E again participated in the national tournaments.

In addition to Rildo Ferreira and Bill Smyth, already cited, the following D&E soccer players have been named to All-American teams: Bill Nuttall, Ekong Etuknwa, Nils Heinke, Hans Wango, Mickey Whelan, Conn Davis, Mike Grayson, Karl Largie, David Ruzicka, and Rod O'Savio. Players selected to participate in Senior Bowls include Hans Wango, Mickey Whelan, Conn Davis, Mike Shue, Tim Murphy, and Rod O'Savio. Besides those already mentioned in 1971 and before, D&E men selected for the All-South team have included Hans Wango, Mickey Whelan, Conn Davis, Al Pagliai, Tim Murphy, Karl Largie, Mike Shue, Michael Grayson, and Rod O'Savio. In recent years, those selected for the All-Tourney NAIA national tournament teams have been Jorge Bergen, Sonny Ideozu, Ove Johansson, Tim Murphy, Karl Largie, Rod O'Savio, Bill Murphy, Lenn Williams, and Mickey Whelan—the last three also being cited as Outstanding Defenders and Whelan as the Most Valuable Player (1973). Since 1972, Bill Smyth, Bill Nuttall, Mickey Whelan, Zlatko Tripkovic, Len Williams, Sonny Ideozu, Tim Murphy, Jim Rippey, Michael Shue, and Rod O'Savio have been drafted to play professionally.

Coach Schmalz also won many honors—South Area Coach of the Year, Coach of the Year in WVIAC, NAIA district and area, and member of the United States Soccer Olympics Committee, among other distinctions. His decision to leave D&E in 1979 was a great loss.

The fame of the D&E soccer teams during the decade inspired

Coach Nancy McFarlane and the 1976-77 Women's Basketball Team.

a renewed interest in intercollegiate athletic competition. Although no coach in the seventies was able to produce a championship varsity basketball team, there were some excellent games and outstanding players. Jim Haynie and Al Hall were especially notable, the latter having gone to play for a Geneva, Switzerland, professional team after leaving college. In women's basketball, however, Coach Nancy McFarlane's co-eds won first place in the conference in 1977 and her teams participated in WVIAA conference tournaments for four consecutive years since 1976 ranking second in 1979. In 1979, Cindy Stinger, Karen Crump, and Cheryl Novoshielski made the All-Tournament team. Cindy Stinger was captain of the All-State team and Karen Crump was named to it. Pam Boyd established the scoring record with 39 points for one game in 1977.

The D&E women's field hockey teams, coached by Dr. Jean Tallman, have been a perennial powerhouse in Division I competition in West Virginia. D&E won the state championship in 1975 and 1976 and was undefeated in scheduled contests in 1976, 1977,

Coach Jean Tallman, *front left,* and the 1978 Women's Field Hockey Team.

and 1978. During those last three years, the teams participated in the Midwest AIAW Region 5 tournaments. Coach Tallman's 1978 team was the first woman's team in any intercollegiate sport from any college or university in West Virginia to qualify and advance from regional to national competition. In that year, D&E defeated Indiana University and Michigan State University to place second in the regional tournament and then competed in the NAIAW national tournament in Ellensburg, Washington. Notable among many outstanding hockey players have been Christine L. Smith (now a coach at Rutgers University), Margaret Yackulics, Peggy Gatewood, Cindy Paulmier, Sherry Phipps, Linda Defiore, Kay Kirby, Joan Vacario, Barbara Barosa, Amy Miese, Cindy Stinger, Leslie Morgan, and Tess Werner.

In 1976, Pam Boyd was named "Athlete of the Year" at D&E, an honor which usually had gone to a male. Cindy Stinger won the title in 1979. Both young women were chosen for membership of the 1980 Olympic Team Handball team. Coach Tallman was chosen in 1979 to be one of twenty field hockey coaches to serve on the national rating board.

In the late seventies, David Barb developed some winning

baseball teams. D&E finished the 1977 season with an 18-5-1 record and Barb was named Coach of the Year. Mark Deutch and Rich Phillips were named to the All-Conference team. In 1979, the D&E team ranked first in the Northern Division. The preceding year a D&E cross-country team participated in a national meet, after a successful season in which Mike Redman placed first in individual awards won at the WVIAC meet. It is notable that D&E teams, in four sports, participated in national competition in the years 1976-78 (soccer, field hockey, cross-country, and baseball).[70]

In 1974, the college established a "D & E Athletic Hall of Fame" to which the first person elected was Senator Jennings Randolph. Others so honored in subsequent years included twenty-four men who had distinguished themselves as D&E athletes or coaches, or who had made a distinct contribution in the field at athletics here or elsewhere.

President Hermanson, *left*, and Coach Edward McFarlane, *right*, with D&E Athletic Hall of Fame "greats" C. A. ("Bill") Gross, Robert N. ("Red") Brown, Frank Wimer, and Harry E. Whetsell.

70. Athletic records and information provided in interviews with Athletic Director Edward McFarlane and Coaches Nancy McFarlane and Jean Tallman, August 30, September 6, 1979.

Interest in drama, always an important aspect of campus life, also continued. Early in the decade, audiences enjoyed performances featuring such talented personalities as Jeff Buckwalter, Katherine Chamberlain, Barbara Cox, Jeff Cronin, John Davidson, David Faunce, Laurie Ross, Lynn Simcoe, and R. Dale Wilson, several of whom subsequently pursued professional careers in the field of theater. Later in the seventies the development of new facilities and an expanded staff greatly enhanced theatrical activities at D&E. In 1975-76, Becky Myers received the award for the "Greatest Contribution made to the Theatre" for the year. The same year, Barbara Fuedale, as Blanche in *Streetcar Named Desire,* gave one of the outstanding performances of the decade. Bruce Fleshman played major roles in each of his undergraduate years and was the first recipient of the "Greatest Contribution for Four Years to the Theatre" award presented in his senior year. George Amos subsequently received that same honor. Nicholas Blanton and Riccarla Hayton were both outstanding, the latter participating in every major production between 1975-79. Tara McKenzie (whose mother, "Tish" Davis, and father, John McKenzie, had been active in D&E drama in their undergraduate years) was the first D&E student to be selected to compete for the Irene Ryan Award.[71] Not to be forgotten were certain faculty members such as Douglas Oleson, Nelson Bard, Ralph Booth, Trevor Owen, Phillips Brooks, Will Gartmann, Cassandra Whyte, and David Seaman who, in some cases, revealed unsuspected talent as thespians during the era.

Professor Douglas Oleson stars in *Merchant of Venice* with Bruce Fleshman and Nicholas Blanton.

With annual enrollments in excess of eight hundred during much of the decade, there were numerous outstanding student leaders in other activities and organizations, in scholarship,

---

71. Interview of Thomas R. Ross with Claire Fiorentino, September 7, 1979; memorandum, Michael Pedretti to Thomas R. Ross, September 6, 1979.

Dean of Women Patty R. Petty with Professors David Seaman and Paul Kradel.

music, campus publications, and student government, as well as in athletics and drama. Among the most eminent in student government were Blaine Steensland, William Humphreys, Arthur Bronk, James Wells, Peter Dougherty, James Garrett, Brian Goodarzi, Bryant Applegate, Diane Ramos, Sara Howard, Richard Dickerson, Andrew McCorkle, Hilary Lutz, Susan Curran, and Susan Byrd. *The Senator* did not prosper as well in the decade as it had in earlier times. It appeared irregularly in some years, was reduced to a four-page tabloid, and only occasionally was of the quality characteristic of the previous decades. There were some exceptions, of course, and editors like Dave Kerr and Barbara Porter brought out some good editions. The *Senatus* staff on the other hand, aided by Professor Patty Petty, produced several excellent yearbooks, especially notable being those edited by Mike Morrison and Diane Tauber in the early seventies and Sherry Jacobs' 1976 edition using the U.S. Bicentennial as a theme.

As President Hermanson observed in his report to the board of trustees on May 6, 1977, "1976 was a watershed year" in D&E's history. That year enrollment exceeded nine hundred, a major bequest made possible the elimination of the cumulative operating deficit and increased the endowment to almost two and one-half million dollars, and the IMPACT program was started.

The chapel with the Hermanson Campus Center in background.

Founders Day (having not been observed for several years) was celebrated again with the award being given to Freeman J. Daniels, and his brother, G. Neal Daniels, both alumni of D&E. The award was presented by Senator Jennings Randolph, the most recent previous recipient. Following that ceremony, the new campus buildings were dedicated. Dr. Lynn Jones, chairman of the board of trustees, presided and former chairmen Dr. Robert A. Pfrangle and Dr. H. A. Stroud participated with President Hermanson in the dedication of the chapel (with its Helen Wehrle organ), the Claude King Davis Plaza, the Gordon E. Hermanson Campus Center and the Harper-McNeeley Auditorium (with the James T. McGranahan Room and the Samuel O. and Celeste Paull Gallery), and the Eshleman Science Center. Later, the large lecture room in the Science Center was named in honor of Dr. S. Benton Talbot.

Of course 1976 was the bicentennial of the birth of the nation, and D&E participated in the observance in various ways. At the suggestion of Senator Randolph and with his financial assistance, the History Department developed a course dealing with "The Signers of the Declaration of Independence" which was said to be unique in the country. Memorable, too, was the winter of 1976, the most severe in at least half-a-century. Fuel was in such short supply that D&E closed for several weeks to conserve energy.

Awareness of the end of the era of cheap energy began in the 1970s. The implications of the energy crisis had to be very significant for D&E as she approached the decade of the eighties. For not only were there twenty buildings to heat (or cool) and light,

Dedicating flags of the nations, Chapel, Plaza, Harper-McNeeley Auditorium and International Residence Hall in background.

but because of the location of the college and the lack of public transportation, the great majority of her students had to depend on automobiles to get to and from Elkins.

Certainly the unprecedented costs of energy and the chronic problem of insufficient endowment combined to confront the college with perplexing challenges as the decade ended. However, the success of President Hermanson's administration in significantly increasing endowment and other financial resources and in markedly improving the plant facilities and the fact that D&E has experienced a steady increase in enrollment during a period when many institutions, both public and private, have experienced a decline, provided bases for optimism. Encouraging, indeed, was a 1978 American Association of Higher Education report based on a study of approximately six hundred liberal arts colleges with enrollments under fifteen hundred. After discussing some of the problems which confront these institutions, the report stated: "Yet there are models of excellence among these colleges . . . (some) are exemplary in the lessons they provide for educational practice and organizational renewal." The first institution to be named as a "model of excellence" was Davis and

Members of the "Founding Families," with Dr. Gordon Hermanson, at the Diamond Jubilee reunion in 1979.

Elkins College. Thus, as Dr. Gordon E. Hermanson completed his fifteenth year as president, he and his associates could take much pride in the remarkable progress made toward the realization of the goals which had been established early in his administration.

In view of the obstacles overcome, the past crises survived, and the achievements made since 1904, there was no reason for despair in 1979. Then, for the most part, faculty and facilities were excellent and the founding families were showing renewed interest in "watering the seed" which their forebears had planted. By then, new relationships with the Synods of the Trinity and of the Virginias had broadened the base for Presbyterian support far beyond anything A. H. Hamilton and the founding Presbyteries of Lexington and Winchester might have dreamed of in the beginning. In 1979, too, able trustees and loyal alumni were demonstrating their concern and affection for the college, and foundations and faithful friends were continuing to promote her further progress as she looked toward her centennial.

When D&E had survived her first decade, a local newspaper editor had written in 1914 that "Elkins feels that the College is one of her institutions and is not a thing separate and apart." Sixty-five years later, when Elkins and D&E had both grown a great deal, all thoughtful persons realized how much the college meant to the community, not only as a center of higher education and culture, but also because the prosperity of the city depended to a significant degree on the millions of dollars poured annually into the economy of the area as a result of the existence of the college.

Only ninety years had passed since the little town had been established in the river valley where before for untold centuries only Indian hunters, roaming through the mountain wilderness, had sped silently along the Seneca Trail. Then for scarcely more than three decades, two wealthy families had dwelt in quiet mansions on the hill overlooking the town, their secluded estates encompassing a segment of the Indians' ancient pathway as well as the lands adjacent. There, in 1979, along that trail and spread over those same lands lay the beautiful campus of Davis and Elkins College, teeming with life and sound and action. For seventy-five years, the aim of the college had been to serve the needs of each generation of students and to provide them an opportunity for sound liberal education in a Christian environment —an education of sufficient breadth and depth to prepare them for effective citizenship and creative leadership in a democratic society. D&E had had her full share of failures and disappointments, but her achievements far outweighed her shortcomings. Thus, as those who loved "the little College on the Hill" looked forward to the future they might well have thought of the Latin motto of an old Presbyterian clan in Scotland: *Spem successus alit* (Success nourishes hope!).

Aerial view of D&E Campus.

Index

Limitations of space preclude the listing in the index of most of the hundreds of names mentioned in the text. See general topics such as "Trustees," "Students," "Staff," "Degrees," "Basketball," etc., for page numbers where individuals may be cited.

A

Abraham, William, 254
Academy, 6, 44, 46, 50, 52, 90
Acta, The, 21, 23, 26, 35, 42, 44, 45, 50
Adum, The, 234
Air Force ROTC, 177, 178, 198, 218, 221, 225, 248, 254
Albert, Charles, 32, 51, 65-66, 72, 75-76, 83, 91, 94, 106, 110, 114-27, 132, 145, 186, 205, 217-20, 258
Albert, Jean Marstiller (Mrs. C. E.), 65, 69, 91, 160, 217, 218, 245
Alexander, Michael, 229
Allaben, Marshall C., 16, 18, 19, 20, 22, 24, 25, 26, 27, 34
Allen, David Kell, 64, 139, 149, 170, 181, 184-218, 226, 229-30, 239-46, 292
Allen, Esther S. (Mrs. D. K.), 176, 187, 190, 200, 242
Allen, James E., 20, 24, 26-31, 36-40, 48, 51, 59-64, 66, 69-75, 80, 83-99, 104-11, 117-18, 121, 139, 172, 186, 202, 220, 246
Allen, James E., Jr., 31, 96, 204, 239, 250, 270, 278
Allen, Robert A., 110, 115
Allen, Russell, 262, 301
Alternative Futures, 285, 286, 293, 294, 295
Alumni Association, 93, 113, 116, 219
Alumni Athletic Committee, 84, 91, 100, 108, 113
American Association of University Professors, 203, 228, 256
American Association of University Women, 230

Anaka, Edward, 254
Anderson, J. Howard, 149, 205, 267
Anderson, Myron S., and Ula Mae Collection, 288
Argonne National Laboratory, 268
Armitage, Jack, 216, 222, 225
Army Air Force College Training Detachment, 139, 140, 144, 150
Arnold, D. H. Hill, 79, 193
Arnold, Eugene, 22, 31
Arthur, William R., 301
Ash, Paul E., Jr., 221
Athletic Hall of Fame, The D&E, 307
Augusta Heritage Workshop, 288, 289
Averill, Lloyd J., Jr., 283-97
Axtell, William B., 231, 235

B

Bader, Robert E., 230
Bader, Robert S., 281
Baird, Robert, 261
Baker, Harriet B., 64, 66, 132, 145
Baker, Mrs. W. E., 94
Baldwin, Donald, 261, 276
Bangham, Joseph F., Jr., 176-78
Barb, David, 306-7
Barb, Natalie, 217, 297
Bard, Nelson, 275, 283, 284, 286, 308
Barnes, Burlin, 79, 145
Barnes, Joseph C., 281
Barron, Frederick H., 7-9, 16-25, 42, 49-53, 60-66, 71, 126-27, 135
Barron, Wallace, 168
Barry, David, 35
Barry, Emily,68
Barry, Richard, 72, 73, 122

317

Baseball, 21, 169, 307
Basketball (players, records), 34-36, 51, 53, 74-77, 81-82, 95, 97, 108, 120, 138, 166-69, 194, 199, 200, 203, 223, 227, 233, 254, 279, 305
Benedum, Michael, 197
Benedum Hall, 108, 209, 237, 259, 261
Benfield, William A., 250, 258
Benjamin, John, 234
Bennet, Richard, 264
Bibbe, Paul C., 237
Bickerstaff, D. D., 300
Biddle, John C., 276
Bird, Andrew R., Jr., 149, 159, 185, 192, 205, 251
Black, Carolyn, 237-38
Blaess, Capt. Robert F., 229
Blakely, Hunter B., 195, 217
Blankenship, Harold, 276, 284
Blankenship, Ira, 218
"Boar's Head Dinner," 202, 236
Book store, 153, 179, 191, 209, 220, 291
Booth, Lucille, 237
Booth, Ralph R., 175, 190, 198, 202, 266, 280, 284, 295, 308
Bowers, E. A., 52, 58, 59, 62, 79, 127, 131, 146, 193
Brady, A. Spates, 59, 62, 91, 101, 128, 131, 148
Brittain, Carrie Lanier, 145, 192, 221, 225
Brock, Cornelia, 231, 237
Brooke, Francis J., 126, 127
Brooks, Allison Cochran, 26
Brooks, Phillips V., 275, 281, 283-87, 290, 308
Brown, John F., 34, 74, 108
Brown, Robert N. ("Red"), 76, 82, 88, 162, 166-69, 307
Brown, William G., 26, 41, 47
Buckwalter, Jeff, 308
Buildings and facilities, 3, 8-9, 11, 21, 42, 62-63, 71, 79, 135-36, 139, 146, 148, 153-55, 171, 178, 191, 196, 201-2, 204, 207, 209, 220, 227, 239, 256, 262-64, 272, 291-92, 310-11
Burns, Russell, 173
Burris, Kenneth A., Jr., 271
Byrd, Robert, 259

C

Caldwell, Frank H., 248
Calendars, 11, 19, 37, 268, 274, 281-82, 285

Camp, William G., 299
Campbell, E. Fay, 149
Campbell, John, 204
Campbell, P. V., 50
Caplinger, John S., 79
Carder, R. H., 201, 229
Carter, Edward M., 284
Catalog, 11-12, 16, 20, 42, 46, 120, 292
Cerrato, Walter, 204
Chamberlain, Katherine, 308
Chandler, Peggy, 204, 217
Channell, Carl W., 250, 301
Channell, E. W., 136
Chapel, 11, 13, 67, 107, 122-23, 134, 171, 278, 310
Christian, Frances, 281
Christian Higher Education Fund Campaign, 207, 209, 229, 271
Christiansen, Norman, 261
Churchill, Sir Winston, 29
Civil Pilots "Flying Training School," 124, 137, 144
Civilian Conservation Corps, 103
Clark, Friend Ebenezer, 160, 190
Claude King Davis Plaza, 291, 310, 311
Cleveland, Eloise, 45
Coberly, B. Jeff, 204
College Aid Club, 94
College Orientation Program, 253
College Song, 34
Commercial Department, 32, 41, 44, 46, 67
Committee to Select a Dean, 283
Committees to Choose President, 8, 16, 112, 126, 185-88, 239
Comprehensive Examinations, 212, 220, 274
Constitution, Faculty, 275
Constitution, Trustees', 39, 257, 275
Converse, Henry A., 20
Cook, W. A., 39
Coolidge, Calvin, 56, 57
Courtney, Lloyd M., 149, 240
Covert, William C., 71
Cox, Barbara, 308
Crawford, Donald K. ("Damper"), 77
Creadick, Nowell, 288
Cromwell, William R., Jr., 88, 193, 205, 301
Cromwell, Mrs. W. R., 288
Cronin, Jeff, 308
Crosier, Alma, 150
Cross Country and Track, 169, 260, 307

Crothers, Betsy, 170
Crouch, Evelyn V., 237
Crouse, Russell, 269
Cuban Missile Crisis, 301
Cullop, Charles P., 229, 231, 235, 239, 269
Cultural Enrichment Programs, 34, 46, 221, 238, 260, 269-70, 280
Cunningham, Allen B., 124
Cuppett, David E., 205, 239
Currence, Velma Belle (Mrs. Clifford Jackson), 42, 44, 56
Curriculum, 12, 15-19, 21, 32, 43-44, 46, 67, 87, 117, 151, 197, 213, 220, 257, 268, 275, 285, 287-88
Currie, A. L., 127
Cutright, Helen, 174
Cutright, Paul, 35, 51

D

D&E Dames, 200
Dailey, C. Wood, 7, 8, 16
Dale, Lorna, 234
Daniels, Daniel, 261
Daniels, Freeman J., 68, 310
Daniels, Joseph, 258
Daniels, W. T. ("Tom"), 267
Darby, Mr. and Mrs. H. M., 139, 147; (House), 140
Davidson, John, 308
Davis, Claude King, 176, 190, 231, 291
Davis, E. H. Hunter, 229, 232, 260, 275, 276
Davis, Henry Gassaway, 1-9, 13-16, 19-20, 24, 30, 38, 40-41, 47-48, 53, 60, 80 (statue), 98, 109, 122, 136, 155, 326
Davis, Henry G., III, 250, 267, 272, 301
Davis, John T., 53, 81
Davis, John W., 80
Davis, Lola S. (Mrs. C. K.), 176, 225
Davis, Patricia Ann "Tish," 165, 200, 308
Davis Memorial Hospital, 50, 96
Davis Memorial Presbyterian Church, 10, 16, 88, 108, 122, 135, 144, 234, 268
Day, Lawrence, 135
Dayton, Alston G., 41
Dayton, Arthur, 146, 149
Debate and Oratory, 30, 37, 44, 78, 88, 107, 228, 254
Deegan, Ken, 216, 225
Degrees, 26, 31-32, 41-44, 51, 60, 67-68, 82, 88, 93, 96, 99, 115, 119, 124, 149, 159, 176, 197, 201, 212, 215, 217, 225, 258, 287
DeHart, Richard, 198, 203
DeNicola, Floyd, 162, 179, 190
Depression, The Great, 57, 85, 86, 88, 105
Derr, Fannie, 32
Development Commission, 213, 224
Development Office, 105, 198, 199, 250, 258, 263, 265, 271, 282, 297
Dickerson, Fred, 138
Dills, Margaret L., 77
DiMario, Michael, 216
Dittmar, Elaine Ann, 267, 279
Dobbins, L. E., 91
Dober, Richard, 263, 264
Dornblazer, George, 91
Douglas, Carol, 216, 227
Dow, James E., 218, 228, 231, 235, 253, 257, 275, 280
Drama and theater, 49, 88, 121, 165, 195, 215-16, 227, 234, 260, 308
Driggs, Lydia, 160
DuBose, S. Wilds, 162, 175, 182, 190, 200, 207, 212, 213, 216, 217, 231
DuBose, Warner, Jr., 201, 267
Duncan, William, 274
Dunlap, Samuel, 244, 246
Dunn, Waldo H., 20
Durfee, Joseph, 145, 152
Durkin, Roseann, 296

E

Elkins, Davis, 30, 41, 53, 120, 149, 152, 301
Elkins, Hallie Davis, 30, 38, 48, 53-61, 79-87, 96-98, 105, 109, 192
Elkins, Stephen Benton, 1-9, 14-16, 19, 24, 30, 38, 40, 43, 53, 60, 122, 152, 215, 326
Elrod, Lloyd M., 266
Elson, Edward L. R., 201
Emm, Marshall, 201, 218
Engert, William F., 258, 262, 271
Enrollment, 12, 23, 31, 34, 68, 73, 88-89, 155-56, 191, 202, 224, 248, 251, 256, 267, 273, 293
Eros, James, 288

F

Faculty, 9-10, 16, 20, 24, 31-32, 37, 45, 51, 64-66, 96, 101, 119, 124, 132, 144-45, 151-52, 158, 160-64, 172, 182, 190, 198, 201-2, 204, 213-15, 218-20, 225, 229, 231, 235, 237, 248,

Faculty (continued)
253-56, 258, 265-67, 269, 275-76, 279-81, 283-84, 293-96, 298-301, 308
Faculty Christian Fellowship, 195
Faculty Committees, 32-33, 128, 133, 157, 191, 196-98, 202, 205-6, 213-14, 221, 228, 238, 244, 261, 268-69, 270, 274-75, 281, 283-84, 285
Farmer, Charles J., 198
Faunce, David, 308
Federovitch, John ("Ace"), 120, 128, 134, 162, 167-69, 175, 190, 198
Ferry, William M., 149, 176, 205, 224, 239, 240, 250, 251
Field Hockey, 169, 254, 305-6
Finney, Chanson V., 284
Fiorentino, A. E., 136
Fiorentino, Claire, 118, 137, 145, 165, 175, 195, 228, 233, 234, 254, 280, 288, 300
Flaningam, Rita R., 301
Fleming, Dewey L., 52, 101, 149
Flemming, Arthur S., 198
Fletcher, Charles, 223
Flynn, Bernard, 302
Football (teams, records), 10-12, 22-23, 34-35, 75-76, 81-82, 94, 97, 102, 115, 120, 128, 134, 138, 166-69, 203, 227, 233
Ford, Raymond, 191
Foreman, Kenneth J., 195
Forest Festival, 90, 91, 118, 137, 171, 175, 206, 238, 259
Forward, 199
Foundation Grants, 202, 230, 236, 239, 264, 272, 278, 290, 292
Founders Day, 258, 272, 277, 278, 310
Founding Families in 1979 (photo), 312
Fox, Fred, II, 216
Francis, David L., 250, 263, 273
Francis, Paul E., 205, 215
French, Harry W., 32, 37
Frost, John, 258
Fund Raising, 7, 38, 48-50, 53, 57, 70, 87, 93, 101, 115, 121, 123, 146-48, 170, 193, 207, 218, 239, 251, 260, 270-72, 292
Fyock, David, 258

G

Gage, Harry M., 149
Gartmann, Will, 276, 279, 284, 295, 301
Gate House, 61, 72
Gates, Charles B., Jr., 205, 239
Gawthrop, Mrs. Flora, 94

Gear, Felix B., 68, 119
General Electric College Bowl, 279
Gilbreath, Truitt, 296
Gilmore, D. Alton, 82, 205
Goddin, Margaret Purdum, 175, 176, 222, 237, 248, 283, 284, 288, 294
Golden, Benjamin I., 66
Golf, 92, 169
Goodwin, Olive, 288
Gore, Howard M., 80
Gould, Eleanor (Cody), 49, 88
Gould, Northam, 88
Gould, Sidney R., 34, 37
Gould, William Roscoe, 52
Gover, Charles A., 225
Graceland Hall, 2, 3, 92, 100, 136, 138, 139, 141, 151, 153, 191, 206, 217, 235
Great Issues Seminar, 228
Green, Bayard, 68, 78, 113
Greer, Mel, 203, 223
Griffith, Richard, 198
Gross, C. A. ("Bill"), 22, 23, 91, 92
Gross, William, 196
Guye, Judith, 237
Gwinn, C. W., 92, 96

H

Hale, Thomas J., 64-66, 91, 119
Hall, N. I., 39, 49, 87
Hall, N. I., Jr., 225
Hall, Stanley, 276
Halliehurst Hall, 2-3, 30, 59-62, 70-72, 76, 91, 100, 104, 118, 123, 134, 136, 138-41, 151, 153, 160, 191, 196, 206, 220, 235, 256
Hamill, Richard, 35
Hamilton, A. H., 6-8, 13, 24, 60; (Honor Society), 61, 313
Hamilton, Bryan, 77, 93
Handbook for Freshman, 137
Hansford, Rowland C., 99
Harper, David, 299
Harrington, B. C., 206, 231
Harris, Vernon B., 68
Harris, Virgie, 64, 66, 68, 75, 105, 106, 128, 132, 208, 216, 219, 220
Hartley, Walter S., 218, 225, 276, 280
Hartman, Carl L., 267, 279
Hartman, Julia F. (Mrs. C. L.), 301
Haught, David L., 160, 190
Hawley, Albert, 81, 95
Hayes, Terry R., 300
Hedrick, Robert E., 153
Henderson, E. Camdem ("Cam"), 65, 73-79, 81, 93, 94, 98, 108-9, 113, 115

320

Henry, Harold R., 198, 219, 258, 284
Henry, James R., 149, 185, 205, 240
Henry, Virginia L., 220, 284
Hensley, Leighton B., 78
Hermanson, Gordon E., 240-50, 258-79, 282-92, 301, 307, 309-13
Hermanson, Mary (Mrs. G. E.), 246, 248, 250, 259
Hermanson, Robert, 246, 248
Herrman, Karl F., 232, 233
Hickling, Anne, 261
Higginbotham, Henry K., 193
Hillick, Susan, 261
Hinkle, Ellery J., 227, 267
Hinkle, Ruth (Mrs. E. J.), 227
Hinkle, Willetta, 288
Hiser, Jonathan Keith, 201-2, 204, 230, 280, 283, 284
Hobart, Calvin R., 265, 284
Hodges, Wiley E., 124
Hodgson, Joseph E., 9-12, 16, 20
Holiday, Norene, 160
Holmes, James D., 283, 296
Hoover, H. L., 4
Hoover, Samuel R., 88, 250
Horne, Geoffrey, 165
Horvath, Gary, 232, 284
Hotchkiss, Jedediah, 8
Hubbell, Minor C., 24
Humphrey, Hubert H., 118, 244, 259, 273
Humphreys, William, 284, 309
Hunter, Roy B., 24
Hutton, Eugene E., 103, 219
Huttonsville Correctional Center, 166, 288

I

Impact Program, 37, 290, 310
Integrated Studies, 286, 299-301
Irons, Abbie, 19, 32
Irons, Robert, 23, 26, 81
Irwin, Robert, 166, 175

J

Jack, Tharon, 223, 271
Jackson, Brenda, 301
Jardetzky, Tatiana, 164, 172, 229, 236, 261
Jenness, M. Ian, 301
Jesse, W. H. (Library Report), 208
Johns, Bertha May, 49, 51
Johnson, David L., 209
Johnson, Dorothy, 301
Johnson, Herman, 11
Johnson, Stuart L., 11
Johnson, Willard F., 301

Johnston, James R., 267, 279
Johnston, Leila, 198
Johnston, Mildred Bryant, 91
Jones, Herman, 105
Jones, Lynn T., 301, 310

K

Kadel, Richard, 300
Keefe, Edward C., 124
Kek, Anna D., 206, 213-14, 227, 264-65, 284
Kek, Evan, 206, 212, 217, 227, 239, 264-65, 268-69
Kelly, Mrs. Charles, 267, 272
Kelly, Mathew J. (Observatory), 79
Kendell, Nevin E., 265-66, 271, 292
Kennedy, Bruce Lee (Mrs. John A.), 2
Kennedy, John F., 230, 235
Kerensky, Alexander, 172
Kessler, Kent, 74
Kessler, Stowell V. ("Bob"), 254, 261
Keyser, Robb, 68, 149
Kibler, Gordon G., 149, 159
Kilgore, Harley, 176
King, Starr, 150
Kirby, David, 96, 101
Kirk, David, 233, 244
Kiser, Raymond W., 161, 213
Kittle, Elizabeth Guye, 164, 165, 297
Knaggs, Nelson S., 215, 221, 250, 262, 263, 290
Knapp, Ron, 203
Kniley, Jesse, 131
Koon, Stanley, 269
Koontz, Louis K., 45, 51
Kradel, Paul F., 299, 309
Kranch, Douglas A., 301
Krizan, Emery, 267
Kump, H. G., 62, 97, 102, 104, 109, 176

L

Lacy, J. M., 122, 137
Laird, Candace, 288
Laird, Mrs. James M., 192, 205
Larson, Lois R., 301
Latham, Lois, 202
LaVoie, Allan, 299
Leahy, Elizabeth, 257
Lee, Grace Davis, 53, 81, 92
Lee, Sue R., 258
Lee, Thomas Davis, 258, 267, 272
Leininger, Albert A., 248
Leist, Bill, 160, 175, 200
Leonard, Charles, 164
Leslie, George C., 207
Levy, Albert G. D., 121

Lewis, Frank Bell, 145
Lexington Presbytery, 3-7, 9, 13, 24-25, 41, 313
Library, 11, 43, 90, 102, 123, 141, 146, 151, 158, 208-9, 222, 225-26, 242, 256, 272, 277
Lin, Han-sheng, 248
Lindberg, Dennis, 276, 281, 284, 288
Lindberg, Sandra, 301
Lingamfelter, C. S., 4
Linhart, A. Lee, 108
Linhart, Louise Sleeman, 108, 109, 198, 200, 238
Liston, Robert T. L., 130-35, 139-41, 143
Little, Jane, 198, 207, 218
Littlefield, Judith, 285
Long, Glen, 254
Long, Richard G., 162-63, 177, 182, 214-15, 218
Loughridge, Gasper A., 161
Lyons, Earl K., 166, 301

M

McAdams, Laura Jean, 101, 105, 225, 229
McCauley, R. L., 150
McCoy, Kenton, 299
McDonald, Jack, 223, 260
MacDougall, Ellis, 165, 176, 301
McFarlane, Edward M., 299, 307
McFarlane, Nancy J., 229, 305, 307
McGee, Fay, 204, 215
McGee, Gale, 270
McGee, James, 165, 175
McGee, Lorrayne Marquette, 173, 175
McGlamery, John W., 50
McKee, Kirkland, 82
MacKenzie, D. M., and Trippett, B. K., (North Central Report), 209
McKenzie, John, 24, 31, 46
McKenzie, John J., 204, 308
McKnight, James S., 276
McLaughlin, George, 175
McLaughlin, Margaret Trickett, 121
McNeill, G. Douglas, 145, 176
McNeish, Edna Warfield, 68, 103
McWhorter, L. E., 205, 223
Maravich, Peter ("Press"), 120, 128-29, 135, 166, 169
Marstiller, Betty (Mrs. R. Gordon Barrick), 122
Martens, Walter F., 62
Martin, James, 277
Martin, John P., 236, 280
Martin, Joseph, 196, 298, 299
Martin, Stephen, 104, 137, 227

Mattison, Louis, 206, 213, 221, 230
Maxon Pilot Study Report, 211, 214, 218
Maxwell, C. W., 74
Maxwell, Earl, 91
Maxwell, Judge Robert E., 8, 270
Meadows, Margaret Isner, 205, 297
Mero, Thomas, 166
Meyer, William G., 196, 198
Mikkelson, David, 267, 296
Miller, Fred A., 145, 151, 212-13, 215, 230-33, 239, 281, 283
Miller, Mrs. Fred A., 225
Miller, Irving, 66, 91, 132, 144, 165, 172, 300
Miller, J. Melvin, 284
Minguez, Teresa J., 266, 296
Montgomery, James Shera, 124
Montoney, Tillie, 238
Moore, Ed, 254
Moore, John Venable, 198
Moore, S. G., 51
Morgan, Calvin, 234
Morgan, Geraldine, 77
Morris, Emery, 53
Morrison, Gerald L., 256, 298
Mullennex, Harnus P., 35, 51, 74, 100, 120, 131, 143, 147, 149, 181
Mumford, L. Quincy, 277-78
Murphy, Margaret Ann, 196
Musical groups, 78, 165, 234, 280, 300
Musick, Ruth Ann, 288
Myers, L. Gregory, 237, 248, 253, 266, 273-74, 303

N

National Student Association, 173 268
National Youth Administration, 89
Nautilus, The, 78
Navy's V-1 Program, 139, 144
Neale, G. H., 131, 149
Neale, Sara V., 278
Nefflen, Louis H., 88, 164
Neill, John B., 295
Nelson, Kenneth S., 276, 279, 296
Netherworld Explorers, 234
New Deal, 89, 97
Nicholson, Jacob E., 181, 186, 198
Nicholson, Walter, 24
Nixon, Richard M., 118, 273
Noble, Hubert C., 248
Noblin, Stuart, 144
North Central Association, 84, 85, 90, 93, 102, 139, 148, 152, 157, 209-12, 217, 228, 281-83
N.S.F. Summer Institutes, 230

O

Oates, James F., 267
O'Conner, R. Emmett, 37, 65
Odor, Susie E., 218, 269
Ogilvie, George, 267-68
Oldenburg, Douglas, 268, 273, 277, 285
Oldknow, J. T., 161
Oleson, Douglas D., 275, 279, 284, 308
Omano, Pres., 172, 265
Opel, Emily Wilmoth, 198, 214, 217-18
Overholt, Mrs. Gilbert, 132
Owen, Trevor, 275, 308

P

Paine, Thomas, 137
Painter, Robert, 267
Palar, L. N., 281
Parents Day, 227, 267
Parmesano, Anna, 64, 113, 164, 206
Partain, Avis L., 237, 279
Pavlos, John, 237
Pavlos, Mrs. John, 245
Payne, Carl, 166-69, 176, 227
Payne, Gloria Marquette, 139, 146, 165, 176, 233, 255, 256, 261, 283, 287
Pedretti, Michael A., 300
Perkins, Edward V., 235, 265, 296
Perry, Mrs. S. Paul (Bess Johnson), 68
Petty, Patty R., 218, 229, 296, 309
Pfrangle, Robert A., 205, 215, 241, 277, 310
Phares, Lindsey J., 116, 250
Phares, Mabel Vanscoy, 175, 231, 297
Phillips, Robert, 166, 201
Phipps, Martha Ann, 206, 245
Phipps, William E., 206, 213, 228, 231, 244, 257, 268, 274, 275, 280, 284
Phoenix, The, 29, 50, 52, 53, 69
Plan of Cooperation, 25-26
Plaut, Thomas, 299
Pledger, Lance, 260, 276
Polino, Sam, 170
Polson, Thomas ("Tam"), 296
Poole, Arnold B., 201, 205
Potter, Charles, 259, 261, 264, 270
Powers, Chester, 103
Prellop, Monroe, 267
Preparatory School, 12-13, 19, 24, 27, 32, 44
Presbyterian Survey of Higher Education (Agnew), 203 ff
Presbyterian Vocational Guidance Center, 195-96, 198, 215, 298
President's Seminar, 228

Pritt, Thaddeus, 87, 131, 148, 152, 156
Purdum, Raymond B., 65-66, 99-102, 104-5, 112, 116-17, 126, 128-29, 132-33, 139, 142-48, 152-53, 156-58, 164, 170-73, 177-80, 182-83, 185-90, 193, 220-22, 292
Purdum, Mrs. Raymond B., 222

Q

Quick Fund Raising Campaign, 48-50

R

Radio Station, 119, 170
Raese, Cleon, 23, 31, 34
Randolph, Jennings, 66, 76, 79, 83, 88, 94, 97, 124, 130, 134-35, 144, 146, 149, 152, 170, 205, 223, 240, 259-60, 270, 272, 277, 307, 310
Reading Period, 245
Rector, James, 173
Rector, John J., 204
Redden, William R., 20
Redmond, Howard A., 190-91
Reed, Elizabeth Millard, 213-15
Reed, Jesse F., 163, 176, 202, 213, 216, 221, 265, 275, 280, 283, 286, 288
Regional Council for International Education, 236, 245, 282
Reith, Roberta, 301
Renneisen, George, 192
Rhoades, C. Cecil, 271
Rhodes, Daniel D., 161, 173, 179, 190
Riddle, Jesse, 31, 37, 90
Rightmire, Frank R., 198, 237
Rippey, Robert, 228, 234
Roberts, Dorothy F., 254, 261, 269-70, 275, 284
Roberts, Margaret Kump, 206
Roberts, Samuel Kump, 298
Robinson, Laurie, 299
Rogers, Frank W., 204
Rohde, Ruth Bryan Owen, 129
Rooker, Harvey, 166
Roosevelt, Franklin Delano, 86, 97, 118, 134, 137, 150
Roosevelt, Mrs. Franklin D., 102-3
Roosevelt, Theodore, 1, 56
Rose, Suzanne, 238, 250
Ross, Laurie, 308
Ross, Thomas R., 65, 162, 182, 192, 195-96, 201, 211-23, 216-18, 222, 226, 230-32, 239, 258, 269, 275, 277, 279, 282-83, 287-88, 297
Ross, Mrs. Thomas R., 245
Roy, Vernie G., 219

S

Sanders, Roger, 218-19
Scarlet Hurricane, 74, 76-77, 81-82, 94, 97, 128
Schilling, Harold K., 248
Schmalz, Fred, 303-4
Schneider, Francis L., 299
Scholarship Dinner, 228
Schoonover, Iri, 101-2
Schwarz, Ernest Thomas, Jr., 229
Scott, Crawford, 102
Scott, Robert, 175
Scott, S. M., Sr., 46
Scott, Samuel W., 37
Seaman, David, 299, 308
See, Mrs. C. M., 46
Senator, The, 69-70, 77, 88, 92, 106-7, 119, 122, 128, 136-37, 141, 150, 162, 166, 172, 174, 186, 222, 230, 245-50, 257-59, 261, 264, 274, 278, 281, 309
Senatus, 69, 78, 108, 115, 150, 166, 298, 309
Shahan, J. Buhl, 87-88
Shannon, Winifred, 218, 229
Sheets, Norman L., 206, 218, 231
Shelton, Harry L. ("Bud"), 95, 97, 102-3, 115, 120, 123, 128, 132, 190, 194, 199, 203, 219, 224-25, 227
Shelton, Kathryn (Mrs. Harry Shelton), 120, 231
Shields, Ellis Gale, 258
Sievert, Guy, 296
Simcoe, Lynn, 308
Simmons, David, 301
Simmons, Mary Elizabeth, 219
Sippola, Rudolph, 179-82, 188
Slater Food Service, 215
Smart, John, 198
Smith, Hulett, 259, 302
Snedegar, Paul, 107, 116, 164
Soccer, 232, 254, 260, 273-74, 276, 278-79, 302, 303, 304
Southwick, Arthur, 226
Spears, Lawrence E. and Jae, 178
Speer, Robert E., 135
Staff (members), 164, 213, 237, 271, 283-84, 296-98
Stary, Georgiana, 145, 151, 157, 172, 198
Steensland, Blaine, 285, 296, 309
Stetson, Mrs. C. E., 192, 205
Stevenson, Adlai, 118, 206
Stevenson, Charles A., 101, 104-6, 126, 128, 132
Stoller, Milan D., 162, 190
Stone, James, 301
Strader, J. Floyd, 173
Strickler, Robert P., 34, 37, 51
Stroud, H. Arthur, 205, 208, 213, 285, 287, 301, 310
Stubblefield, Frank, 145, 157
Studenmund, W. Russell, 276, 284
Student Government, 37, 123, 129, 150, 173-74, 200, 204, 277, 309
Student Organization, 21, 77-79, 92, 117, 119, 165, 175, 200, 222, 233, 268, 280-81
Students, 11-12, 19, 23, 26, 31, 52, 68, 77, 79, 82, 88, 99, 103, 107, 109, 115-16, 121, 139, 173-76, 200, 204, 215, 217, 225, 238, 276, 279, 309
Summer School, 26, 73, 155-56, 282
Sutherland, Howard, 41, 43, 49-50, 71, 99, 149
Sutherland, Richard K., 52, 149
Swanson, Carl, 296
Swimming, 161, 169, 233, 253, 254
Sycamore Street Trees, 122
Sylvia Inn, 191

T

Talbot, S. Benton, 66, 69, 88, 93-94, 101, 104, 121, 128, 131-32, 137, 142, 144, 157-58, 179, 183, 189-90, 219-20, 310
Talbott, Richard H., 69, 79, 145, 243
Talbott, Mrs. Richard H., 162-63, 189-90
Tallman, Anna Jean, 236, 254, 286, 305-6
Tarr, Edward E., 35
Tedford, Barbara (Mrs. S. H.), 225
Tedford, Sidney Hamilton, 225, 234, 280, 284, 300
Tennis, 169, 216
Thayer, C. R., 196, 215
Thompson, Franklin, 229
Thompson, Harry, 269, 295
Thompson, John Grant, 172
Thorne, Nelson H., 131, 143
Tierney, Glady J., 297
Toadvine, Stephen P., II, 162, 203
Tolstead, William, 215, 287, 291
Towler, James A., Jr., 198
Troxell, Richard, 263
Truman, Harry S., 118, 176, 185, 238
Trustees, 7, 26, 40-41, 131, 148-49, 192, 205, 240, 241, 250, 301-2
Tuition, 13, 19, 24, 46, 68, 89, 105, 151, 156, 159, 201, 236
Turner, James M., 225
Tygart Valley Homestead project, 89, 102

U

Underwood, Carl, 162, 180, 190
Urban, Robert E., 200

V

Van Gundy, James J., 300
Vaughan, Carrie B., 218
Vaughn, Silas M., 198
Vazquez, Alfonso, 237, 280
Vazquez, Georgiana, 237, 286
Vest, Marvin Lewis, 79, 115
Vick, George H., 149, 176, 205
Viehman, Harold H., 314
Vosburgh, Donald, 201

W

Wagener, Jean, 237, 248
Wagener, Jerald, 237, 248, 276
Wallace, Herbert, 216
Walter, Donald M., 254-56, 283-84
Wands, Cynthia, 234
War, 44-45, 50-52, 129, 135, 137-38, 143, 153, 176-77, 244, 257, 261, 278
Ward, William, 137
Warner, David E., 161, 169, 190
Wartenburg, Carl, 261, 279, 299
Washington Semester Program, 226, 230, 282
Watring, Denver, 166
Watring, Glen, 94
Weaver, Priscilla ("Pat"), 222
Weber, Robert C., 300
Wees, Boyd, 109
Weese, Frances, 176, 301
Weist, Scottie Roberts, 288
Welshonce, James, 201, 236
West Virginia Federation of College Students, 173
West Virginia Foundation of Independent Colleges, 183
West Virginia Intercollegiate Press Association, 135
Whetsell, Clay, 150, 193, 224
Whetsell, Harry E., 35-36, 49, 51, 64-66, 72, 75, 91, 99-100, 104, 108, 122, 125-29, 131-32, 307

White, Kenneth A., Jr., 268-69, 295
White, Stanley, 161
Who's Who in American Universities and Colleges, 119
Whyte, Cassandra Bolyard, 284, 299, 308
Whyte, William, 284
Wilcox, Paul, 194, 199, 223, 227
Wilcox, Willis H., 51, 64-65, 67, 76
Wilkey, David, 296
William James House Program, 253, 299
Wilson, E. D., 101, 131
Wilson, Frank E., 131, 148, 169, 192
Wilson, George W., 127-28, 131, 148
Wilson, James L., 173-74
Wilson, John Russell, 275, 283-84, 293-94, 297
Wilson, Mrs. J. R. (Claire), 276, 293
Wilson, Knox, 162, 215, 258, 275
Wilson, Mrs. Knox ("Boots"), 162, 215
Wilson, Lewis W., 198, 234
Wilson, R. Dale, 288, 308
Wilson, Robert, 267
Wimer, Frank C., 35-36, 51, 97, 114, 307
Winchester Presbytery, 4, 7, 24-25, 41, 313
Winters, C. L., Jr., 180; (report), 180-81, 188
Witherspoon, James W., 149, 205, 239, 247, 248, 258
Wolverton, John Calvin, 10, 16, 20
Wood, William, 206
Woodward, Mabel, 99, 256
Woodward, Mary Margaret, 149, 237
Woodsworth, Malcolm B., 10, 16, 20

Y

Yount, G. A., 127-28

Z

Zuboy, John, 301